# In the
# Early Hours

## REFLECTIONS ON
## SPIRITUAL AND SELF DEVELOPMENT

## KHURRAM MURAD

### EDITED BY RIZA MOHAMMED

Revival

ISBN 0 9536 768 0 3


*Published by*
Revival Publications
Markfield Conference Centre
Ratby Lane, Markfield, Leicestershire LE67 9SY
United Kingdom

TEL: 01530 244944 • FAX: 01530 244946
E-MAIL: revival@islamic-foundation.org.uk


*Printed by*
Interprint Limited, Malta


*Cover/Book design & typeset*  Imtiaze Ahmed Manjra
*Cover photograph* Assiakhatun Imtiaze

*In the Name of Allah the Beneficent, the Merciful*

———⊷⊷⊷———

## REVIVAL PUBLICATIONS

The process of change always starts with postulation of fresh ideas to challenge the status quo. It is only through innovative thinking that problems can be solved and progress can be made. The hallmark of the Islamic Movement has always been to produce stimulating literature covering all aspects of life – social, political, economic and legal as well as moral, spiritual and religious. This dynamic literature has inspired and motivated a large section of the Muslim *Umma* and prepared them to struggle to bring about change in the society.

There is no doubt we require literature for the Islamic Movement that reflects the needs of this country. It should take into account the problems faced by the society in the West. The launching of *Revival Publications* is to meet these needs. We will endeavour to publish literature by the pioneers of the Islamic Movements as well as by young intellectuals and scholars so that a forum of discussion can be initiated to portray the message of Islam to society at large.

It is appropriate to launch this programme of publications by a collection of inspirational advice on the subject of spiritual and self development by the late Brother Khurram Murad.

We are grateful to Allah (*Subhanu wa Tala*) for His help and guidance in enabling us to undertake this task. Without His Help and Mercy we cannot accomplish anything.

We also very gratefully acknowledge the moral and financial support provided by the Islamic Foundation and the UK Islamic Mission. We pray that Allah may accept our humble efforts and reward all those who are working in His cause.

The Editorial Board,
*Leicester, October 1999*

# Contents

# Preface

THE title of this book, *In the Early Hours,* has been carefully and specifically chosen to highlight that precious but often neglected time during the night that Allah is closest and most receptive to His servants. The Messenger of God said:

Our Lord descends each night to the nearest Heaven when only the last third of the night remains, and says: 'Is anyone praying that I may answer him? Is anyone seeking forgiveness, that I may forgive him? Is anyone asking, that I may give to him?', and this continues until dawn. (*Tirmidhi.*)

The later part of each night is the most conducive period for reflection and self development. It is the occasion with the most potential for the heart to be present, alert and free of worldly concerns as the Quran declares: *Lo! The vigil of the night is* [a time] *when impression is more keen and speech more certain.* [al-Muzzammil 73: 6.]

This book is a collection of inspirational advice by a dear and beloved teacher, *Ustadh* Khurram Murad on the subject of spiritual and self development. In it he sets out the goal of the Believer – the single-minded desire to seek the good pleasure of Allah and Paradise. He then outlines the methods and instruments which must be used in the attainment of that ultimate goal.

The spiritual exhortations that follow were originally delivered in the early hours of Summer 1993 just after *Salat al-Fajr* as part of a course entitled *Self Development for Islamic Workers* at The Islamic Foundation, Leicester. That course represented one of many similar courses *Ustadh* Khurram conducted for young Muslims, both male and female. He recognised that it was in the young generation's eagerness, strength and enthusiasm that the future of the Muslim *Umma* lay.

Each of the seven sections in this book represents one *Nasiha* or Advice. Each *Nasiha* was delivered in a presentation of approximately 45 minutes. This time allotment was not, of course, sufficient for *Ustadh* Khurram to discuss the subjects in detail. I have therefore drawn material from several of his other speeches and works for 'thoroughness', coherence and to provide clarity on the topics discussed. I have also added Quran and *hadith* references wherever I felt they were relevant and added to the richness of the text. Only Allah knows how close I have come to making clear the Message of the Quran and the *Sunna* as expressed by *Ustadh* Khurram.

Let me emphasise that this book merely represents an introduction to spiritual and self development. I hope that each of the topics exposed here will lead you to further study so that you can continue to grow and progress along the path of attaining closeness to Allah, our Lord and Master. A selection of suggested readings is given at the end of this text to assist in further study.

The task of preparing this text has certainly been a challenge for me, but one which I have enjoyed and benefited from immensely. I am grateful to Muhammad Abdul Aziz, Alyasa Abdullah, Asim Abdullah, Sharifa Abdullah, Fazeela Mollick,

Wajid Mollick, Hashim Mohammed and Lucy Bushill-Matthews who all read the manuscript and offered valuable comments and advice during the initial phase of this text's preparation. My deepest appreciation, however, goes to Abdul Wahid Hamid, whose literary skills, advice and motivation were instrumental in finalising this work. Ultimately, though, any mistakes this book contains are my own – may Allah forgive me and have mercy on me. Whatever good is derived from it, all praise is due to Him, for without His help and guidance, nothing is possible.

I would like to end with a *dua* or supplication of the Prophet which epitomises the sole objective of this work and our goal in life:

O Allah, You change hearts, so change our hearts to be obedient to You. (*Muslim.*)

**Riza Mohammed**
*Leicester, October 1999*

## CHAPTER ONE

# The Process of Self Development

THE path to God is only illuminated when a person recognises the central place of God in his life and strives to develop his self accordingly. The Messenger of God said:

> If someone wants to know what position he enjoys in the eyes of God, he has only to look at what place he gives to God [in his heart and life]. (*Hakim.*)

The term nearest in meaning to self development in the Quranic vocabulary is *tazkiya*. *Tazkiya* means purification and refers to the cleansing of the human self from all that is unwholesome, undesirable and unwelcome. It also refers to the nurturing and strengthening of all the qualities within the human self that are essential for growth and development, for blossoming and flowering.

## THE GOAL IN LIFE

Success and happiness in this world and the Hereafter depend on *tazkiya*, the purification and nurturing of our personality. The Quran states that true success is only reserved for those who seek to purify themselves:

*Successful indeed is the one who purifies his whole self.* [al-Shams 91: 9.]

Our personality comprises not only the physical body but also the mind and the heart, feelings and attitudes, character and behaviour. Proper nurturing and development of these elements of the personality will achieve desirable goals. When goals are desirable, the process of aspiring to, working towards and achieving them also becomes desirable. This is part of human nature. It is critical, therefore, that we recognise and understand the true nature of our ultimate goal in life.

For the Believer, the most coveted goal in life is to seek the good pleasure of Allah and *Janna* or Paradise. Our Creator has set this goal for us: *And surely Paradise – it is the goal* [al-Naziat 79: 41]; *Indeed the Next abode – it is truly the life!* [al-Ankabut 29: 64]; *The companions of Paradise – they are the triumphant ones.* [al-Hashr 59: 20.]

Know, however, that attaining the pleasure of Allah takes precedence over seeking *Janna* but the two are closely connected. Paradise can only be attained through seeking Allah's pleasure, and when Allah's pleasure is gained, we will indeed be granted Paradise. Reflect upon the following two verses in the Quran:

*And there is a kind of person who would willingly give up personal interests, seeking Allah's pleasure; and God is Most Compassionate towards His servants.* [al-Baqara 2: 207.]

*Indeed Allah has purchased from the Believers their lives and their possessions, promising them Paradise, in return.* [al-Tawba 9: III.]

The alternative to attaining Paradise in the Hereafter is to be placed in *Jahannam* or Hell-fire and to receive its punishments. The Quran states: *But in the life to come*: [it is either] *severe suffering, or God's forgiveness and His goodly acceptance.* [al-Hadid 57: 20.] What is it that makes a person deserving of such a suffering? The answer is to be found in the second part of the same verse: *for the life of this world is nothing but an enjoyment of self-delusion.* [al-Hadid 57: 20.] *Jahannam*, therefore, is for those who seek as their ultimate goal in life, not the pleasure of Allah or Paradise, but the enjoyment of worldly gains.

The pursuit of worldly gain is but a mirage. All worldly gains are left behind when you die. All that is on earth is bound to perish while Allah and His good favour will remain forever. It is for this reason that the Quran advises:

*Vie with one another in seeking to attain to your Sustainer's forgiveness, and to a Paradise as vast as the heavens and the earth, which has been readied for those who have attained to faith in God and His messengers: such is the bounty of Allah which He grants unto whomever He wills – for Allah is limitless in His great bounty.* [al-Hadid 57: 21.]

All your efforts in this world should therefore be focused only on seeking Paradise. It is the Promise of the Almighty that:

*You will only be rewarded fully for all your good deeds on the Day of Resurrection, and [on that Day] whoever will be drawn away from Hell-fire, and admitted into Paradise, will indeed have triumphed.* [Al Imran 3: 185.]

## THE FIRST STEP TO PARADISE

The first step in self development, then, is to concentrate single-mindedly on Paradise. Indeed, the one who is unsure of his destiny in life, torn between this world and the Next, like one standing with his feet in two separate boats – will be thrown off balance. Many of the difficulties that we face are due to this lack of commitment and inability to focus on the real and ultimate goal. If you can keep your focus on *Janna*, then everything else will be possible.

The selection of the ultimate goal of Paradise must be made consciously and may involve an absolute break with the past. To choose this new goal as the ultimate goal in one's life is in fact to choose a new life, to begin a new journey. Embark on this new journey by refreshing your *wudu* (ablution) and offering two *rakas* (units) of *Salat* or Prayer reminding yourself of all the punishment of Hell-fire you have just resolved to avoid at all costs and all the rewards of Paradise that you will strive to achieve. Remind yourself also of the important stations and landmarks on the journey: imagine death as near; imagine the moment when the Angel of Death will declare, 'your time is over, now you must follow me'; imagine that moment when you will be made to stand in the presence of Allah, Most High, so that the final judgement of life may be passed on you and imagine the consequences of that judgement. When you have completed the two *rakas* then resolve once more that all efforts will be directed towards achieving Paradise, beseech Allah and pray with humility:

O Allah, I ask for Your mercy and whatever brings me closer to it, in word and deed.

O Allah, I ask for a faith that will never vanish, a blessing that will never diminish, a pleasure that will never abate, and the most elevated position in Paradise distinguished by the companionship of Your Messenger, Muhammad.

While improvement in your habits and actions is a life-long process, the desire to achieve it can thus be sparked in a moment. This desire will provide the momentum for attaining your goal – the good pleasure of Allah and Paradise.

## YOUR MISSION

Having taken the first step and resolved to attain Paradise, you may ask yourself, what does Allah require from me in order for me to succeed?

What Allah requires of you, in Quranic vocabulary, is for you to be a *mumin* and *mujahid*. A *mumin* is one who is true and firm in his faith in God. A *mujahid* is one who strives his utmost, with all the means at his disposal, to gain God's pleasure. If you are a *mumin* and a *mujahid*, Allah, the Most Exalted in Power and yet the Most Compassionate, will assist you to rise to higher stations both in this world and in the Hereafter. Allah has promised this to those who possess the qualities of *iman* or faith and the active resolve for *jihad* or struggle. The Quran states:

*The Believers are only those who have attained to faith in God and His Messenger and have left all doubt behind, and who strive hard in God's cause with their possessions and their lives: it is they, they who are true to their word.* [al-Hujurat 49: 15.]

You now have a mission: to become a *mumin* and *mujahid*. As you embark upon this mission you may come to feel that your knowledge of Islam is somewhat limited or perhaps that you are unable to attain those heights of submission and purification that you desire or others expect of you. This is only natural. You must not, however, allow these feelings of personal shortcomings to undermine your efforts to practise Islam. Remember that Islam is a state of becoming not a state of being. Each day you must strive to improve and better yourself – and you will improve.

*Tazkiya* or this new programme for self-improvement that you now find yourself in, is a process that unfolds itself step by step. You cannot expect to change all at once. This is against the laws of nature. The Prophet was always aware of this when he was dealing with his Companions. Whenever someone embraced Islam, the Prophet would not ask that person to do everything immediately. Instead, he would teach and expect that person to start fulfilling his obligations only as much as he could bear at a time. This gradual process of change is also clearly reflected in the manner in which the Quran was revealed over a period of 23 years. In all your efforts towards becoming a better Believer, you must bear in mind this principle of gradualism, otherwise you may try to attain the impossible, and when you do not achieve it, you may become frustrated.

At this stage, what matters most is that your bargain with Allah, *iman,* remains sound and firm. This definition of *iman* is perhaps a little different from the definition you usually hear. It is, however, a definition that we find in the Quran [al-Tawba 9: III]. Furthermore, attainment of such *iman*, allows you to be counted among the true and sincere servants in the eyes of your Lord. The Quran states:

*Behold, God has bought of the Believers their lives and their possessions, promising them Paradise in return, they fight in God's cause, and slay, and are slain: a promise which in truth He has willed upon Himself in the Tawra, and the Injil, and the Quran. And who could be more faithful to his covenant than God?* [al-Tawba 9: III.]

Once you have committed yourself to Allah, all that you have must be spent in His way. This is the ideal. Ideals, however, are always difficult to achieve – and this you must understand and accept. Ideals are always to be pursued; if they are easily and always achievable, they can hardly remain as ideals. Keeping to your side of the bargain then, is an ideal that you must always seek to maintain. It is this seeking and this striving to spend all that we have in the way of Allah that is known as *jihad* and alternatively, in this instance, as *tazkiya*.

## PREREQUISITES OF *TAZKIYA*

As you proceed on your journey along the new path, in quest of the ultimate goal of Paradise, you will encounter difficulties and hardships. These may often seem insurmountable. Overcoming them may be made easier by a good early grasp of the prerequisites of *tazkiya*. These are as follows:

### 1. Tazkiya – *Your Personal Responsibility*

You must accept that *tazkiya* is a highly personal process and that it demands taking personal responsibility for carrying it forward. You can only see the results of *tazkiya* through your own realisation, your own personal efforts and your own exertions. No one else can perform *tazkiya* for you. No organisation, no leader and no teacher can replace your own responsibility. God says: *And no bearer of burdens shall be made to bear another's burden; and if one weighed down by his load calls upon* [another] *to help him carry it, nothing thereof may be carried* [by that other], *even if it be one's near of kin.* [al-Fatir 35: 18.]

This sense of personal responsibility is basic to the whole purpose and approach of Islam. Ultimately, we are judged individually for discharging our own responsibilities. If someone else fulfils your obligations, then it should be he that is rewarded, not you. To be rewarded you must do what is expected of you by Allah by yourself:

> *Whoever strives hard in God's cause does so only for his own good: for, verily, God does not stand in need of anything in all the worlds! And as for those who attain to faith and do righteous deeds, We shall most certainly efface their bad deeds, and shall most certainly reward them in accordance with the best that they ever did.* [al-Ankabut 29: 6-7.]

Some people allow themselves to be dictated to by others. The Quran states that the weak will say on the Day of Judgement that they were coerced into following the dictates of others, but that Allah will reply that the excuse is not legitimate for the decision to deviate from the Straight Path was their own. [Qaf 50: 26-28.] Even Shaytan will stand up on the Day of Judgement, saying: *'I invited you and you responded to me, so don't blame me, blame yourselves'.* [Ibrahim 14: 22.] Ultimately, then, the blame and the reward will be yours, because the responsibility was yours:

*On that Day all people will come forward, cut off from one
another, to be shown their deeds. And so, he who shall have done
an atom's weight of good, shall behold it; and he who shall have
done an atom's weight of evil, shall behold it.* [al-Zalzala 99: 6-8.]

Taking charge of your own affairs may certainly seem a
daunting task, but one which you will accomplish with
distinction if you appreciate and take advantage of the
tremendous human potential that Allah has blessed you with.
Allah says in the Quran:

*Verily, We created man in the best conformation, and thereafter
We reduced him to the lowest of the low – excepting only such as
attain to faith and do good works: and theirs shall be a reward
unending!* [al-Tin 95: 4-6.]

*Tazkiya* does not consist simply of ideas, but of life,
behaviour and conduct. The key to success, according to the
Quran, lies in having true faith. To inculcate true faith you must
start by acquiring a sound knowledge of Islam through a
dedicated study of the Quran and *Sunna*. You must then
translate your knowledge into practice. For this to occur, you
need to have firm resolve and determination. This, in turn, will
produce *amal salih* or righteous conduct.

To aid you in your task, you must seek the company of those
who are also striving to please Allah. They will encourage you
towards righteousness and correct you when you deviate from
the true Path. Your company also includes your mental and
psychological company – the ideas you entertain, the ambitions
you nurture, the sensitivities and sensibilities you develop and

the books you read. All of these represent a form of company because they are your companions in solitude.

## 2. Genuine Effort

In order to succeed, you must have a deep desire to make a genuine effort to fulfil your obligations as a Muslim:

> But as for those who strive hard in Our cause – We shall most certainly guide them onto paths that lead unto Us: for, behold, God is indeed with the doers of good. [al-Ankabut 29: 69.]

With desire, of course, come actions. But know that it is not solely the results of your endeavours that count; what matters most is that you made your best effort. This is a very important point to appreciate because without genuine effort nothing can happen. Those who think that Prayer alone can work miracles are not living in a realistic world. Prayers are part of the effort, but Prayers are not the whole answer. If you pray, 'Allah! Guide me and make me good', it is not going to bring you any benefit unless you are also determined to become good and make an effort towards becoming good. Once you have done the latter two things, then, of course, Prayer will be a source of *baraka* or Divine grace that will further inspire and strengthen your efforts.

The initial desire and the ensuing effort to do and become good, is part of the continuing process of self development, a process that may begin at any point in life that you choose and continue till your last breath:

*O you who have attained to faith! Be consciou*
*the consciousness that is due to Him, and do not a*
*overtake you until you have surrendered yourselves unto*
[Al Imran 3: 102.]

There will never be a point when you will be able to say that you are now a perfect person or that you have achieved your full potential. If at any point you feel so, then be sure that is the starting point of your downfall. On the other hand, you may find that the greater your desire to fulfil your obligations as a Muslim, the more you feel beset or plagued by frustration, despondency and despair in your heart and mind. All of us, whether young or old, have experienced these diseases, and often just give up. What we should try to remember at such times is that it is the intention and effort that matters, not the result. This effort must be a continuing process:

*Be not, then, faint of heart, and grieve not: for you are bound to*
*rise high if you are believers.* [Al Imran 3: 139]

## 3. Sustaining Will-power

To achieve the ultimate goal in life requires a sustained determination to do so, a will-power that is forever responsive and strong. In Quranic terminology this is called *irada*. *Irada* is basic to all our efforts. Without willing to do something you cannot do anything.

*Irada* is very different from desire. You always hear people reflecting upon unfulfilled aspirations. One of the main reasons why aspirations and dreams remain unfulfilled is that they are no more than desires which failed to assume the status of *irada*.

... of the basic weaknesses in
... development is the weakness
... y of Adam, Allah informs:

*...de Our covenant with Adam; but he*
*...ness of purpose in him.* [Ta Ha 20: 115.]

...gth and consistency and is indeed the
a... ...esitation or lethargy. Once *irada* is firmly
in plac... ...must have no doubts and you must not
hesitate.

Now, what purpose should *irada* serve? The Quran makes it clear that this will-power must be a firm resolve to seek the pleasure of Allah because this is the part of the bargain that you must deliver:

*And whoever desires* [arada] *the Life to Come, and strive for it as it ought to be striven for, and are* [true] *Believers withal – they are the ones whose striving finds favour* [with God]. [al-Isra 17: 19.]

### 4. Reliance on Allah

Self-confidence is borne from the Believer's intimate knowledge and understanding that Allah is ever ready to assist those who strive and struggle in His way. Self-confidence comes from depending upon Allah and knowing that He is there to help you, protect you and shower His mercies upon you:

*So he who gives* [in charity] *and fears* [Allah] *and* [in all sincerity] *testifies to the best – We will indeed make smooth for him the path to Bliss.* [al-Layl 92: 5-7.]

Self-confidence also emanates from knowing that Allah in His infinite mercy has equipped you with all that you require to undertake the tasks set before you. It is not characteristic of the One that is Most Just and Most Merciful to prepare you for a task without equipping you with the necessary tools.

Self-confidence is thus borne of total reliance and trust in Allah. It is knowing that at every step of your journey Allah is there assisting you. If you constantly hold yourself back believing that you are weak and incapable and blame your incompetence on minor inadequacies, then you are bound to fail. You must never allow yourself to believe or feel that Allah has treated you unfairly or that He has placed upon you a burden you cannot shoulder for *on no soul does Allah place a burden greater than it can bear.* [al-Baqara 2: 286.]

Likewise, hope is central to your efforts and your success. You must sincerely hope and believe that everything you do to earn the pleasure of Allah will lead you to fulfilment. A superiority complex negates the task of self development. An inferiority complex is derived from a lack of confidence in Allah and oneself. You should never allow yourself to believe that you cannot fulfil your obligations nor should you despair of the mercy of Allah. Confidence, hope and determination are all important ingredients for your success:

*Those unto whom men said: Lo! The people have gathered against you, therefore fear them. But it only increased them in faith and they cried: Allah is sufficient for us! Most Excellent is He in Whom we trust!* [Al Imran 3: 173-174.]

You must be wary, however, of the kind of self-confidence that causes a person to proclaim himself self-sufficient. Modern concepts of self-sufficiency are indeed an evil form of *shirk* or polytheism. To ascribe self-sufficiency to one's self is to assume for oneself an attribute reserved only for Allah. For the Muslim, self-confidence is wholly dependent upon the trust one places in Allah; it is not an arrogant proclamation of complete independence from Allah. Allah alone is Self-Sufficient. All else is reliant upon Him for existence.

## 5. The Best Use of Time

Time is not money or gold; it is life and it is limited. You must begin to appreciate every moment of your life and always strive to make the best use of it. With all the demands of worldly life on your time, you will yet need to find time for self development and maximise its potential. The better route towards self development is, of course, to integrate all your efforts into a structured daily life. *Imam* al-Ghazali, may God have mercy on him, in his great work, *Ihya Ulum ad-Din*, gives the following advice:

> You should structure your time, arrange your regular devotions and assign to each function a set period of time during which it is given first priority but which it does not overstep. For if you abandon yourself to neglect and purposelessness, as cattle do, and just do anything that may occur to you at any time it happens to occur to you, most of your time will be wasted. Your time is your life, and your life is your capital; it is the basis of your

transactions [with God], and the means to attain to everlasting felicity, in the proximity of God the Exalted. Each of your breaths is a priceless jewel, and when it passes away it never returns.

Remember also that 'the deeds most loved by Allah [are those] done regularly, even if they are few.' (*Bukhari, Muslim.*) While you must always strive to make the best use of your time, you must always aim for excellence in everything you undertake, whether at school, at home, at work or at play. Indeed, the Prophet has said, 'Verily Allah has prescribed *ihsan* (proficiency and excellence) in all things.' (*Muslim.*)

## 6. Tazkiya – *All-embracing Process*

Islam does not subscribe to the type of asceticism where we purify our hearts and yet remain immersed in political, economic or social corruption. *Tazkiya* must encompass our entire life – the privacy of our thoughts as well as their social manifestations in our daily life. Everything must be in conformity with Allah's will.

This will of God also requires you to seek and maintain a delicate balance between the various obligations that demand your attention; between your obligations to Allah, your obligations towards others and your obligations towards yourself. The Prophet advised us against extremism of any kind. It is reported that he said to Abdullah ibn Amr:

'Have I heard right that you fast everyday and stand in prayer all night?' Abdullah replied, 'Yes, O Messenger of

God.' The Prophet said, 'Do not do that. Fast, as well as eat and drink. Stand in prayer, as well as sleep. For your body has a right upon you, your eyes have a right upon you, your wife has a right upon you, and your guest has a right upon you.' (*Bukhari, Muslim.*)

Unless you approach *tazkiya* as an all-embracing process, you will find that your life is compartmentalised, certain parts impeding the development of others. This can only result in a life of disharmony and unhappiness. Approached as a comprehensive and all-embracing process, however, you will find that each part of your life will complement some other part. This should, God willing, make your struggle on the path to God and *Janna* easier and full of grace.

As you struggle to make headway on the path to God, always remember that you have an excellent example before you. This is the example of the Prophet Muhammad, may God bless him and grant him peace. Often we would like to emulate our sports heroes, our parents, our teachers, our friends or others who attract our attention. For your spiritual development, however, the most beautiful example is that of the Prophet. Allah says in the Quran:

> *You have, indeed, in the Messenger of God an excellent exemplar, whoever places his hopes in God and the Final Day, and who remembers Allah much.* [al-Ahzab 33: 21.]

### BLESSINGS AND BENEFITS

The decision to purify and develop yourself requires that you clearly define the path and consider the ways and means to achieve Paradise. This whole process will not only purify your heart, but also affect your entire life and the will of Allah will become so much easier for you to follow. Following the Divine Will is, of course, *tazkiya* itself. Soon, all your efforts will be directed towards the ultimate goal – the pleasure of Allah and Paradise.

Know that every sin can be effaced through forgiveness, and forgiveness is a sure way to Paradise. As you strive to better yourself, then, simultaneously and continuously pray for forgiveness for all your shortcomings. God says: *And whoever repents and believes and works righteous deeds, God changes evil deeds into good ones, and God is Ever-Forgiving, Merciful.* [al-Furqan 25: 70.]

It is a misconception to believe that simply by setting up Paradise as the ultimate goal, one can get there without any further effort. It is also a misconception that Paradise can solely be achieved by concentrating only on certain aspects of life, the 'religious and the spiritual'. The very fact that Paradise is the ultimate objective means that *tazkiya* must be pursued in all aspects of life, and in life as a whole. Consider, for example, the following:

- Is not honesty a means to enter Paradise?
- Will not a sense of responsibility enable me to enter Paradise?
- Will not striving to fulfil the needs of fellow human beings make me deserve Paradise?
- Will not abstaining from vain talk and aimless actions, bring me closer to Paradise?
- Is not consciousness of the best use of my time a key to Paradise?
- Will not keeping promises and offering *Salat* on time, which

are distinguishing traits of the righteous, put me on the highway to Paradise?
• Must not all of the above be sought to attain Paradise?

Every effort that is legitimate and is aimed at attaining Paradise is also an integral part of the process of *tazkiya*.

*Insha Allah* (God-willing), if you take heed of all the prerequisites, blessings and benefits of *tazkiya*, you will surely find the right environment, the true companionship and brotherhood and the most appropriate training programmes to make the task of self development easier and more rewarding.

> *So give the good news to My servants who listen to the word* [of God], *then follow the beauty in it. Such are they whom God has guided. And such are they who are endowed with understanding.* [al-Zumar 39: 17-18.]

## SUMMARY

The most comprehensive goal for a Muslim is the single-minded desire to attain Paradise. This desire to seek Paradise is a life-long process which can be sparked in a moment – and this desire will provide the means and the momentum to reach the goal.

Your model for self-development is that of the Prophet Muhammad. In your quest for Paradise, you must personally take charge of your responsibilities, develop the will-power to perform and make a genuine effort to fulfil your obligations, ensure that you make the best use of your time and adopt a balanced approach to life.

Remember that every effort that is legitimate and is aimed at attaining Paradise is also an integral part of the process of *tazkiya* and that every sin can be effaced through forgiveness – and that forgiveness is the sure way to Paradise. *And as for the one who fears to stand before his Lord and who restrains himself from base desires, the Garden is surely the abode.* [al-Naziat 79: 40-41.]

May Allah enable us to be among those who purify themselves for *it is God Who causes whomever He wills to grow in purity; and none shall be wronged by as much as a hair's breath.* [al-Nisa 4: 49.] *Were it not for God's favour upon you and His grace, not one of you would ever have remained pure. For it is God who causes whomever He wills to grow in purity: for God is All-Hearing, All-Knowing.* [al-Nur 24: 21.]

## CHAPTER TWO

# A Life of Remembrance

IN a verse of the Quran that I love very much, Allah, Most Gracious and Loving, commends:

*Remember Me and I shall remember you. Be grateful unto Me and deny Me not.* [al-Baqara 2: 152.]

Can you imagine a more gratifying state than this, where, when you remember Allah, the Creator, Sustainer and Lord of the Universe, He remembers you in return? The same exhortation has been beautifully conveyed in a *hadith qudsi:*

I treat My servant as he hopes that I would treat him. I am with him whenever he remembers Me: if he remembers Me in his heart, I remember him in My 'heart'; if he remembers Me in a gathering, I remember him in a gathering far better than that gathering; if he draws near to Me a hand's span, I draw near to him an arm's length; if he draws near to Me an arm's length, I draw near to him a fathom's length; and if he comes to Me walking, I go to him running. (*Bukhari, Muslim.*)

Those who remember Allah standing, sitting and reclining and who reflect on the creation of the heavens and the earth are highly commended in the Noble Quran. They are wise in that they fill their hearts with the remembrance of God in every moment, in every circumstance and in every posture of their lives. [Al Imran 3: 191.]

The exhortation to remember Allah at all times is a reflection of Allah's all-embracing and overwhelming love for us. The door to Allah is always open to us: *Remember Me and I will remember you*. We need only find our way to and through that door.

## THE SIGNIFICANCE OF *DHIKR*

Regarding the significance of *dhikrullah* or the remembrance of God, Allah says in the Quran, itself the ultimate reminder (*dhikr*) to all the worlds [Sad 38: 87], the following:

*Remember Allah, for He has guided you.* [al-Baqara 2: 198.]

*O you who believe! Remember Allah often with much remembrance. And glorify Him morning and evening.* [al-Ahzab 33: 41-42.]

*And men who remember God much and women who remember – God has prepared for them forgiveness and a vast reward.* [al-Ahzab 33: 35.]

*Hadith* literature is similarly replete with references to the remembrance of Allah:

The servant cannot perform a better deed which will save him from God's punishment than the remembrance of God. (*Malik.*)

Whoever wishes to feast in the gardens of Paradise, let him remember God often. (*Tirmidhi.*)

Indeed, with regard to *dhikr*, the Quran concludes: *And the remembrance of Allah is the greatest deed, without doubt.* [al-Ankabut 29: 45.]

The significance of *dhikr* lies in the fact that it is God's own chosen and recommended mode by which the *muminun* or Believers show gratitude for having been shown the straight path. In addition, it is indeed the surest way of attaining God's forgiveness and achieving the ultimate reward of Paradise.

The importance of *dhikr* then is not difficult to understand. It is *dhikr* that purifies your *qalb* or heart and makes it sound. And you can only attain salvation and true success by having a pure and sound heart.

The *qalb* or 'heart' referred to here is not the pump in your breast that pushes blood around your body but rather the centre or locus of your personality which pumps out your desires and motivations and which makes you conduct yourself as you do. It is this *qalb* that lies at your centre and dictates your actions which is the key to your ultimate success. Thus, with reference to the Day of Judgement, the Quran declares:

[It will be a Day] *when neither wealth nor children shall profit,* [and when] *only he* [will be saved] *who comes before God with a sound heart* [free of evil]. [al-Shuara 26: 88-89.]

This point is more elaborately made in a *hadith* in which the Prophet says:

Listen [to me] carefully. There is a lump of flesh in the body – if it is set right and made good, the entire body becomes good and healthy; but if it becomes diseased, the entire body becomes diseased. Remember well – it is the Heart. (*Bukhari.*)

If the heart is the key to ultimate salvation and success, it may, likewise, be the seat of much corruption and open doors to many evils. It may facilitate the corruption of political and economic activities and ultimately the social institutions of a society. Where such a state prevails, the Quran suggests that it is because people, individually, have become diseased in their hearts. [al-Baqara 2: 10.] In this state, people stop seeing and doing what is right. The Quran explains that this is not because they have become blind in their eyes but because their hearts have become blind. [al-Hajj 22: 46.] This blindness only draws them nearer to the ultimate chastisement.

It is the heart, as the decider of our ultimate fate, that must then be the starting point of any *tazkiya* programme to purify this heart and then summon it to the service of mankind.

Ibn al-Qayyim, one of the great scholars of Islam, states in his *Kitab al-Adhkar* (The Book of Remembrance), that 'the heart which is devoid of the remembrance of Allah is a heart that is dead'; it is dead even and long before the body carrying the heart reaches its grave. Indeed, this living body that carries the heart is the heart's grave. Ibn al-Qayyim's statement is reminiscent of the *hadith* of the Prophet which states: 'The difference between someone who remembers his Lord and someone who does not is like the difference between the living and the dead.' (*Bukhari.*) The statement is also reminiscent of the following verse of the Quran: *Do not become like those who forget Allah and Allah makes them forget themselves. It is they who are truly deprived.* [al-Hashr 59: 19.]

The purpose of *tazkiya* is to ensure that the heart never falls into a sorry state of being and that it is always alive with the remembrance of God. *Prosperous indeed is one who purifies himself and remembers the name of his Guardian-Lord, and prays* [unto Him]. [al-Ala 87: 14-15.] The Prophet further emphasised the importance of *dhikr* when he said to his Companions: 'Shall I not inform you of the best of your actions, the purest in the sight of your Lord, which raises your rank to the highest, which is better for you than spending gold and silver, better than meeting your enemy so that you strike at their necks and they strike at yours?' They replied: 'Yes, indeed,' and he said: 'It is the remembrance of Allah.' (*Tirmidhi.*)

Strive then, to fill all your moments, all your thoughts and all your actions with His remembrance. Recite *tasbih* or words of glorification and praise to punctuate all your actions and achievements.


### THE MEANING OF *DHIKR*

What is the precise meaning of '*dhikr*'? What is its scope and what does it entail? Does it simply involve certain utterances of the tongue, like *Subhanallah* (I glorify Allah's absolute perfection), *Alhamdu lillah* (All praise be to Allah), *Allahu Akbar* (Allah is the Greatest), *La ilaha illallah* (There is no god but Allah) and the recitation of some other selected verses of the

Quran, or is there more to it? Of course, such utterances of the tongue and recitation of verses of the Quran are important. In fact they are very important forms of *dhikr* for, indeed, the best forms of remembrance are those that involve both the heart and the tongue. You must understand, however, that the scope of *dhikr* is considerably wider.

*Dhikr* must not only be felt by the heart and uttered with the tongue, but must also effect *amal salih* or good deeds. Significantly, Ibn al-Qayyim suggests that *dhikr* encompasses 'any and every particular moment when you are thinking, saying or doing things which Allah likes'. Hence, if your conversation is filled with the words of God, this is *dhikr* and if all your actions are in accordance with His will, this is *dhikr*. Indeed Allah commends that we remember Him while standing, sitting and even while reclining. This is only possible if *dhikr* embraces every single aspect of life. Consider for example the following verse of the Quran where *dhikr* is emphasised in both Prayer and business activity:

> *O Believers, when the call to Prayer is sounded on the Day of Congregation, hasten to Allah's remembrance and leave all worldly commerce. This is for your own good, if you but knew it. And when the Prayer is finished, then disperse through the land, and seek of the bounty of Allah; and remember Allah frequently that you may prosper.* [al-Jumua 62: 9-10.]

Attending the *Salat al-Jumua*, listening to the *khutba* or sermon and performing the congregational Prayer are all well known as forms of *dhikr*. But in our worldly pursuits as well we are urged to remember Allah even more often.

We may thus conclude, that attending to your personal needs, earning a livelihood and spending on your family are all forms of *dhikr*. But of course, they can only be *dhikr* if, alongside with the relevant *adhkar* or supplications in the heart and on the tongue, they are done in obedience to Allah, for His pleasure, to attain *Janna*. Otherwise, as the Quran warns us, far from being *dhikr*, they may have the opposite effect:

> *Let not your worldly possessions and your children make you neglectful of Allah's remembrance. But spend in the way of Allah.* [al-Munafiqun 63: 9-10.]

## THE METHODS OF *DHIKR*

We have thus far discussed the significance, meaning and scope of *dhikr*. Let us now turn to the various forms and methods of *dhikr*. How do we remember Allah in the morning and evening, during the day and at night and while standing, sitting or reclining? There are basically two forms of *dhikr*. The first involves continuous and sustained inner awareness of Allah in all that we say and do in our daily lives. The second involves mechanisms, whether performed individually or collectively, that help to develop the first.

### 1. Sustained Awareness of Allah

Let us begin with a discussion of the first form and its methods. How can you remember Allah throughout the normal course of your day without withdrawing from the routine of your daily worldly life? How can you ensure that your personal life, family life, professional life and other activities all continue in full swing, and yet, at the same time, ensure that your life as a whole – every moment of it – is permeated with remembrance of Allah? Such an all-pervading *dhikr* can be an onerous task, but one you can accomplish – with some ease. Let me remind you of four states of consciousness that you must strive to develop by remembering certain things, absorbing them and reminding yourself of them often.

ONE: *Say to yourself*: I am in Allah's presence; He is watching me.

If ever you are alone, He is the second and that if you are two, He is the third. *He is with you wherever you are.* [al-Mujadala 58: 7.] *He is nearer to you than your jugular vein.* [Qaf 50: 16.] He is watching everything that you do and hearing everything that you say. He is ever present and His knowledge is all encompassing. Remind yourself of this as often as you can, and throughout the day – every time you begin a new task, and every time you speak. Indeed, your aim should be to impress this on your heart in such a way that it ultimately becomes your very breath. When the Prophet was asked by a Companion about the best method of purifying himself, he replied: 'You should always remember that Allah is with you wherever you are.' (*Tirmidhi.*)

TWO: *Say to yourself*: Everything I have has been given to me by Allah.

All that there is – surrounding you, on you and in you – comes from Allah alone. There is none that creates or gives anything but Allah. [al-Nahl 16: 78; Ya Sin 36: 33-35.] Therefore, reflect upon all the *baraka* or blessing that He has created you with and be thankful to Him. In all the *adhkar* that the Prophet has taught us, *hamd* or gratefulness to Allah is a constant theme. Many of these *adhkar* are simple to learn, and indeed, it was the most simple of his *adhkar* that he used most frequently. When the Prophet rose in the morning, he would say *Alhamdu lillah*; whenever he ate or drank he would say *Alhamdu lillah*; and even when he relieved himself he would give thanks to Allah. Learn as many of the *adhkar* as you can, and throughout the day, as you witness all that Allah has blessed you with, punctuate your day with these *adhkar*.

If ever you appear to be short of things to be thankful for, recall the *hadith* of the Prophet: 'There are 360 joints in the body and for each joint you must give a *sadaqa* [thanks or charity] each day.' (*Bukhari*.) You must give a *sadaqa* for each one of them because without any one of them you will be incomplete and handicapped. You must do this on a daily basis for should any one of them become damaged one day, you will similarly become incapacitated.

Additionally, you may remind yourself that, as we now know from our knowledge of human physiology, your heart beats 72 times a minute. Every time it beats, it does so with the permission of Allah. The moment He withdraws that permission, the heart will stop beating and your life will certainly come to an end. If you feel that there is nothing else to thank Allah for, then thank Him for the life that He has given you – for, so long as there is life, there is hope.

**THREE:** *Say to yourself:* Nothing in this world can happen without His permission.

Everything lies in the hands of Allah. No harm can befall you and no benefit can reach you except as Allah ordains. It is as the

Quran informs us: *If God should touch you with misfortune, none can remove it but He; and if He should touch you with good fortune, He has power over all things. He alone holds sway over His creatures; He is the All-Wise, the All-Aware.* [al-Anam 6: 17-18.]

The Prophet Muhammad would supplicate to Allah after each Prayer:

O Allah, whatever You want to give me, no one can stop it from coming to me and whatever You want to prevent from coming to me, nobody can give to me.

Prayer after Prayer, you should recite these beautiful words. And beyond that, remind yourself as much as you can and throughout the day, especially as you expect something to happen, or not to happen, that everything happens only as He commands, and by His permission.

FOUR: *Say to yourself*: I am going to return to Allah one day and that day could be today.

You do not know when you will leave this world. It may be that the coming morning is your last morning, or perhaps the coming evening is your last evening. Indeed, it may be that this hour is your last hour, or even, that this moment is your last moment. Such an uncertainty does not, of course, justify a complete withdrawal from this life so as to prepare for the Next in some monastic fashion. It is important, however, that you are always conscious of this uncertainty, to the extent that it motivates you to spend every moment of your remaining life seriously, considering it as a gift from Allah and spending the resources He has blessed you with – time, ability and energy – as He has advised. Then, and only then, will your life have achieved what is required of it, and your return will achieve what is required of it. To help you attain this state of consciousness, recall and reflect upon the following Quranic verse as much as you can and throughout the day: *from Allah we came and to Him we shall return.* [al-Baqara 2: 156.]

These are the four states of consciousness that can help us achieve a life completely devoted to the remembrance of Allah. To try to reach these four states simultaneously, and with sincerity, can only purify you. To try in a determined fashion to reach these four states will lead you inevitably to Paradise.

## 2. Specific Methods of Dhikr

For us to achieve a continuous and sustained awareness of Him, Allah, in His Wisdom and Mercy, has taught us some very specific mechanisms of *dhikr*. These include: the formal *ibada* – *Salat, Sawm, Zakat* and *Hajj*; *tilawa* of the Quran, *dua, istighfar* and *tawba*, seeking the company of the righteous and *dawa*. Together these mechanisms or methods constitute what we have classified above as the second form of *dhikr*, but here we may sub-divide them into two groups: those that can be performed individually and those that are performed collectively.

## 3. Methods of Individual Dhikr

The foremost of the specific methods pertaining to individual *dhikr* include the *fard* or obligatory *ibada*. Allah has said in a *hadith qudsi*:

My servant does not draw near to Me with anything more loved by Me than what I have made obligatory. (*Bukhari.*)

Each specific formal *ibada* or act of servitude to God, has been ordained as an instrument of self development. When we observe our *Salat* regularly at the proper times, together in congregation whenever possible, with clear intentions and sincerity; when we fast in the month of *Ramadan* with awareness and resolve; when we give *Zakat* as soon as it falls due with a generous heart; and when we fulfil the obligations of *Hajj* as soon as we have the means, we will gain that special closeness to Allah that He has promised. Indeed, we may get even closer to God through additional observance of these specific formal acts of servitude, for Allah continues in the *hadith qudsi*:

My servant continues to draw nearer to Me with additional devotions until I love him. When I love him, I become the hearing with which he hears, the sight with which he sees, the hand with which he strikes and the foot with which he walks. Were he to ask for something I would surely give it, and were he to ask for refuge, I would surely grant him refuge. (*Bukhari.*)

For each specific *fard ibada*, there is an additional *nafl* or supererogatory equivalent. These are as follows:

- The *Sunna Salat* – these include the additional Prayers before and after the five obligatory ones, but just as importantly the *Tahajjud* Prayer.
- The *Sunna* Fasts – as recommended by the Prophet and to be practised on Mondays and Thursdays of each week, the

thirteenth, fourteenth and fifteenth day of each lunar calendar month, and other recommended days in the Islamic year.

- *Sadaqa fi sabilillah* – the giving of voluntary charity, however much and whenever one can afford, for the pleasure of Allah.
- The *Umra* – performance of the voluntary short pilgrimage.

In addition to the *fard* and their related *nafl ibada*, there are two further specific methods of individual *dhikr*: the first is the daily recitation of the Quran, and the second, frequent *dua* or supplications to Allah for forgiveness, guidance and fulfilment of needs.

Let us explore each of these specific methods pertaining to individual *dhikr* in more detail, particularly as instruments of *tazkiya* and *dhikr*.

## A. Salat

*Salat* is the foremost form of *ibada* that Allah Himself has prescribed for us. In His own words He commands: *Establish regular Prayer that you may remember Me.* [Ta Ha 20: 14.] The whole purpose of *Salat* is to be ever-conscious of Allah, the Creator, Lord and Sustainer of all things. When we perform *Salat* we involve our tongue, our heart, our mind and indeed our whole body. In this sense, *Salat* is indeed, one of the most comprehensive forms of *dhikr*. It is perhaps for this reason that Allah states in a *hadith qudsi*: 'Out of all the ways through which My servant gets closer to Me, *Salat* is the dearest to Me.' (*Bukhari*.) It is unfortunate, therefore, that we do not always take full advantage of this gift. We may pray five times each day but few of us remain conscious for long that in Prayer we have the best means to develop a strong connection with Allah. We may compare the obligatory *Salat* to bathing five times a day. If after such frequent bathing, your body remains dirty, then we may question the usefulness and efficacy of such bathing.

Similarly, if after regular observance of Prayer your heart remains unmoved, your morals remain corrupt and your conduct remains unaffected, we may question the usefulness and efficacy of your Prayer? If you enter into *Salat* and come out of it the same person, then you have missed something, and you may have missed a golden opportunity to achieve something great.

Remember, though, *Salat* is an obligation. Whether your heart is attentive or not, it must be performed. You cannot give up Prayer because to you it appears useless. Don't give up the obligation but try to infuse it with the purpose it seeks to serve – remembrance of Allah.

How can you improve the quality of your *Salat*? Remember, first and foremost, that as soon as you commence your *Salat*, Shaytan makes it his duty to fill your mind with anything and everything but thoughts of Allah. [al-Araf 7: 16–17.] For, Shaytan is aware that your remembrance of Allah will draw you closer to Him, so he tries ceaselessly to disengage your mind and heart from such remembrance, so that you may never achieve that closeness. The most important hurdle to overcome from the outset, therefore, is absentmindedness. It is this that destroys the quality of your Prayer, for Allah does not accept the Prayers of a wandering mind. The Prophet Muhammad said:

> God does not accept the Prayers of an individual until his
> heart achieves in it what his body has achieved.[1]

The ability to concentrate in Prayer may be improved by undertaking adequate psychological, mental and physical preparation before the Prayer and by utilising certain techniques whilst performing the Prayer. Below we discuss some of them.

### i. Psychological and Mental Preparation

- The planning of your daily activities should revolve around the five daily *Salat*. [al-Ma'arij 70: 22-23.] Do not plan everything else and then try to fit Prayer into your busy schedule.
- Ensure that you are conversant with all the rules and regulations governing your Prayer. Research in depth the Quranic verses and *ahadith* relating to the virtues of *Salat*.
- Be punctual with your Prayer. [al-Nisa 4: 103.] Get into the habit of praying at the earliest hour. Do not procrastinate. The Prophet said, 'The deed most loved by Allah is Prayer performed on time.' (*Muslim.*)
- Pray as much of your *fard Salat* in *jama'a* or congregation as is possible. [al-Baqara 2: 43.]
- Avoid praying in a state in which you are mentally and physically fatigued. [al-Nisa 4: 43.]
- Rid your mind of all evil thoughts and ideas. [al-Maun 107: 4-6.]
- Keep your mind free of worldly worries and engagements.
- Plan what *ayat/duas* you are going to recite.
- If you do not understand Arabic learn the meaning of what you recite in your Prayer.
- Remind yourself that engaging in Prayer offers you an opportunity to release yourself from the pressures and tensions of this world. The Prophet has said that in Prayer was placed the comfort of his eyes. Therefore cherish the opportunity to remove the shackles and burdens of this world from your shoulders. [al-Baqara 2: 45.]

- Use your Prayer to remain focused on your mission in life – to bring your entire being to serve only Allah.
- Use your Prayer as a source of strength, inspiration and enthusiasm for your life and activities.

## ii. *Physical Preparation*

- Fulfil all your personal needs before you commence your Prayer, for example, thirst, hunger and calls of nature.
- Pray in a pure physical state. Perform your *wudu* with care and perfection. [al-Maida 5: 6.]
- Although the whole earth is a *masjid* or a place of worship, choose a place that is clean.
- Pray in an environment free of noise and one where there is no distraction.
- Adorn yourself with clean and respectable clothes for Allah has said: *O Children of Adam, wear your best clothes at every place of worship.* [al-Araf 7: 31.]

## iii. *Performing Your Prayer*

- Assess your mental readiness for Prayer before its commencement, during the various postures with its attendant recitations, after each *raka* and ultimately at the end. Try to make improvements at each stage.
- Pray with humility both in your mental state and in your physical manner. Pray with hope and awe, asking Allah for His mercy and forgiveness.
- Remind yourself continually that you are talking to the most important 'Being' in your life – your Creator and Sustainer.

He is in front of you. You are facing Him and you are involved in a dialogue with Him. [al-Alaq 96: 19.]

- Commence your Prayer by seeking Allah's help and protection from the influences of Shaytan. [al-Nahl 16: 98.]
- Lower your gaze while praying and do not allow the physical environment to distract you. Anas related that the Prophet said: 'My dear son, be sure to avoid being distracted during Prayer, for, to become distracted while praying is a disaster.' (*Tabarani*.)
- Use a variety of Quranic verses and *duas* in your Prayer to achieve greater concentration and awareness.
- Adopt a whispering technique in your recitation. This will increase your ability to remain focused on what you are saying. [al-Isra 17: 110.]
- As you recite the Quran, translate it into your own language so that your attention is held. As you concentrate upon the meaning and implications of the words, *insha Allah*, all thoughts of worldly ideas will disappear.
- On each occasion that you recite the *Sifat* or attributes of Allah in *ruku* and *sajda*, consider how indebted you are and how grateful you should be to Allah and express your true emotions.
- Utilise the occasion of *sajda* to make additional *dua* to Allah. The Prophet said: 'A servant is nearest to his Lord when he is in *sajda*, so increase your supplication when in *sajda*.' (*Muslim*.)
- Make your Prayer of moderate duration so that you do not become physically and mentally tired but be aware that while in Prayer you must take your time praying.
- Give due regard to the proper performance of all the physical postures.
- Pray as if it is your last Prayer. The Messenger of God said: 'When you stand up to pray, perform your prayer as if it were

your last, do not say anything you will have to make excuses for tomorrow, and resolve to place no hope in what is in the hands of men.' (*Ahmad.*)

Performing your Prayer in a satisfactory manner should lead to a radical change in the way you lead your daily life. *Salat* must be as the Quran states: *Surely, Salat prevents indecency and evil.* [al-Ankabut 29: 45.] Your improved and more disciplined life will in turn help the quality of your Prayer to increase even more. The two should feed one another and continuously reinforce each other.

Note that there is punishment for a Prayer not performed satisfactorily. It will be a witness against you rather than a witness for you on the Day of Judgement. However, the reward for a Prayer well performed is immeasurable. The Prophet said: 'If a man performs two *rakas* of *Salat* without the distraction of any worldly thought, all his previous sins will be forgiven.' (*Bukhari.*)

## *iv.* Tahajjud Salat

Even though it is not obligatory, try to establish *Tahajjud Salat* as part of your nightly activities. The Prophet said: 'The best Prayer after the *fard* Prayer is the night Prayer.' (*Muslim.*)

One of the characteristics of the *Ibadur Rahman* or Servants of the Most Merciful, is that they get up at night and perform *Tahajjud Salat.* [al-Furqan 25: 64.] *Qiyam al-layl* or night vigil is a source of great spiritual energy. The Prophet has said:

Keep up *qiyam al-layl.* It was the way of the virtuous who came before you, it draws you nearer to your Lord, atones for your sins, forbids you from evil and protects the body from sickness. (*Tirmidhi.*)

When a man wakes up his wife at night and they pray two *rakas* (units) together, they are written down among the men and women who remember Allah. (*Abu Dawud.*)

The Quran also commends the one who utilises the early hours of each day to engage in remembrance of Allah: *Is one who worships devoutly during the hours of the night prostrating himself or standing* [in adoration] *and who places his hope in the mercy of His Lord* – [like one who does not]? *Say: 'Are those equal – those who know and those who do not know?' It is those who are endowed with understanding that receive admonition.* [al-Zumar 39: 9.]

## B. *Sawm*

*Sawm* or fasting is another important instrument of *tazkiya*. It holds a unique status among all other forms of *ibada*. In a *hadith qudsi* we are told:

Every good deed of a man is granted manifold increase, ten to seven hundred times. But Allah says: Fasting is an exception; it is exclusively for Me, and I will give reward for it as much as I wish. (*Bukhari, Muslim.*)

The fruit of fasting ought to be that rich inner quality which the Quran calls *taqwa*:

*O Believers! Fasting is ordained for you, even as it was ordained for those before you, that you might attain taqwa.* [al-Baqara 2: 183.]

*Taqwa* is the most basic prerequisite for being guided by Allah. It entails God-consciousness, a sense of responsibility, accountability, dedication and awe. It is that which prompts and inspires us to fulfil our responsibilities towards the Creator. *Taqwa* is the main criterion by which Allah values the deeds of a Muslim. The Quran states: *Surely the noblest among you in the sight of God is the most God-fearing of you. Verily God is All-Knowing and All-Wise.* [al-Hujurat 49: 13.]

We must strive to the utmost to inculcate *taqwa* in our lives as Allah has ordained: *Take provisions with you, but the best of provisions is taqwa. So remain conscious of Me, O you who are endowed with insight.* [al-Baqara 2: 197.]

Fasting teaches us to remember Allah. It helps to instil in us certain attributes and qualities which develop our *taqwa*. We discuss some of these below.

### i. Fulfilling Allah's Wishes

While fasting, the most basic physical needs – food, water and sleep – are readily and joyfully sacrificed. Hunger and thirst are no longer harmful; Allah's displeasure is harmful. Physical pleasures no longer hold any lure; Allah's rewards do. The scale of values is turned upside down. The measures of comfort and pain, success and failure are radically changed. However, whatever the physical discomfort, the mortification of the flesh is certainly not the desired object. The gifts of Allah are there to be enjoyed but limits by Him must also be strictly observed. Once the sun has set, the fast must be broken and the sooner the better. All that was forbidden during the fasting hours, at His command, becomes permissible again, at His command. Similarly, eating before dawn is strongly encouraged even though the hour is early for it provides the necessary strength for the rigours of the day ahead. Fasting and praying are obvious acts of worship but eating also constitutes a form of worship.

### ii. Will-power

Fasting strengthens our will-power. The Prophet has said: '*Sawm* is a shield [or a screen or a shelter from the Hell-fire].' (*Bukhari*.) The regime of dawn-to-sunset abstinence from food, drink and sex, for the sake of Allah alone, internalises the lesson that we must never enter, acquire or even touch that which does not belong to us under the law of Allah. A man can no longer remain a slave to his own self-indulgence as he prepares for the arduous journey on the road to His Lord.

For many, it is difficult to see the value of long hours of hunger, thirst and sleeplessness. Productivity losses are difficult to accept in an age that has tried to promote economic growth at all costs. According to Islam, however, we are created to live a life of total submission to the One and Only Allah, and this purpose must be paramount in all scales of values. Fasting is crucial to this understanding. It shows that its purpose, like Allah's guidance through His Prophets and Books and all the rituals of worship, is to train us how we must live totally and unreservedly in submission to Allah.

### iii. Protection From Shaytan

Fasting enables us to protect ourselves from the evil influences of Shaytan. While fasting: 'Eyes should refrain from seeing evil, ears from hearing evil, tongues from speaking evil and hearts from reflecting evil.' (*Bukhari*.) The Prophet also said: 'Five things break a man's fast: lying, backbiting, scandal-mongering, perjury and a lustful gaze.' (*Azdi*.)[2]

## C. *Tilawa* of the Quran

The most important nourishment for the *qalb* or heart is the Quran. Those who lived in the time of the Prophet received their training and inspiration from the Quran. It was their guide, their light and their leader. Likewise, it must be your constant companion.

The Quran contains a treasure house of soul-stirring inspiration and wisdom. We can and should spend hours in understanding the Quran. There are thousands of pages of *tafsir* or Quranic exegesis to read. But we must know that the real test of benefiting from the Quran lies somewhere else. The Quran says that when people really listen to it, their faith must increase:

> *Believers are those who, when God is mentioned, feel a tremor in their hearts, and whenever His Messages are conveyed to them their faith is strengthened.* [al-Anfal 8: 2]

Where there is a fire, there is smoke. If the 'fire' of *iman* has been lit inside the heart, there must be smoke, and you will see that those who truly listen to the Quran, their eyes begin to well up with tears which trickle down their cheeks.

Nowadays, when we listen to the Quran or read it, our hearts are not moved, nor do our lives change. It is as if water is falling on a rock and flowing away. Our task is to replace this hard rock with soft absorbent soil so that the Quran may nourish the seed that has been planted. We should always study the Quran as if it is being revealed to us today. One of the greatest injustices we do to the Quran is that we read it as if it were something of the past and of no relevance to the present.

Remember that the whole purpose of the Quran is to guide you and to change you by bringing you into submission to Allah. As you read it, also try to live by what it invites you to. If it does not have any impact upon your actions and if you do not observe what it enjoins and avoid what it prohibits, then you are not getting nearer to the Quran. In fact, one who reads the Quran and does not try to act upon it may be more likely to be cursed and punished by Allah. The Prophet said:

> Many of the hypocrites in my *Umma* will be from among the reciters. (*Ahmad.*)

> He is not a Believer in the Quran who makes *halal* or lawful what has been made *haram* or prohibited. (*Tirmidhi.*)

It is also narrated that many Companions, like Uthman and Abdullah ibn Masud, once they learnt ten verses from the Prophet did not move further unless they had 'learnt' it fully – both in understanding and in action; that is how they sometimes spent years in learning only one *sura* or chapter.

If you sincerely start changing your life according to the Quran, Allah will certainly help you and make the path easy for you. Allah reassures us in the Quran:

> *Those who say, 'Our Lord is Allah,' and continue upon the straight way, the angels descend upon them: 'Do not fear, nor be grieved, and receive glad tidings of the Garden which you were promised. We are your supporters in this world and in the*

*Hereafter. And for you therein is whatever your souls desire, and for you therein is whatever you ask for.'* [al-Fussilat 41: 30-31.]

### i.   The Method of Tilawa

*Tilawa* or recitation is an act in which your whole person – soul, heart, mind, tongue and body – should participate. Thus, to recite the Quran, as it deserves to be recited, is not a light task; but neither is it impossible nor difficult. Otherwise, the Quran could not have been meant for everyone; nor could it be the mercy and the guidance that it surely is. There are a few obligations regarding recitation of the Quran which you should keep in mind.

- Read the Quran every day; in fact do not consider a day complete without it. It is better to read regularly, even if it be a small portion, than to read large sections, but only occasionally.
- Every day you must also find time to memorise as much of the Quran as you can. You can start with small *Suras* and short passages and then move on to longer portions.
- Read as much of the Quran in Prayer as you can, especially during the night, after the *Isha*, before the *Fajr* and in the *Fajr*, as nothing is more effective in making you attuned to the Quran and ensuring you absorb it than reading it in the night or in the morning. Indeed, the early hours of the morning is a particularly blessed time to recite the Quran: *Indeed, the recitation of the Quran at dawn is ever witnessed.* [al-Isra 17: 78.]
- Read the Quran in a good voice, as we have been told: 'Beautify the Quran with your voices' (*Abu Dawud*); but also remember that the real beauty is the beauty that comes with

44

the fear of Allah in the heart: 'His recitation and voice are the most beautiful so that when you hear him, you think he fears Allah.' (*Darimi.*)

• Read the Quran with concentration and understanding. The Prophet told Ibn Umar not to finish reading the Quran in less than a week. He also said that one who finishes it in less than three days does not understand any of it. One Companion said that he preferred to read a short *Sura* like *al-Qaria* with proper understanding than to hastily finish long ones like *al-Baqara* and *Al Imran*.

### ii. Your Constant Companion

The Messenger of Allah, peace be upon him, has said, 'I am leaving you with two *murshids*.' The term *murshid* refers to the one who guides to the right path. The first is the talking *murshid*, the Quran, and the second is the silent *murshid, mawt* or death. As much as you keep in touch with the Quran and as long as you keep in touch with the idea that you are going to return to Allah and give an account of your actions, so you will stay on the right path. You don't need any other training programme or another 'person' to guide you. These two *murshids* are enough and everyone has them at his disposal.

### D. Dua

*Dua,* supplicating to Allah, is 'the spirit of *ibada.*' (*Tirmidhi.*) Indeed, it is a demand of Islam. The Prophet has exhorted us: 'Allah is angry with him who does not ask [anything] from Him.' (*Tirmidhi.*)

Each of your *duas* must capture the spirit of your goals and ambitions. You must offer them with humility and sincerity. The Prophet Muhammad has taught us some of the most beautiful supplications – said in beautiful words, encapsulating beautiful ideas, through beautiful ways of asking. Reflect upon the following *dua* as an example:

I am Your servant, I am at Your door. I am a poor man, I am at Your door. I am a helpless man, I am at Your door. I am a sinner, I am at Your door. I am Your guest, You invited me to come, I am at Your door. So have mercy on me.

There are many similar *duas* that move the heart and make tears flow from one's eyes. Additionally, there are *duas* that were part of the Prophet's daily routine: Prayers said while eating, drinking, sleeping, entering and leaving home. All of these *duas* must be memorised and utilised, for they remind us of Allah and His Omniscience.

But how exactly can these *duas* be used by us to remember Allah? Allow me to share with you one method, which can be utilised on a daily basis. The Prophet Muhammad taught us in one *hadith:*

After performing the dawn [*Subh*] Prayer, before you utter another word, say: O Allah, save me from Hell-fire [*Allahumma ajirni min an-nar*], seven times. If you die that day, Allah will decree that you be saved from Hell-fire. After performing the sunset [*Maghrib*] Prayer, before you utter another word, say: O Allah, save me from Hell-fire, seven times. If you die that night, Allah will decree that you be saved from Hell-fire. (*Abu Dawud.*)

Whenever I recite this *dua*, I use a method of recitation and reflection which helps me remember the final meeting with my Lord. For each of the seven times I recite this *dua*, I reflect on one of the stages from the Quran of the *Akhira*: the time of death; the sojourn and questioning by the angel in the grave; the time of rising and standing before Allah; the time of giving an account of all that has been done and seeing our actions displayed before us; and the passage over the *Sirat* or Bridge, then entering either Paradise or Hell.

All of these are stages of the journey. Each time that I bring to my mind one of those stages, even for the briefest moment, I supplicate to Him: 'O Allah save me from the fire.'

This exercise in supplication takes me about five minutes after both *Salat al-Fajr* and *Salat al-Maghrib*. There is, however, no prescribed format to follow. You can select and form your own short course of *duas* based on the Prophetic traditions and use this as part of the regular way in which you remember Allah.

Finally, it is important for us to observe the etiquette of *dua* so that we may derive maximum benefit from them. These have been beautifully summarised by *Imam* al-Nawawi, where he lists ten prime conditions and dispositions that we should observe:

- Seek out the blessed times of Prayer: The Day of the Standing on the plain of Arafat [during *Hajj*]; the month of fasting [*Ramadan*]; Fridays [days of congregational prayers]; and during the night [especially the last third of it].
- Seek out the blessed moments for Prayer when the heart is receptive and tender: immediately after the five daily prescribed Prayers; between the call to Prayer (*adhan*) and the final call to Prayer (*iqama*); when breaking fast; while on the field of battle; when rainfall occurs; and when bowing down [*sujud*] in Prayer,

for the Prophet said, 'The worshipper is closest to his Lord while bowing down. So pray much then.' (*Muslim.*)

- Face the direction of Makka and raise the hands [with palms spread upward] to the level of the shoulders.
- Voice supplications in a moderate tone that is neither too loud nor too soft.
- Prayers need not be said in a forced rhymed prose [an often natural form in Arabic].
- Implore God with humility and reverence.
- Be fervent in Prayer and optimistic of the answer. Sufyan ibn Uyayna stated: 'What a person knows of himself should never stop him from supplicating to God for He answered the most evil of creatures, Iblis [Shaytan], when he said, "Give me respite until the Day they are resurrected." God said, "You are of the respited ones." [al-Araf 7: 14.]
- Repeat requests, preferably three times, and don't be impatient or despondent in waiting for an answer.
- Begin supplication with the mention of God [His Names, praises and attributes] before asking of Him, and entreat God to send His blessings and peace upon the Prophet.
- Strive for inner purity with repentance and sincere devotion.

### E. *Istighfar* and *tawba*

The process of *dhikr* must involve the recognition and confession of our faults, mistakes and aberrations and turning to Allah in asking for forgiveness with the expectation of His *rahma* or mercy. *Istighfar* is seeking forgiveness while *tawba* is turning away from our faults and returning to Allah, to His Path. When Allah desires good for a Believer, He gives him awareness of his faults. The Messenger of Allah when questioned about the nature of virtue and sin replied: 'Virtue is to have good morals, sin is what pricks your heart and you dislike what people come to know about it.' (*Muslim*.) Likewise, whenever we are faced with a dilemma or uncertainty in our daily life we have been exhorted by the Prophet to observe the following guidelines:

> Seek a verdict from your heart. Virtue is that which your soul and heart feel satisfied with. Sin is that which troubles the soul and about which the heart is uneasy and confused, even though people may give their legal opinions in its favour. (*Muslim*.)

But what exactly does the process of *istighfar* and *tawba* entail? Ali ibn Abi Talib, may Allah be pleased with him, once saw a Bedouin repeating words of repentance in a great hurry. 'This is fake repentance', remarked Ali ibn Abi Talib. The Bedouin asked, 'What is true repentance?' Ali ibn Abi Talib explained that there are six elements in an act of true repentance:

- You should regret what has happened.
- You should discharge the duty which you have neglected.
- You should restore the right that you have misappropriated.
- You should apologise to the one whom you have caused injury.
- You should resolve not to repeat the act.
- You should dedicate yourself entirely to the service of Allah so that you may experience the rigours of obedience as you may have relished the pleasure of transgression.

We may now ask the question – when is the best time during the course of the day to perform *istighfar*? There is of course no special time to seek the forgiveness of Allah. But perhaps one of the best occasions is the early hours of each day which the Quran declares is the time utilised by true Believers to draw closer to their Lord: *they forsake their beds to cry unto their Lord in fear and hope.* [al-Sajda 32: 16.] The significance of this early part of each day has also been explained by the Prophet as follows:

> Our Lord descends every night to the nearest Heaven when only the last third of the night remains, and says: 'Is anyone praying that I may answer him? Is anyone seeking forgiveness that I may forgive him? Is anyone asking that I may give to him?' And this continues until dawn. (*Tirmidhi*.)

You should therefore start each day by taking an account of yourself: seek forgiveness for the wrongs you have done and make the intention not to repeat these mistakes. In this way you shall become free from these sins. Every day you may commit a sin, but if every day you come sincerely to Allah, then every day He will forgive you. Such is His love and blessings for us. Allah reminds us:

> *When My servants ask you concerning Me, I am indeed close [to them]. I listen to the Prayer of every supplicant when he calls on Me. Let them also, with a will, listen to My call, and believe in Me so that they may walk in the right way.* [al-Baqara 2: 186.]

While seeking the forgiveness of Allah, you must place your full trust and confidence in Allah for He always listens and answers the Prayers of His servants. In one *hadith qudsi,* Allah has reassured us:

> Son of Adam, so long as you keep calling upon Me and hoping for good from Me, I shall forgive you whatever you have done, and I do not mind. Son of Adam, were your sins to rise as high as the sky, and were you to ask Me for forgiveness, I would forgive you. Son of Adam, were you to come to Me with sins as large as would fill the earth, and meet Me having ascribed no partner to Me, I would bring you forgiveness as great as your sins. (*Tirmidhi.*)

### 4. Methods of Collective Dhikr

### A. Seeking the Company of the Righteous

*Dhikr* can also be performed collectively. The Prophet told us that the *baraka* or blessing of Allah is with those who gather and work as a unified *jama'a* for the cause of Islam: 'Allah's hand is upon the *jama'a*.' (*Tirmidhi.*) Indeed engaging in remembrance of Allah collectively is encouraged in many *ahadith.* The Prophet is reported to have said:

> If a group of people sit together remembering Allah, the angels will circle them, mercy will shroud them, peace will descend onto them and Allah will remember them among those with Him. (*Muslim.*)

*Dhikr* in a group may help teach those who do not know the desired *adhkar* and bring hearts together and strengthen their noble ties. To ensure that our company is always filled with remembrance of Allah, it is of paramount importance that we continuously seek the company of the righteous if we wish to be elevated in the eyes of Allah. Hasan al-Basri said in this regard:

> Sit in the company of scholars. They will be pleased to see your virtues and will forgive your mistakes. They will not rebuke you when you commit mistakes; rather, they will provide clear guidance. When it is necessary to testify, they will bear true testimony to your advantage.

You must be careful with the selection of friends, for your companionship can and must be a form of *dhikr*. The Messenger of God said: 'The best friend is the one who makes you remember Allah when you see him.' Also: 'Whosoever Allah wishes good for, He will grant him a righteous friend who will remind him if he forgets and aid him if he remembers.' And the Quran says: *Bind yourself with those who call upon Allah morning and evening.* [al-Kahf 18: 27-28.] As soon as you see the seed of *iman* planted in your heart and you recognise it in someone else's and you find that he agrees with you, you will feel ten times stronger. Social scientists have also discovered that group life is one of the most powerful forces to stimulate and improve the human being.

## B. *Witnessing Unto Mankind*

Life can only be filled with *dhikr* if you strive and invite others to the path of Allah, the same path that you have found. This is a necessary outcome of your faith in Allah. The Quran advises: *Make it* [the truth] *known to mankind, and do not conceal it!* [Al Imran 3: 187.] *Help one another to righteousness and taqwa and do not help one another to sin and transgression.* [al-Maida 5: 2.] *Encourage one another in the truth, and encourage one another in patience* [al-Asr 103: 3.] *Remind* [others of the truth] *in the event that this admonition profits. The reminder will be received by he who stands in awe* [of God]. [al-Ala 87: 9-10.]

As your *iman* increases, you will yearn to share with everybody what you think and know is right and call upon them to join your mission and the *jama'a* for *who is better in speech than one who calls to God, acts righteously and says: 'I am of those who surrender* [unto Him].' [al-Fussilat 41: 33.] Moreover, as the *jama'a* grows, your commitment to Allah will grow as well, each reinforcing the other. That is how the whole of life will become integrated in finding a path to Allah.

## ORGANISING YOUR *DHIKR*

To benefit fully from all of the specific methods of *dhikr* whether individual or collective that we have discussed, you must strive to implement them in a daily programme of devotions, study and reflection. Set aside some periods each day to devote yourself completely to these tasks and do not allow anything to interfere with them. Spending even a small amount of time each day will bring within you a feeling of closeness to Allah and familiarity with His *Din* or way of life.

You should begin each day with some *dhikr* after *Salat al-Fajr* and make the intention that your whole day will be spent in serving Allah. Follow up the *dhikr* with a *dua* seeking provisions for the day. Allah Himself has exhorted us in the Quran:

*O you who believe, celebrate the praises of Allah and do so often;
Glorify Him in the morning and the evening.* [al-Ahzab 33: 41.]

After the *dhikr* and *dua* spend some time reciting,
memorising and studying passages from the Quran for *indeed the
reading* [of the Quran] *at Fajr is witnessed.* [al-Isra 17: 78.] If it is
not possible to perform this task just after your *Fajr* Prayer then
you may do it later, but you should make an effort to ensure that
no day passes by without at least some reading and study of the
Quran. Allocate some time also to study from a comprehensive
syllabus which covers all the major aspects of Islam including
Quran and *hadith* sciences, *Sharia* or Islamic law, *Fiqh* or Islamic
jurisprudence, *Sira* or the life history of the Prophet Muhammad
and Islamic history.

Perhaps the best way to learn about Islam is to learn from
those who have more knowledge than you. You should therefore
strive to attend Islamic study circle sessions, camps and courses
whenever you can. At the same time, as much as you learn and
improve your understanding of Islam, do not forget your
obligations towards your family and those around you. Set aside
a period also to teach them about Islam.

As night falls just after the *Salat al-Maghrib*, it is again
recommended to make *dhikr*, seeking protection for the coming
night. And then to complete the day, just before retiring, reflect
on what you have accomplished – where you have succeeded
and where you have failed. As for your successes, thank Allah
that He has enabled you to do whatever you may have
accomplished. For your failures, you must ask for His
forgiveness with humility and sincerity. Close the day with
Prayers for help and guidance to overcome your weaknesses and
to develop your strengths.

**SUMMARY**

Your salvation and true success lies in the purification of your heart. The key to gaining a sound heart is remembrance of Allah.

There are basically two forms of *dhikr*. The first involves continuous and sustained inner awareness of Allah in all that we say and do in our daily lives through development of certain states of consciousness. They include a continuous realisation that Allah knows everything, that everything you possess has been given to you by Him; that He has power and control over everything; and ultimately, that you are going to return to Him. The second involves specific methods of *dhikr,* some of which may be performed individually and others which must be done collectively. Each of these specific methods helps to develop the other. When they are implemented in an organised programme of daily devotions, they will, *Insha Allah,* lead to a life of continuous remembrance of Allah.

May Allah enable us all to remember Him often and much and may He enable our hearts to find the satisfaction that we seek for *without doubt, in the remembrance of Allah hearts do find satisfaction.* [al-Rad 13: 28.]

## CHAPTER THREE

# *Relating to Allah*

EACH day in our *Salat*, we repeatedly make one humble request to Allah, our Creator and Sustainer: 'Guide us to the Straight Way.' [al-Fatiha 1: 6.] It is only by seeking and staying on the Straight Way, that we can ever hope to attain true salvation and success. What then must we do to ensure that Allah accepts and grants our Prayer? The Quran explains: *Whosoever holds on to Allah, he has already been guided onto a Straight Way.* [Al Imran 3: 101.]

### CHARACTERISTICS OF 'HOLDING ONTO ALLAH'

What exactly is *itisam billah* or 'holding onto Allah'? How do we develop a close attachment to and a close relationship with Allah? Let us explore the answers to these questions by reflecting upon the characteristics needed to 'hold onto Allah' and thus be among those who are shown the *Sirat al-Mustaqim* or the Straight Way.

### 1. *Thankfulness to Allah*

The first characteristic is being ever grateful and thankful to Allah for everything that you possess including your wealth, health, status, intellectual abilities and life. You should recognise that your very existence and your continuing sustenance are dependent on Allah. Whatever praise is due, therefore, it is due to Him alone, for nobody has the power or the resources to give you anything except by His will. His bounties and blessings are countless. Allah says:

> *Is, then, He who creates comparable to any that cannot create? Will you not, then, take heed? For should you try to count Allah's blessings, you could never compute them. Allah is, indeed, All-Forgiving, All Compassionate; and Allah knows all that you keep secret as well as all that you bring into the open.* [al-Nahl 16: 17-19.]

It is for this reason that Allah commanded the Prophet Ibrahim to say: *It is He who has created me, and so it is He who guides me; it is He who gives me to eat and drink, and whenever I am sick it is He who heals me; and it is He who makes me die and then will bring me to life. And upon Him, I pin my hope that He would forgive my sins on the Day of Judgement.* [al-Shuara 26: 77-82.]

In many places in the Quran, Allah compares the terms *shukr* and *kufr*. [al-Baqara 2: 152, Luqman 31: 12.] *Iman* implies *shukr* or gratefulness as opposed to *kufr* or ungratefulness. A *kafir* or unbeliever is ungrateful to the Being who has given him everything, whereas a *mumin* or Believer is one who is ever thankful for all that Allah has given him, for he recognises that *his Lord is Merciful and Loving.* [Hud 11: 90.]

*Iman*, therefore, requires due praise and thanks to Allah. If you are ungrateful, Allah is unaffected. If you become grateful, then you have taken the first step towards becoming a true Believer. It is for this reason that the Prophet exhorted us to 'love Allah as we benefit from His grace'. (*Tirmidhi.*)

In every moment and in every situation we see our Creator and Sustainer actively involved. He has not retired from this world. He is on His throne creating, distributing and administering everything. He governs and sustains all in the Universe. Not even a leaf can fall without His knowledge, His permission and His command. The Quran declares:

*He knows all that enters the earth and all that emerges therefrom, and that which comes down from the sky and all that ascends therein; and He is with you wherever you may be.* [al-Hadid 57: 4.]

Everything that happens to us – even events that we may consider to be personal afflictions or natural disasters – are from Him. So even in times of calamity and distress, there will be some good for us, provided we respond appropriately. The Prophet said:

How wonderful is the case of a Believer! There is good for him in whatever happens to him – and none, apart from him, enjoys this blessing. If he receives some bounty, he is grateful to Allah and this bounty brings good to him. And if some adversity befalls him, he is patient, and this affliction, too, brings good to him. (*Muslim.*)

Look again at the Quran; you will see that the very first introduction to Allah is *ar-Rahman ar-Rahim*. [al-Fatiha 1: 1.] Allah Himself is saying that He is the Most Merciful, He is the Most Compassionate. He shows and gives mercy to all, even those who continue to be ungrateful and rebellious towards Him: *Indeed God is the possessor of bounty for all people but most people do not give thanks.* [al-Baqara 2: 243.]

Reflect upon your own life and you will find innumerable occasions when Allah's 'hand' has been holding you and helping you. So often, we subconsciously use the expression 'thank God for this and that', without realising the full implications of our words. The Quran even reminded the Prophet Muhammad, peace be upon him, that in his early life, Allah's 'hand' was holding him and guiding him:

*Did He not find you an orphan and gave you shelter* [and care]? *And He found you wandering and He gave you guidance. And He found you in need and made you independent. Therefore, treat not the orphan with harshness, nor repulse him who asks.* [al-Duha 93: 6-10.]

This exhortation is not only for the Prophet but for all people. From the moment that we open our eyes in this world until the moment our souls leave our bodies, and even beyond, Allah's mercy, compassion and protection remain with us. Continuously remind yourself then that your entire existence is dependent on Him. He is your Lord and Sustainer. He is nourishing and sustaining all that exists. From morning until evening, your tongue must be moist with continuous praise of Allah. In return, Allah has promised increased *rahma* or mercy for you: *If you are grateful, I will surely give you more and more.* [Ibrahim 14: 7.]

This is the cornerstone of your faith and the Islamic way of life. If you learn this first lesson, you will begin the process of 'holding onto Allah'. *And whoever is grateful, he is only grateful for the benefit of his own self* [Luqman 31: 12] *for surely if it was not for the grace of God on you and His mercy, you would have been among the losers* [al-Baqara 2: 64].

## 2. Worshipping Allah

Out of that sense of receiving everything from Allah, comes another important character trait of those who 'hold onto Allah' – exclusive worship of Allah. The Quran states that true *taqwa* cannot be attained until all your actions in life are done exclusively to earn the pleasure of Allah:

> *O mankind, worship your Lord alone, who has created you and those before you, so that you may attain taqwa or righteousness.* [al-Baqara 2: 21.]

You must ensure that your *qalb* or heart submits totally and wholeheartedly to the Creator. Allah says: *O you who believe! Enter into Islam wholeheartedly, without reservation.* [al-Baqara 2: 208.] *The only* [true] *way in the sight of Allah is Islam* [submission to the will of God]. [Al Imran 3: 85.]

Your *qalb* cannot be compartmentalised. You cannot dedicate one piece of it to Allah and another to some other god, like wealth, status, career, spouse and so on.

There is a beautiful verse in the Quran which throws light on the absurdity of such a situation. It tells about some of the *mushrikin* or idol-worshippers who sacrifice animals and then say that one part of the animal is for Allah and another is for their idols. The verse then states quite clearly that whatever is assigned to Allah is also, in reality, assigned to the idols, for Allah does not accept something divided between Him and others. He is One, indivisible and wants the human being to be undivided in service to Him. So long as our heart lies in a hundred places, so long as our eyes are set in a hundred directions, so long as we have many loyalties, we shall never be able to achieve that condition of 'holding onto Allah'.

Why should we allow divided loyalties to capture parts of our heart? Nothing in this world is going to be of use to us when we breathe our last, however hard we may have striven for it and however valuable it may seem to us. We must recognise that the prizes we seek are not the worldly possessions received from human beings like ourselves. It is only our Creator who can put a real value on our striving and bestow on us a real reward. *Shall I tell you of a business that will deliver you from a tormenting punishment?* [al-Saff 61: 10.] This 'business' amounts to you committing your whole undivided being to Allah alone, and selling yourself in order to earn His pleasure.

### Sincerity in Worship

What does it mean to do everything *fi sabilillah*, for the sake of Allah, which should be the crux and substance of our lives? People are in the habit of classifying life's activities into those which are mundane and those which are religious. Remember, though, only those things done for the sake of Allah are the 'religious' things. Everything that is done for other than Allah – however 'religious' it may seem – is a worldly act. If a person prays ostentatiously, it is a worldly act; if he fasts to expose his spirituality, it is a worldly act; but if he earns thousands of pounds to support his family and to spend for the cause of Islam, seeking only Allah's pleasure, it is a highly spiritual act. The Prophet reminded us:

> Many people fast but gain nothing from their fasting except hunger and thirst; and many people pray all night but gain nothing from their night Prayers except sleeplessness. (*Darimi.*)

What is of most importance to us is not the outward form of our actions. Although we perform all our duties and conform to all the protocols, it is the sincerity of purpose and intention behind our actions that really matters. The Prophet Muhammad, upon whom be peace, emphatically stated: 'Actions are judged only by intentions and everyone shall have what he intended.' (*Bukhari, Muslim.*)

Remember that purpose and intention are like the soul of a body or the inner capability of a seed. Many seeds look alike, but as they begin to grow and bear fruit, their differences become manifest. The purer and higher the motive, the greater the value and yield of your efforts. For all your daily actions, remind yourself of the motives behind your deeds. This may be the best way to ensure the purity and exclusiveness of purpose and intention.

## 3. Love of Allah

The next character trait of those who 'hold onto Allah' is that they love Allah. The Quran says that *those who have iman, love Allah more than anything else.* [al-Baqara 2: 165.] It does not say that one must love only Allah. Love is a blessing given to us by Allah and is manifested in many aspects of life. In Islam, however, it must be foremost for Allah, our Creator and Sustainer.

What is love? Perhaps it cannot be defined in terms which adequately reflect its nature and importance in a person's life. It is not possible to define it by a formula in a manner we define a scientific fact. But still each one of us knows what love is and can tell from our own experience the powerful force that it is. It

IN THE EARLY HOURS

is the overpowering force in life. It captivates you, it grips you, it moves you and you are prepared to do anything for the sake of it. Once love is there, what you do is not something which has to be imposed upon you, because you need imposition only for the things you do not love. *Iman* is something which must penetrate deep into your heart and generate love for Allah and His Prophet more than anything else. Unless this happens, you cannot experience the real *iman*.

To develop this love for Allah does not require us to retire to or seclude ourselves in a monastery. This love makes us do our duty to Allah while we are out in the street, at home or in the office. With this love, we live as servants of Allah everywhere, willingly making every sacrifice required of us. In fact, it propels us to share actively in the service of Allah's other creatures. True love of Allah makes us care for people and their needs.

Whether or not you have that love is something for you to examine closely. If you love someone, one of your most intense desires will be to get closer to that person. In Islam, you have a way in which you can get closer to Allah and talk to Him and that way is through *Salat*. The Prophet said that when a person performs *Salat*, he actually comes nearer to Allah and talks to Him. If you look at how you pray five times a day, you will have a barometer in your hand to find out how much you love Allah.

Once you are praying to Him, you are in front of Him, you are near to Him, you are talking to Him, you are responding to Him in gratitude and you are asking for His forgiveness. Prayer is not just a ritual in which you go through certain postures. The soul has to surrender itself exclusively to Allah and love Him. This love is like a seed which, as it grows, envelops the entire personality.

## Ihsan – *The Essence of Worship*

To entice us to remember Him and to love Him even more, Allah has used the beautiful words in the Quran: *Wajh Allah* or the Face of Allah. He says:

> *All that is on earth will perish, but the Face of your Lord will abide forever – Full of Majesty, Bounty and Honour.*
> [al-Rahman 55: 26-27.]

Everything on this earth will perish except the 'Face' of your Lord. His is the 'Face' you must desire. The expression 'Face of Allah' does not, of course, mean that Allah has a face like ours. But, again, if you love someone, you desire to look upon his face all the time, you always want to be in his company and you will make all the necessary sacrifices to earn his pleasure. So, when the Quran uses the expression 'Face of Allah' it is really to make us conscious that Allah is looking at us and we should do the things which will please Him and abstain from things which will displease Him. Thus, when the Prophet was questioned about the true meaning of *ihsan*, he replied:

> *Ihsan* is that you worship and serve Allah as though you are seeing Him; for even though you do not see Him, He surely sees you. (*Bukhari, Muslim.*)

If you continuously remind yourself that Allah is looking at you when you are praying, when you are studying, when you are doing your job, when you are with your family and friends, when you are involved in *dawa* – then you are well on your way to attaining *ihsan*, the most excellent form of worship. *Ihsan* takes us to the highest station of nearness to Allah. This is what gives real worth to everything we do and makes our actions acceptable in the eyes of our Creator and Sustainer.

### 4. *Becoming* Hanif

Those who 'hold onto Allah' must also strive to become *hanif*. Literally translated, it refers to one who is inclined or one who cuts himself away from everything that is false and belongs only to Allah. The term is used in the Quran in ten places, six times with reference to the Prophet Ibrahim, on whom be peace, and the rest for anyone who is sincere and sound in faith. The term connotes sincerity, uprightness and single-mindedness in one's dedication and commitment to Allah.

### A. The model of Ibrahim

The example of a *hanif* is beautifully expressed in the life of Prophet Ibrahim, on whom be peace. Let us ponder upon two of his outstanding qualities.

### B. Love for Allah

Ibrahim loved Allah. He forsook all loyalties and obedience to any object other than Allah. He said: *'I have turned my face [my entire being] to Him who is the Creator of the heavens and earth, having turned away from all else.'* [al-Anam 6: 79.]

He brought his entire life and being under Allah's rule, ensuring that he worshipped Him with heart and body. Ibrahim understood that Allah must rule everywhere: in homes as well as in hearts, in manners as well as in minds, in public life as in private. For him, the decision to surrender was personal and free. A ceaseless striving towards that end became the substance of his life so much so that Allah endowed him with the worthy title, *Khalil Allah* or Friend of God. [al-Nisa 4: 125.] With utmost devotion and concentration, Ibrahim supplicated:

> *My Prayer and all my acts of worship, my living and my dying are for Allah alone, the Lord of all the worlds. He has no associate: Thus I have been commanded, and I am foremost among those who surrender themselves unto Him. [al-Anam 6: 162-163.]*

## C. Complete trust in Allah

Ibrahim was tried and tested in every conceivable way. Whenever his Lord called upon him to surrender, he would readily respond: *'I surrender to the Lord of all the worlds.'* [al-Baqara 2: 131.] 'If You want me to go into the fire and be burnt alive, I am ready for that! If You want me to leave my home, I am ready for that! If You want me to take my son and wife and put them in a place where there is no shelter, no food and no one to protect them, I am ready for that! And if You want me to make the supreme sacrifice and put a knife to the throat of that which I love best, my son, I am ready for that!'

It is following in his footsteps that millions of people go to the *Baytullah*, the House of Allah, during the *Hajj* echoing the words of Ibrahim:

> Here I am, O Lord, here I am!
> Here I am; no partner hast Thou; here I am!

Surely to Thee is all Praise, all Goodness and all Sovereignty;
No partner has Thou!

*Labbayk! Allahumma labbayk!* I am here! O Allah I am at Your
command! I am always at Your command! I am always ready to
surrender! I am always ready to sacrifice!

Ibrahim accepted Allah as the only Lord and the only source
of guidance. He had absolute conviction in the commandments
of Allah. He was prepared to surrender and sacrifice everything
at a moment's notice without any hesitation whatsoever. His
*tawakkul* or trust in Allah was absolute. His example is
reminiscent of the verse in the Quran: *If anyone puts his trust in
Allah, sufficient is* [Allah] *for him.* [al-Talaq 65: 3.]

To become true servants of Allah, we must continuously echo
and abide by the words of the Quran: *Hasbunallah wa nimal
Wakil [Allah is sufficient for us and He is the best Provider]* [Al Imran
3: 173] in every circumstance of our lives.

To become a *hanif,* as exemplified in the life of the Prophet
Ibrahim, on whom be peace, you must love Allah as he did,
everything in life must be done to please Allah and you must
trust and rely on Allah completely:

*To each is a goal to which Allah turns him: So strive together as
in a race towards all that is good.* [al-Baqara 2: 148.]

## 5. Jihad – *Striving in the Path of Allah*

The next characteristic of 'holding onto Allah' is to strive with
all the means at your disposal to make the Word of Allah
supreme within your heart and in the hearts of those around

you. You must therefore bring all of mankind to Allah by witnessing to His guidance, *so that you be witnesses unto mankind and the Messenger be a witness unto you.* [al-Baqara 2: 143.]

In the *Sira*, we note that when the first ray of Divine Revelation reached Muhammad in Hira [al-Alaq 96: 1-5], the command of '*Iqra*' or Read was impregnated with world-shaking forces. He trembled. The second Revelation made things clear: *Arise and warn! And your Sustainer's greatness glorify!* [al-Muddaththir 74: 2-3.] The Prophet Muhammad, may God bless him and grant him peace, then took up his task with a single-minded dedication and encountered stiff opposition. The call to *let Allah be the Greatest* implied that all false claimants – and every claimant is false – to greatness, to unlimited power, authority and lordship to obedience, loyalty and servitude from Allah's creatures, must be challenged and dethroned. It is not difficult to see that this requires *hijra*, supreme sacrifices in 'giving up' everything one loves and fighting with all that one possesses for the sake of that love of Allah which must be greater than all else. Allah says:

> *And strive hard in God's cause with all the striving that is due to Him. It is He who has elected you* [to carry His Message] *and has laid no hardship on you in* [anything that pertains to] *religion* [and make you follow] *the creed of your father Ibrahim.* [al-Hajj 22: 78.]

> *The Believers are only those who* [truly] *believe in Allah and His Messenger, and then they doubt not; and who struggle hard with their wealth and their lives in the way of Allah; it is they who are the truthful ones.* [al-Hujurat 49: 15.]

A life of *jihad* necessarily requires important qualities: knowledge of and devotion to the Quran, *iman* or deep and strong faith, *sabr* or resolve and steadfastness. Read the Quran and you will find every promise of success here and in the Hereafter conditional upon these qualities.

## A. Acquiring knowledge

In order to fulfil your mission in life as the *khalifa* or ambassador of Allah in the establishment of His way of life, you need to arm yourself with *ilm* or knowledge of Islam. The Prophet Muhammad has said: 'Whoever Allah wishes good for, He bestows upon him a deep understanding of the *Din.*' (*Bukhari, Muslim.*) The Quran also exhalts those who possess useful knowledge and use it as an instrument to develop their closeness to Allah: *Are those who know equal to those who do not? Only those with insight can keep it in mind* [al-Zumar 39: 9]. *God will exalt those who believe among you and those who have knowledge to high ranks* [al-Mujadala 58: 11]. *Of all His servants only those who know fear God.* [al-Fatir 35: 28]. The Prophet also said that there are countless rewards both in this world and the Next for one who seeks to educate and purify himself:

If one travels in search of knowledge, Allah will make him travel to Paradise. The angels, being highly pleased with him, spread their wings over the seeker of knowledge. Everything in the heavens and on earth, even the fish in the depths of water, seek forgiveness for a scholar. And the superiority of a learned man over one engaged in ritual worship is like that of a full moon over the rest of the stars. (*Ahmad.*)

Consider the following guidelines as you set out on the path to educate yourself.

- Seek to have a sound understanding of the Quran and *Sunna*. May Allah bless the renowned Islamic scholar al-Muhallab, who advised his children: 'Acquire knowledge before you become leaders so that leadership does not keep you preoccupied from acquiring knowledge.'[3]
- Try to improve your reading, writing and oratory skills.
- Be well versed in the issues of the day by reading current newspapers, magazines and journals.
- Strive to have a good understanding of contemporary issues and problems affecting society.
- Strive also to understand the problems of the Muslims in such depth as to develop your own solutions in the light of the Quran and *Sunna*.
- Develop a personal library even if it is a small one and most of all cherish your Islamic books.

## B. Practising what you preach

'Real' *iman*, once lodged in the heart and embedded at the centre of life, must flourish into a mighty tree of righteous deeds. True *iman* which resides in hearts, shapes lives, and finds acceptance with Allah is always differentiated in the Quran from outward, 'legal' *islam*.

> *The Bedouins say, 'We believe.' Say: You do not believe, rather say, 'We have surrendered', for [true] faith has not yet entered their hearts.* [al-Hujurat 49: 14.]

Similarly, mere verbal professions of faith, which are contradicted by actions, are rejected.

*O Messenger, let not those grieve you who vie with one another in [the cause of] kufr from among those who say 'We believe' with their mouths, but their hearts believe not.* [al-Maida 5: 41.]

Even Believers are often called upon 'to believe', that is, to attain true faith: *O Believers, believe in Allah and His Messenger, and the Book He sent down before.* [al-Nisa 4: 136.] Or, *Believe in Allah and His Messenger, and spend out of that in which we have made you vicegerents.* [al-Hadid 57: 7.]

The connection between *iman* and actions is clearly manifest in the way both are almost always linked together: *al-ladhina amanu wa amilus-salihat* [those who believe and do righteous deeds].

The bond between true faith and ritual worship on the one hand, and a life lived totally in worship, which leads to justice and compassion in society on the other, is firmly established in many places in the Quran:

*Have you seen him who denies Judgement? That is the one who repulses the orphan and urges not the feeding of the needy. Woe to those that pray and are unmindful of their Prayer, those who want to be seen, and who refuse small kindnesses.* [al-Maun 107: 1-7.]

When we examine the body of *hadith* literature, we will also, immediately realise how the Prophet links a wide range of values and actions with *iman* in a very clear and defined manner. Just look at some of them:

No one among you believes until all his desires follow what I have brought. (*Sharh al-Sunna*.)

What lies between a man and *kufr* is the abandonment of Prayer. (*Muslim*.)

While one fornicates he is not a Believer, while one steals he is not a Believer, while one drinks he is not a Believer, while one takes plunder which makes men look at him he is not a Believer, and while one defrauds he is not a Believer. (*Bukhari, Muslim*.)

Flesh which has grown out of unlawful earnings will not enter Paradise, for Hell is more fitting for all flesh which has grown out of the unlawful. (*Ahmad*.)

Finally, remember that as a *daiya* or caller to Islam you need to set an excellent example and you need to practise what you preach. Those who do not follow their own advice have been strongly condemned by Allah. Keep close to you the following verses of the Quran:

*O you who believe! Why do you say that which you do not do? Grievously hateful is it in the sight of Allah that you should say what you do not do.* [al-Saff 61: 2-3.]

*Do you enjoin righteousness upon mankind while you yourselves forget* [to practise it]*? And you are readers of the Scripture! Have you then no sense?* [al-Baqara 2: 44.]

## C. Developing patience and perseverance

There will be many obstacles and hardships that may prevent you from fulfilling your obligations to Allah and you therefore need to develop *sabr* or patience and perseverance. The Quran states: *So [O Believers] endure hardship with beautiful endurance.* [al-Maʿarij 70: 5.] *So, patience is beautiful.* [Yusuf 12: 83.] *And God is with those who patiently persevere.* [al-Anfal 8: 66.]

Know that life is filled with tests and trials. Allah reminds us in the Quran:

*Do men think that they will be left alone on saying, 'We believe', and that they will not be tested? We did test those before them and Allah will certainly know those who are true from those who are false.* [al-Ankabut 29: 2-3.]

The best of people therefore are those who bear their tests and trials with fortitude and optimism and who see in every difficulty an opportunity to turn to Allah in remembrance and Prayer. Remind yourself constantly that *Allah shall make ease after hardship* [al-Talaq 65: 7], *and that on no soul does He place a burden greater than it can bear* [al-Araf 7: 42]. Remember that He has all the power. He gives everything. No harm can come to Him, and no benefit can come to Him. Everything that is happening in life is because of Him and comes from Him for no power is there save with Allah, the Most High, the Great.

### IMPEDIMENTS IN 'HOLDING ONTO ALLAH'

There are some character traits that you must take care to rid yourself of as you strive to 'hold onto Allah'.

## 1. Pride

One such evil and impediment is *kibr* or pride. This represents the antithesis of humility and is a devastating moral ailment. The efforts which we make for *tazkiya*, it is hoped, will make us successful. But if one is successful, the greatest cancer that can eat everything away, is *kibr*. The Messenger of Allah said:

> 'No one will be admitted into Paradise who has even a tiny grain of pride in his heart.'
> A man asked him: 'But what if someone likes to dress well and put on good sandals?'
> He replied: 'Truly Allah is beautiful, and He loves beauty. Pride is to disdain the truth, and to belittle and despise other people.' (*Muslim.*)

The day you feel that you have attained something special is the day of your spiritual death. Thus, the entire effort which you make should continue to be permeated with humility. Always remember that whatever you have achieved is by the grace of Allah, not through your own efforts.

Secondly, know that the ideal for you to emulate is the *uswa* of the Prophet. His example is so high and exalted: *And you* [Muhammad] *stand on an exalted standard of character.* [al-Qalam 68: 4.] One of the reasons the 'ideal' standard is so high, is to ensure that we always strive to better ourselves. If the ideal is easily reachable, then once a person has attained it, he will feel content, and contentment will set him off on a downward slide. Because our ideal is high, we are always in a state of aspiration. We are perpetually in a state of effort, striving and spiritual development. Should *kibr* arise in this state, it can only be an act of Shaytan, who is there just to test whatever one has achieved in the field of knowledge or action. *Kibr* will destroy whatever you have achieved, so protect yourself against it. Remember that it comes in very attractive, very concealed and very deceptive channels and forms. So, be ever vigilant.

The characteristics of a Believer whose heart is free of pride and filled with *ikhlas* and humility are described in a *hadith qudsi*. Allah Most High has said:

> Truly, of those devoted to Me, the one I most favour is a believer who is of meagre means and much given to Prayer, who has been particular in the worship of his Lord and has obeyed Him inwardly, who was obscure among people and not pointed out, and whose sustenance was just sufficient to provide for him yet he bore this patiently.
>
> Then he [i.e. the Prophet] rapped with his hand and said: Death will have come early to him, his mourners will have been few, his estate scant. (*Tirmidhi.*)

You should thus strive to become like one who doggedly keeps on working for the cause of Allah. You may not necessarily read details of him in newspaper columns, nor does he appear on television screens, nor does he win applause by making beautiful speeches in large gatherings and commendations for writing good pieces. He is not plagued by doubts. He does not waver in the face of defeat and failure. He does not calculate the chances of success but he knows very well that the only chance of success for him is to do his duty, and do it to the best of his ability. He is the backbone of the Islamic work and the Muslim *Umma*.

## 2. Hypocrisy

Another evil that destroys all that the Believer has achieved, or is trying to achieve, is *nifaq*. *Nifaq* entails hypocrisy, showing off, and pretending to have what one does not possess. The Prophet condemned this in the strongest terms. He said:

> Whoever prays to show off, he is [a sort of] idolater, for he makes a god beside Allah; whoever fasts to show off, he also makes a god beside Allah; and whoever gives charity to show off, he too makes a god beside Allah. (*Ahmad.*)

He also said:

> Three characteristics are the signs of a hypocrite, even if he fasts, performs the Prayer and claims that he is a Muslim: when he speaks, he lies; when he makes a promise, he breaks it; and when he is trusted, he betrays his trust. (*Bukhari, Muslim.*)

Hypocrisy serves only to cloud your consciousness of Allah. It is a moral ailment which eats away one's character as a moth eats away cloth. *Nifaq* is the opposite of *ikhlas* whereas *ikhlas* is the most essential ingredient of faith and good deeds. You should therefore assess your motives and actions frequently.

## 3. Pessimism

A third danger is that of *qunut* or pessimism. You must try to rid yourself of *qunut*, the feeling of hopelessness and pessimism.

Allah calls *qunut* an act of *kufr* or disbelief and rejection: He says: *who despairs of the mercy of his Lord, those who go astray?* [al-Hijr 15: 56.]

If you have tried and failed a hundred times, your efforts would still have won incalculable gains. The feeling of disappointment and pessimism and of losing heart should never occur. The promise of Allah is true and will come to pass: *And those who strive in Our way, We will certainly guide them to Our paths.* [al-Ankabut 29: 69.] Always adopt a hopeful and positive outlook. Be an eternal optimist.

### 4. Uncontrollable Anger

A fourth danger is that of uncontrollable anger. Once you begin to truly 'hold onto Allah' you will find that life becomes pleasant and easy. To work for the cause of Islam becomes a joy. Inter-personal disputes, family problems and organisational problems will be resolved amicably. Most problems which persist in affecting our social relationships and organisations are due to lack of sincerity and lack of exclusiveness for Allah.

If you begin to do everything for Him, there is no need to be angry if somebody insults you since he or she cannot harm you at all. Only Allah's displeasure can harm you. Remember the words of Allah:

*Never let your enmity for anyone lead you into the sin of deviating from justice. Always be just: that is closest to being God-fearing.* [al-Maida 5: 8.]

Why should you become angry? Uncontrollable anger and unnecessary rudeness and disputes that take place are counterproductive especially when you are working in a *jama'a*, hand-in-hand with your fellow Muslim brother and sister for the cause of Islam. Remember that we are working only to seek the pleasure of Allah. Do not ruin your good deeds by corrupting your heart with *kibr* and letting your *nafs* or selfish desires get the better of you. Identifying a practical method of controlling anger, the Prophet advised:

> When one of you gets angry while he is standing, he should sit down. Then the anger [will] leave him, and if not, then he should lie down. (*Ahmad, Tirmidhi.*)

The Prophet also used to make *dua* constantly in order to avoid negative emotions and behaviour:

> O Allah, Purify my heart from hypocrisy and my actions from ostentation. (*Bukhari.*)

> O Allah, Sustain me with Your love and the love of one who loves You, and the love of that which will draw me near to Your love, and make Your love more dear to me than cool water. (*Bukhari.*)

There are many more Prayers and supplications of the Prophet for similar things. They are food for the soul, food for the *qalb* and a source of sustenance for living this worldly life, for doing business, for studying, for working, for bringing up children and for *dawa*. Remember, if we do things for worldly objects, these objects will perish and our own actions will also perish.

*The parable of those who reject their Lord is that their works are as ashes on which the wind blows furiously on a tempestuous day. No power have they over what they have earned. That is the straying far, far* [from the goal]. [Ibrahim 14: 18.]

## 5. Abuse of the Tongue

A fifth danger is abuse of the tongue. We should be careful how we use our tongue for its misuse is the fastest way to Hell-fire. Lying, slandering, backbiting and obscenity should never be part of our speech. We should be exceedingly careful with what we say about others. The Prophet said:

> None of my Companions should tell me anything about anyone, for I like to meet [any one] of you with a clean heart. (*Abu Dawud.*)

*Janna* has been promised for those who are careful with their speech. The Prophet said:

> Whoever can promise me that he will be virtuous with what is between his lips, and what is between his thighs; I promise that he will go to the Garden. (*Muslim.*)

The key to control of the tongue is to infuse our conversations with remembrance of Allah. The Prophet said in this regard:

> Do not talk for long without remembering Allah, for talking much without remembering Allah is hardness of the heart. The most distant among man from Allah is one with a hardened heart. (*Tirmidhi.*)

## 6. Lustful Sexual Passions

The sixth and last impediment I wish to highlight is that of lustful sexual passions. Sex is a powerful driving force that Allah has blessed us with. In the Quran, Allah praises *men who guard their sex organs* [al-Nur 24: 30], and *women who guard their sex organs* [al-Nur 24: 31]. Despite great temptations, true Believers are able to control their sexual desires and in the process preserve their chastity.

The abuse of one's sexual organs leading to either fornication or adultery (*zina*) is described in the Quran as a great abomination:

> *Do not come near zina, for it is a foulness and an evil way.* [al-Isra 17: 32.]

The verse warns against approaching any avenue which excites passions, opens ways for illicit relations between a man and woman, and promotes indecency and obscenity. For this reason we are advised by Allah and His Prophet to observe the following regulations:

- We should seek to get married if we are in a position to do so. The Prophet said: 'O young men! Those of you who can support a wife should marry for it keeps you from looking at women and preserves your chastity.' (*Bukhari.*) If you are unable to get married, you should fast regularly for this will assist in controlling your sexual desires. The Prophet said: 'O young men! You should marry. Whosoever cannot marry should fast, for fasting will lessen his desire.' (*Bukhari.*)
- We should strive to control all the parts of our body not just our genitals from *zina* or fornication. The Prophet said: 'Every son

of Adam has his share of fornication. The eyes fornicate and do so by looking. The hands fornicate and do so by touching. The feet fornicate and do so by walking [to an immoral act or place]. The mouth fornicates and does so by kissing. And the heart forms thoughts and wishes which the genitals confirm or deny.' (*Bukhari, Muslim.*) Thus the Prophet used to make *dua* continuously: 'I seek refuge in Thee from the evil which may be in my ears, my eyes, my heart and my semen.' (*Abu Dawud.*)

- We should avoid looking at members of the opposite sex *with desire*. The Prophet considered lustful looks as the *'zina* of the eye', according to his saying: 'The eyes also commit *zina* and their *zina* is the lustful look.' (*Bukhari*). He also said: 'A gaze is a poisoned arrow from Shaytan. Whoever abstains from it in fear of God shall receive from Him an increase in faith, the sweetness of which he will feel in his heart.' (*Musnad* of *Ibn Hanbal.*)

- We should avoid looking at the *awra* or private parts of others. The Prophet forbade looking at the *awra* of another, whether of the same or the opposite sex, and whether with or without desire. He said: 'A man should not look at the *awra* of another man, nor a woman of a woman, nor should a man go under one cloth with another man, nor a woman with another woman.' (*Muslim.*)

- We should observe the rule of *khalwa*. *Khalwa* or privacy denotes a man and woman being alone in a place in which there is no fear of intrusion by anyone else, so that an opportunity exists for sexual intimacy. Islam prohibits *khalwa* between a man and a woman who are outside the degree of *mahram* relationship. The reason for this is not a lack of trust but rather to protect ourselves from sexual temptation arising when we are alone with a member of the opposite sex. The

Prophet said: 'Whoever believes in God and the Last Day must never be in privacy with a woman without there being a *mahram* with her, for otherwise Shaytan will be the third present [with them].' (*Ahmad.*)

## SUMMARY

The Quran has laid down certain guidelines for staying on the Straight Way. The first is to 'hold onto Allah' and life's journey will be easy.

'Holding onto Allah' means that you must be grateful to Him for everything, worship only Him, love Him more than anything else, strive to become a *hanif*, and make *jihad* only for Him.

Likewise, be aware of the following impediments in 'holding onto Allah': pride, hypocrisy, pessimism, uncontrollable anger, abuse of the tongue and lustful sexual passions.

May Allah guide us to the Straight Way for *He guides whom He wills to the Straight Way.* [Yunus 10: 25.]

## CHAPTER FOUR

# *Relating to Allah's Messenger*

THE Quran's major claim upon us is to put its teachings into practice for Allah demands the whole of our lives:

> *O you who have attained to faith! Surrender yourselves wholly unto God, and follow not in Shaytan's footsteps, for, verily, he is your open foe.* [al-Baqara 2: 208.]

The only way to live by the Quran is to live life as the Prophet Muhammad, may God bless him and grant him peace, lived it, for his life was the Quran in practice. His example is the surest guide to its meaning and Message. If you want to 'see' the Quran then look at the Prophet's life. For, as Sayyida Aisha said, 'his conduct was nothing but the Quran.' (*Muslim.*)

The best way to understand the Quran and follow its Message is to learn what the Prophet said, spend hours and hours in his company, follow in his footsteps and cast yourself in the mould that he left behind.

The Quran provides the essential framework for human life. But the Prophet and his *Sunna* provide us with the details of that framework. The manner in which that structure is to be given shape in actuality, the method to be adopted in order to live by

Divine guidance, and the wisdom that enables one to rise to all occasions and live through all situations in accordance with Allah's guidance.

If you desire to know what type of person the Quran wants you to be and what type of society the Quran wants you to create, you only need to look at the Prophet's life history.

Knowing, however, is not enough. We require inner strength to follow the Quranic teachings. We need to have the real flavour of faith inside our hearts. This strength comes out of the love that a Believer must have for Allah and His Messenger. Anas, may Allah be pleased with him, reported that the Prophet said:

> There are three types of people who will experience the sweetness of faith: he to whom Allah and His Messenger are dearer than all else; he who loves a human being for Allah's sake alone; and he who has as great abhorrence of returning to unbelief after Allah has rescued him from it as he has of being cast into hell. (*Bukhari, Muslim.*)

This love is not merely the profession of faith. It is a love that supercedes all other types of love and a love that makes faith penetrate into the heart. It is through this love for God and His Messenger that one tastes the real sweetness of faith. The way to that love and the symbol of that love lies in following in the footsteps of the Prophet who was commanded by Allah to say:

*If you love Allah, follow me; Allah will love you and forgive you your sins. For Allah is Oft-Forgiving, Most Merciful.* [Al Imran 3: 31.]

## THE POSITION OF THE *SUNNA* IN A BELIEVER'S LIFE

By the time the Prophet, peace be on him, departed this world, there were thousands of people whose lives mirrored his life. He left behind a society whose every aspect carried his stamp. His guidance, his teachings, his actions and his sayings not only fashioned that society during his time, but also continued to influence it after he had died. He created a new society and led the creation of a new civilisation and culture out of the teachings of the Quran. This he did in accordance with the task given to him by Allah Himself.

> *O Messenger! Convey all that has been sent to you from your Lord. If you did not you would not have delivered His Message.* [al-Maida 5: 67.]

## THE PROPHET'S MISSION

Muhammad, upon whom be peace, was not simply a 'Messenger' who brought a 'Message'. His responsibility and his task went beyond merely conveying the word of Allah to mankind. He was assigned the duty of teaching the Book, the Law, and the Wisdom to people, purifying them and making them develop into the human beings that the Quran desired them to be.

In many places in the Quran, these duties have been explicitly mentioned. In the very first part of *Sura al-Baqara*, Prophet Ibrahim, on whom be peace, prayed for a new Messenger:

> *Our Lord! Raise up in the midst of our offspring a Messenger from among them who shall recite to them Your verses and instruct them in the Book and in Wisdom and purify their lives. Verily, You are Mighty, Wise.* [al-Baqara 2: 129.]

In the above verse, four duties of the Prophet are mentioned:

- to convey the Message of the Quran to people;
- to instruct them in the Scripture which means the 'code of law' for human life;
- to teach them wisdom, through which life can make its journey in the light of the Quranic teachings;
- to train them in self-purification

His mission, therefore, was not merely to convey the Quran. He was designated to explain it and provide the guidance for day-to-day situations as the movement he led progressed from one stage to another.

In other places in the Quran,[4] Allah has described his mission and duty as:

- *Indhar* (warning)
- *Tabshir* (bringing glad tidings)
- *Dawa* (inviting and calling)
- *Tabligh* (communicating)
- *Tadhkir* (reminding)
- *Talim* (teaching)
- *Tilawa* (conveying and propagating)
- *Amr bil-maruf wa nahi anil-munkar* (enjoining and promoting what is good and right and forbidding and eradicating what is bad and wrong)
- *Iqama* (establishing the *Din* or way of life)
- *Qist* (establishing justice)
- *Izhar* (making Divine guidance prevail)
- *Shahada* (witnessing)

All these expressions pertain to the same mission, though from different perspectives and with different emphases.

The Prophet was also given the authority to make things permissible and to make things prohibited: *Adopt what the Messenger gives you and refrain from what he prohibits you.* [al-Hashr 59: 7.] And he had this authority from none other than Allah.

It was to accomplish these duties assigned to him that the Prophet Muhammad spent his whole life in changing people's behaviour and establishing a new society. The Quran accords him a unique position which no one else can ever have. *Whoever obeys the Messenger, indeed, he has obeyed Allah.* [al-Nisa 4: 80.] *Those who gave their hands in pledge to you, indeed, they gave their hands in pledge to Allah.* [al-Fath 48: 10.]

Once the Prophet has given his decision and his judgement, no believing man or woman has any right to question, doubt, disobey, or harbour any feeling of disapproval. They must submit totally and willingly to him.

> *It is not fitting for a Believer, man or woman, when a matter has been decided by Allah and His Messenger, to have any option about their decision. If any disobeys Allah and His Messenger, he is, indeed, on a clearly wrong path.* [al-Ahzab 33: 36.]

In the life of the Prophet, according to the Quran, lies the most beautiful and the most perfect example to follow:

> *You have, indeed, in the Messenger of Allah an excellent exemplar, for whoever hopes for Allah and the Last Day and remembers Allah much.* [al-Ahzab 33: 21.]

## GUIDELINES IN STUDYING THE *SUNNA*

One may ask where can the *Sunna* be found for there are so many books and traditions circulated. What the Prophet has left behind however, is not merely a record of what he did or what he said. He left behind him living human beings and a living society. It is through these living human beings and through this society that one can find the *Sunna*. The degree of homogeneity, conformity, and consistency that you find in this *Umma*, even after 1,400 years, are because of this *Sunna*.

You may walk into any *masjid* from Indonesia to Washington and you will find the rites and rituals of the formal acts of worship and the language of Prayer almost identical. You may walk into any Muslim home and you will find every Muslim eating with his right hand. Why? Because that is the *Sunna* left behind by the Prophet.

These examples may seem trivial but my purpose in citing them is to point out that even on the minutest of details, uniformity exists in the Muslim *Umma* and this is due to the *Sunna*. If the *Sunna* is given up as a source of guidance and if the Quran is separated from the *Sunna*, then this Muslim society that has existed for over fourteen hundred years, through many periods of severe strains and tests and tribulations, would disintegrate. It would then be relatively easy for foreign cultures and societies to assimilate it. What gives Muslim society and Muslim communities a distinct identity and colour of their own is the pattern left behind by the Prophet.

## THE *SUNNA* IN THE CONTEXT OF WESTERN SOCIETY

Muslims in Western societies live in a culture which is 'alien' in its spirit. To live in this type of culture is your own choice and your own decision. In many instances, you have no other option for the West is your home. Unfortunately, the same can be said for people living in Muslim countries since Western culture is slowly weaving its way and replacing genuine Islamic culture in these countries also.

To survive and prosper in Western society requires great courage to stand up for your beliefs and ideals. You need to have a clear appreciation of the true nature of Islamic culture. The true spirit of Islamic culture lies in an understanding that the 'real' realities of life are all beyond the perception of physical senses. The beginning of *Sura al-Baqara* states that its guidance is for: *Those who believe in al-ghayb* [what lies beyond the perception of physical senses]. [al-Baqara 2: 4.]

So all that is 'real' – Allah, His Angels, Prophethood, the Day of Judgement, Heaven and Hell – are all beyond any measure of physical testing. They all lie beyond human capability to see them, to smell them, to measure them, or to find their real situation.

Western culture as it exists and as it has spread now throughout the world, in this 'global village', has perpetuated the view that, only that which can be materially measured or found out is 'real'. Whatever cannot be measured has no value. Therefore, both Islamic and Western cultures are diametrically opposed.

Once you have chosen to live in a 'Western type' society, the only source of light for you is the Messenger of Allah. He was also faced with an almost similar situation. As he came down from the cave of Hira, after his experience of receiving the light of Divine guidance, he re-entered a culture and society which were quite 'alien' to his Message. His Message began by linking the whole of life to the name of Allah. That was the starting point. All knowledge, all culture, all civilisation and all human action must be centred on one pivot and that is the name of Allah. This was a totally strange Message for the society in which he had to operate. So, we need to look at the Prophet's *Sunna* in the context of operating in an 'alien' society and see how we can practise a genuine Islamic culture.

## THE REAL MEANING OF THE TERM *SUNNA*

The technical definition of *Sunna* is all that the Prophet did, said, or approved. When the term *Sunna* is used, our minds are diverted immediately to the manners and morals which we are so careful to observe, while dressing and eating, walking and praying.

I have no intention of belittling the importance of these relatively minor acts that he left behind. It reminds me of a beautiful incident from his life. A man and his son came to meet the Prophet. As he came out of his house, the buttons of his shirt were open. Both of them shook his hand and went away. That was the only occasion in their lives when they came face to face with the Prophet. But, for their entire lives they always kept the buttons of their shirts open – not because it was obligatory, but once you fall in love with someone, each and every action that he does, and each and every thing that he says, becomes dear to the heart. It has to be followed.

If, however, you consider the technical definition of *Sunna*, and if you look at the life of the Prophet from the moment he received revelation in the cave of Hira till he breathed his last in Madina, what is it that stands out as his most dominant concern and his main activity? The most outstanding feature of his life was that every moment was spent in *dawa*, in inviting his fellow human beings to live in submission to their Creator. He lived every moment of his life in purifying individuals and making them grow in their love and submission to Allah. Every moment of his life, he talked about and carried out his mission. In the streets of Makka, in the valley of Taif, on the battlegrounds of Badr and Hunayn, and in the totality of affairs of Madina – *dawa* was his essential concern. That was his essential *Sunna*.

## YOUR MISSION

*Dawa* is the first and most important duty for Muslims today. In your daily affairs, it is the *Sunna* that must be uppermost in your mind and heart. It must make the greatest claim on your time and wealth.

Secondly, while living in an 'alien' culture, you have to preserve your Islamic identity – not only through rational arguments, but through emotional, cultural, and civilisational symbols. It is only the *Sunna* that can provide these emotional and civilisational symbols through which you will not only preserve your identity but strengthen and advance it.

Thirdly, it is the youth who must claim your major attention for that is also the *Sunna* of the Prophet. They were the people who had the energies and capabilities to carry the burden of his mission.

Fourthly, in a society where so many misgivings about Islam prevail, where Islam has been misrepresented and distorted so widely, your conduct must be a living example of that mercy to mankind, just as the Prophet was *rahmatun lil-alamin*, a mercy to the worlds.

*We sent you not but as a mercy for all the worlds.* [al-Anbiya 21: 107.]

The Prophet Muhammad was such a model of mercy that he declared that removing an obstacle from another's path leads one into Paradise; to quench the thirst of a dog entitles one to enter Paradise; and to tie up a cat without food or water until he dies makes one deserve Hell-fire. Such was the mercy of his *uswa*, his living example. You will only be able to invite people to Islam if you follow his example.

### SUMMARY

We must recognise the unique position that the Prophet must occupy in our lives as a focus of our love and obedience and as an ideal we must follow.

Our biggest challenge is to fulfil our role as ambassadors of the last Ambassador of Allah to mankind for all times. By our words and deeds, by our example of integrity and compassion, we must make our neighbours understand who Muhammad, peace be upon him, was and what his Message for mankind was.

In this process, we must be the embodiment of mercy that the Prophet was. In this way we will create a new future by making the new generation a living example of his *Sunna*. Then, perhaps, our presence in this world will prove a great blessing, not only for the Muslim community, but for all mankind.

## CHAPTER FIVE

# Spending in the Way of Allah

WHATEVER you give or spend in the way of Allah will be returned to you in manifold increase. Allah, the most Bountiful and the most Loving, commends:

> *Lend unto God a goodly loan. Whatever good you shall forward on your behalf, you shall find it with God, as better and richer in reward.* [al-Muzzammil 73: 20.]

Be generous, therefore, for whatever you spend on yourself is only for your temporary sustenance while whatever you spend in the way of Allah is an investment in your future for which will provide everlasting sustenance. Seek to invest in others for your own benefit with whatever Allah has endowed you.

*Sadaqa* or charity, of course, is not compulsory. What is obligatory, however, is *Zakat*, a fixed percentage of your *halal* or lawful savings which is meant to purify your wealth by recognising that the needy has a right over a portion of it. Indeed, the very meaning of the term *Zakat* signifies purification. Allah says: *Of their wealth take alms to purify and sanctify them.* [al-Tawba 9: 103.] Furthermore: *He that spends his possessions* [on others] *so that he might grow in purity.* [al-Layl 92: 18.]

Love for worldly possessions is primarily a disease of the heart while the purpose of *sadaqa* is to act as its antidote or cure. *Sadaqa* serves as a form of *dhikr* to remind us that all forms of wealth come from Allah and what we possess is simply a short-term loan for which we will be held accountable when our contract expires. This loan is meant to cater for our personal needs and family needs and those of the wider society.

## SPENDING ON FELLOW HUMAN BEINGS

Spending on those in need is a highly commendable form of *ibada* or worship. The Prophet Muhammad declared:

> A generous person is close to Allah, close to Paradise, close to people, and far from Hell. However, a miserly person is far from Allah, far from Paradise, far from people, but close to Hell. Allah loves more an ignorant man who is generous than a worshipper who is miserly. (*Tirmidhi.*)

We should not, of course, expect any favours from those who receive our *sadaqa*. Neither should we expect that they will be grateful and kind to us and give something to us in return, nor should we be motivated by a desire for any other worldly reward. Concerning our attitude to giving, Allah reminds us: *O you who believe, make not your charity worthless by reminders of your generosity, and by causing vexation.* [al-Baqara 2: 264.] Our *sadaqa* should be *qard hasan*, a loan given for the sake of Allah without expectation of profit. The Quran describes the attitude of those who give to the needy as follows:

*And they feed, for the love of Allah, the indigent, the orphan, and the captive* [saying], *'We feed you for the sake of Allah alone: No reward do we desire of you nor thanks.'* [al-Dahr 76: 8-9.]

Their reward is sought from Allah rather than mortals. And whose gratitude and return can be greater for us than Allah's, given out of love and mercy for us?

Instead of hoping for some worldly benefit from our *sadaqa*, we should be grateful to those who accept our *sadaqa*, for they have given us an opportunity to invest our wealth in a 'business venture' with Allah who has promised in return a reward 'seven hundred times greater'. *The parable of those who spend their wealth in the way of Allah is that of a grain, out of which grow seven ears, in every ear a hundred grains.* [al-Baqara 2: 261.]

Just imagine if such an investment was offered to you by a company – you would rush to put every penny you possess into it when you consider the magnitude of profit to be made. To invest in Allah's 'business venture' requires the certainty of faith, which affirms that there is a 'real' reward available for you to receive. Of this reward, the Quran declares: *Allah has purchased of the believers their persons and their goods; for theirs* [in return] *is the Garden.* [al-Tawba 9: 111.]

When a Believer attains the certainty and faith that his real reward lies in the Life to Come, his heart becomes enlarged with generosity and love for his fellow men and his giving knows no bounds. In return, Allah promises ease for him in all his efforts until he reaches eternal bliss.

*Surely, your striving is to diverse ends. And for him who gives, is God-conscious and believes in the Truth – for him shall We make easy the path towards ease. But, as for him who is niggardly, behaves as if he is self-sufficient and denies the Truth – for him shall We make easy the path towards hardship.* [al-Layl 92: 4-10.]

The Prophet, upon whom be peace, was the most generous person in his community. It was his unique sense of generosity and affection which captivated the hearts of the people and brought them into the fold of Islam. His example was the most important form of *dawa*. *Imam* Bukhari has recorded that the close Companion of the Prophet, Jabir, testified that he never observed the Prophet refusing anyone who requested something from him. The Prophet, upon whom be peace, has himself testified: 'If I had a mountain of gold, I would not like to save any of it for more than three days, except something I put aside to pay debts.' (*Bukhari.*) The magnanimity of the blessed Prophet is the example we must strive to follow.

## SPENDING FOR THE CAUSE OF ISLAM

Spending on fellow human beings – family, relatives, the needy, the orphan, the destitute – is one aspect of *infaq fi sabilillah* or spending in the way of God. There is also another – that is, spending for the cause of Islam. When you spend for the cause of Islam, Allah adopts another manner of asking for it: *Who is there who will give a loan to Me?* [al-Hadid 57: 11.] Just imagine His generosity. It is His wealth, it belongs to Him. Even if He asks us for it without offering any reward, He will be justified in doing so but yet He is prepared to buy back His own property so that you may again reap its benefits and gain a noble reward.

Consider our attitude when we are asked to contribute for the cause of Islam. We are miserly. We will spend one-hundredth of what we spend on our homes, our children, our clothes and food for the cause of Islam. *Sura al-Hadid* goes on to invite those who claim to be Muslims to become true Believers and to give their lives and their possessions and belongings in the way of Allah. Finally, it invites Muslims to give a good loan to Allah which He will multiply many times and return with a noble reward:

*One day we shall see the believing men and believing women with their Light running before them and on their right. A glad tiding for you today, gardens underneath which rivers flow, therein to abide forever. This is the supreme triumph.*

*On that day hypocrites, both men and women, shall speak unto those Believers: 'Wait for us. Let us have light from your light.' But they will be told: 'Turn back and seek a light of your own.' And thereupon a wall will be raised between them with a gate in it. Inside it will be mercy and outside the wall will be suffering and punishment.*

*Those who will be outside will call out to those who would be inside 'Were we not with you?' To which the others will answer: 'Yes, indeed, but you allowed yourself to be tempted and you were hesitant and you were in doubt and your wishful thinking deceived you until Allah's command came to pass. For, indeed, the deceiver deceived you concerning Allah. And so, no ransom shall be accepted today from you and neither from those who disbelieved. Your abode is the fire. It is your only refuge, and how evil a journey's end.'*

*Is it not time that the hearts of all those who have believed should feel humbled at the remembrance of Allah and of all the truth that has been given to them, lest they become like those who were granted revelation before and whose hearts have hardened with the passage of time, so that many of them have now become iniquitous?*

*But, know that Allah gives life to the earth after it has been*

IN THE EARLY HOURS

*lifeless! We have, indeed, made Our Messages clear unto you, so
that you might use your reason.*

*Verily, as for men and women who accept the Truth as true,
and who offer up unto Allah a goodly loan, they will be amply
repaid, and shall have a noble reward* [in the Life to Come].
[al-Hadid 57: 12-18]

The above verses describe a vivid and graphic scene
concerning the Last Day, *Yawm al-Qiyama*. It concerns two
groups of people, those who are true Believers and those who are
shaky, hesitant and doubtful in their commitment to their faith
and to our Creator.

The first verse describes the group of believing men and
women. They will have a *Nur* or Light which will be in front of
them and on their right. With that Light they will journey to
their destination and they will be greeted with glad tidings of
beautiful gardens in which they will live forever – that will be the
highest possible achievement for which they can hope.

The first point we may note is that both men and women are
mentioned in the verse separately. This means that as far as the
demands and duties of this world and eligibility for the rewards
in the Life to Come are concerned, there is no difference
between men and women. Both men and women will possess
the Light for their journey.

Then, the Quran focuses the narrative on the second group,
the hypocrites and miserly ones – both men and women – who
will not possess the Light. Those who were niggardly and did not
believe in the promises made by Allah will cry out to the true
Believers for their bounty – but, it will be too late to benefit
from the generosity of others. A wall will arise separating the

generous ones from the miserly. The generous ones will find shelter in Allah's *rahma*, while the miserly ones and the hypocrites will be on the side of Allah's wrath. A dialogue will then commence between the two groups. Ibn Kathir elaborates the conversation in a very vivid manner. The miserly and the hypocrites will be saying:

> 'Were we not with you? Did we not go with you to the Friday Prayers? And did we not attend with you the congregations? And did we not do other things with you? Did we not fight side by side with you in the battles? So, why are you now leaving us behind?' The true Believers will reply, 'Yes, indeed, you were with us. But you were with us only outwardly, with your bodies, but not with your intentions and with your commitments. And you allowed yourselves to be tempted away by these worldly things which you considered to be dearer, more valuable for you in life. You were more concerned about your families, you were more concerned about amassing wealth, you were more concerned about making life comfortable and you were more concerned about building up a good life in the world. And so, all these worldly things, once they became the medium and vehicle for taking you away from the Right Path, led you to this position. And you waited and you hesitated.'

If we reflect on the whole scene, we will find that there is mention of a gate in the wall. If we believe that all that is going to happen in the *Akhira* is a result of what happens today, it means that although there is a wall which separates the sincere from the insincere, and the true Believers from the hypocrites – there is always a door between the two groups that can be opened.

If, today, someone makes a decision to step inside that door it requires two things: a will and a step, and then you are inside, near the mercy of Allah. The time to walk through that door is today and not tomorrow, because tomorrow that door may not be open. But today, despite all the walls that may separate the sincere from the insincere and the generous from the miserly, the door for *istighfar* and *tawba* is open. The door for turning back is open and the door to make a decision and so become sincere to your commitment is also open.

Now is the time to commit yourself to Islam and to become sincere. You must ensure that your whole life is based on spending for the cause of Islam by giving your time, attention, heart and mind – utilising the faculties of speaking, writing, reasoning and intelligence that Allah has bestowed on you for the establishment of His *Din* or way of life. Only then will you attain the highest station of faith:

> *Never will you attain the highest degree of virtue unless you spend* [freely] *in the cause of Allah out of that which you love; and whatever you spend, Allah surely knows it well.* [Al Imran 3: 92.]

### THE SMALL CHARITY

We should never consider any charity too small or not worth doing or giving. Even meeting your Muslim brother or sister with a smiling face or giving a good word of encouragement and praise are acts of *sadaqa*. Adi bin Hatim has related that the Prophet Muhammad said:

Every one of you will certainly meet Allah. On the day that he meets Him, there will be no curtain between them, nor any interpreter. He shall then say, 'Did I not send you a Messenger who was conveying the Message to you?' He will reply, 'Certainly'. He shall then say, 'Did I not give you property and show favour on you?' He will reply, 'Certainly'. Then he will look to his right and see only *Jahannam* and he will look to his left and see only *Jahannam*. [Then the Prophet said] Guard against the fire, even though it be with half a date. And, if anyone does not have even that much, he should do so with a good word. (*Bukhari*.)

Some people have so narrow a view that they cannot bring themselves to even utter a kind and pleasant word. The Messenger of Allah has said: 'Do not belittle even the smallest act of kindness, even if it were no more than meeting your brother with a smiling and cheerful face.' (*Muslim*.)

It will not cost a penny to say a good word, but so miserly have we become that we are not even prepared to utter a word of kindness, praise and encouragement. It will make a lot of difference to our spouses, siblings, and neighbours – be they Muslim or non-Muslim – if we were to be loving and kind in all our inter-personal relationships.

## MODES OF LIVING

Your *din* or way of life can be one of two types: one way of life is to look after your own self-interests and the other way is to seek to improve the welfare of others, even at your own expense, in order to earn the pleasure of Allah. These are two diametrically opposed ways of thinking, behaving and living. Now the way to Allah is the way of giving. The Prophet made a comparison of the two different personalities as follows:

> The case of a miser and a generous one is like that of two people who are clad in steel armour from their breasts up to their collar bones. When the generous one spends, his armour expands until it covers his fingers and his toes. When the miser makes up his mind to spend something every ring of the armour sinks into his flesh. He tries to loosen it but it is not loosened. (*Bukhari, Muslim.*)

Wealth and possessions are a *baraka* or blessing from Allah when used in a productive way to earn the pleasure of Allah. Otherwise, it can be our worst enemy, a curse. As soon as we realise that everything belongs to Allah and that the things that we are going to receive in the *Akhira* depend on how much we spend in the *Dunya*, it will become easier to give *freely* from our pockets. Giving and sacrificing will become a pleasure rather than a burden.

For most of our life, we work hard to earn money in order to build bank balances and to buy houses. These are all commendable acquisitions – in moderation. Remember that you may have a house with one hundred rooms, but you can sleep in only one room. You may have one hundred dresses in your wardrobe, but at any one time you can wear only a single dress. You may have one hundred dishes laid on the table, but you cannot eat more than will fill your one stomach. Even that may be difficult for you to digest. Always remember the *hadith:* 'Self-sufficiency does not mean plenty of provisions; it means self sufficiency of the spirit.' (*Bukhari*.) All those extravagant things that deceive you are not worth pursuing or living for.

> *Say: If it be that your fathers, your sons, your brothers, your mates, or your kindred; the wealth that you have gained; the commerce in which you fear a decline; or the dwellings in which you delight are dearer to you than Allah, or His Messenger, or the striving in His Cause – then wait until Allah brings about His Decision: and Allah guides not the rebellious.* [al-Tawba 9: 24.]

## LOVE OF THIS WORLD

I am not saying that you should not enjoy the 'good things of this world'. Rather, we must work hard for them because nothing good comes without genuine effort. Abu Bakr as-Siddiq said: 'Your religion is your future and your money is your livelihood; there is no good in a man with no money in his name.' We should therefore live this life fully. We should be interested in it. As Allah encourages us:

> *Seek, by means of what Allah has granted you, the life to come, and forget not your share of the present world; and do good as Allah has done good to you; and seek not to spread corruption on earth.* [al-Qasas 28: 77.]

In addition, the Prophet informed us that wealth can also serve to increase our *taqwa*: 'What a good helper is wealth in maintaining God-consciousness.' (*Kanz al-Ummal*.) He also said: 'Anyone who acquires it [wealth] lawfully and spends it lawfully, for him it is the best helper.' (*Muslim*.)

Thus, all the good things in life must be pursued, but not the love of this world. There is no true enjoyment of the good of this world if we do not adequately prepare our home in the Next world. Umar ibn Abd al-Aziz used to repeat the following verse unceasingly: 'There is no good in the life of a man for whom Allah has appointed no share in the everlasting abode.'

The love that we should desire is the love of the *Akhira*. For this to be achieved, *the love of Allah and His Messenger must be dearer to you than all else* [al-Baqara 2: 165]. This will earn you the pleasures of this world and of the Next. When the Prophet was requested by one Companion to tell him of some deeds which will make him earn the love of Allah, as well as that of other people, he replied, 'Do not covet this world, and Allah will love you; do not covet what people possess, and people will love you.' (*Bukhari.*)

It is not the amount of money that you possess which matters in the eyes of Allah. Rather, He wants you to rid yourself of the love for that money. If a person has one pound only, but his heart is in that one pound, then he is a man of this world. On the contrary, if he has £100,000 and his heart is not in those pounds and he is prepared to part with it whenever it is required, then he is not a man of this world; he is a highly spiritual man. Similarly, if you earn £10 and give £5 in charity, this is much more precious in the eyes of Allah than someone who earns £100,000 and gives £1,000. The first person has given half of his wealth while the second has given one-hundredth of what he has earned.

In the time of the Prophet, those who possessed firm conviction in Allah's promises would bring everything they had in their homes and put it at the feet of the Prophet. It is of the *Sahaba* and their selfless sacrifices that the Quran says: *They give preference over their own selves, even when they themselves are destitute.* [al-Hashr 59: 9.]

If you truly seek the pleasures and rewards of the Hereafter, spend, *infaq fi sabilillah!* This is one of the most effective ways of ridding ourselves of the love for the *Dunya* and acquiring a love for the Hereafter. It is indeed an important instrument of *tazkiya* as the Quran declares:

> *And the likeness of those who spend their substance, seeking to please Allah and to strengthen their souls, is as a garden high and fertile: heavy rain falls on it, but makes it yield a double increase in harvest.* [al-Baqara 2: 265.]

While spending in the way of Allah, you must give as much as you can give, but do so with moderation. The Quran exhorts us to be like *those who are neither extravagant nor niggardly in spending, but keep a balance between the two.* [al-Furqan 25: 67.]

There are also two important things you must take care to avoid when giving to those in need. One is that of *kibr* or pride and the other is *riya* or show. Giving with pride in your heart and actions will only consume your good deeds while spending to seek the attention of others will corrupt your pure intentions and make your actions worthless in the eyes of Allah.

The battle to part with what you possess is one that you will experience each day until your meeting with your Lord. It is an ongoing war between the temptations of this world and our conviction in the rewards of the *Akhira*.

This world is filled with beauty and attractions but the *Akhira* is filled with beauty unimaginable. The Quran has made a comparison between both worlds.

*Alluring has been made for people the love of desires for women, and children, and heaped up treasures of gold and silver, and horses of high rank, and cattle, and farms. But all this may be enjoyed only in the present life – whereas, the best resort is with Allah. Say: Shall I tell you of better things than these [earthly joys]? For the God-conscious there are, with their Lord, gardens through which waters flow, therein to abide for ever, and pure spouses, and Allah's good pleasure.* [Al Imran 3: 14-15.]

### FORGIVING OTHERS

*Sadaqa* also has no value without love and sympathy. The Quran states: *Kind words and the covering of faults are better than charity followed by injury.* [al-Baqara 2: 263.] Those who are generous forgive people for their mistakes. The Prophet reminded us: 'If one gives charity it does not diminish his wealth; if one forgives others, Allah bestows more honour on him; and if one humbles himself for Allah's sake, He exalts him higher.' (*Muslim.*) The Quran also mentions both giving and forgiving together: *And compete with one another for your Lord's forgiveness and a Paradise as vast as the heavens and earth prepared for the God-fearing, who give generously whether in times of plenty or in times of hardship, and hold in check their anger, and pardon their fellow human beings; Allah loves such doers of good.* [Al Imran 3: 133-134.]

Spending in the way of Allah is closely related to controlling anger and forgiving people. All come from a big heart. The Prophet said: 'Two of the qualities which Allah loves are gentleness and endurance.' (*Bukhari.*) When your heart becomes big enough to forgive the faults of others, Allah has promised for you the reward of *Janna.*

*The wronged one who endures with fortitude and forgiveness indeed achieves a matter of high resolve.* [al-Shura 42: 43.]

**SUMMARY**

Whatever you can give, spend. Spend on your family and those in need, but be even more generous in spending for the cause of Islam. Remember that the time to commit yourself to Islam is now. Utilise all the resources at your disposal: time, attention, heart and mind, faculties of speaking, writing, reasoning and intelligence that Allah has bestowed on you for the establishment of His *Din*. Do not let the love of this world beguile you. Be forgiving and accommodating to your fellow human beings if you want to earn the forgiveness and mercy of Allah.

May Allah enable us to detach ourselves not from this world, but from the love of this world. May He help us to spend of that which He has bestowed on us for our own benefit.

## CHAPTER SIX

# *Relating to Allah's Creation*

ALLAH has laid down certain rights and duties between people and between all of His living creation. Parents and children, wife and husband, brother and sister, neighbours, Muslim and non-Muslim, employer and employee, even animals are all included in this wide range of rights and obligations. In this interdependent world, every person is responsible for those under his care. The Prophet Muhammad said:

> Every one of you is a shepherd and every one of you is responsible for his flock. A ruler is shepherd over his people and he is accountable for their welfare. A man is shepherd over his family and he is accountable for their welfare. A woman is shepherdess over her husband's household and children and she is accountable for their welfare. A man's servant is shepherd over his master's property and he is accountable for it. Be careful! All of you are shepherds and all of you shall be accountable for your flocks. (*Bukhari, Muslim.*)

The Quran also informs us that we must be compassionate with each other and generous in our giving:

*Worship and serve Allah alone and make no gods beside Him;*
*and do good to your parents, relatives, the orphans, the needy, the*
*neighbour who is a relative, the neighbour who is a stranger, and*
*the companion by your side, and the wayfarer, and those you*
*rightfully possess; for Allah does not love the proud and boastful,*
*those who are niggardly and urge others to be niggardly.* [al-Nisa
4: 36-37.]

The injunctions of the *Sharia* or Islamic moral and legal code
relating to rights and duties are usually divided into two
categories: the rights of Allah together with our duties towards
Him and the rights of Allah's servants together with their duties
towards mankind. This classification is meant to simplify our
understanding of our obligations but the Prophet Muhammad,
peace be upon him, taught us that Allah would Himself be
claimant on behalf of those whose rights have not been
honoured on the Day of Judgement. A *hadith qudsi* states:

The Messenger of Allah said: Allah will say, 'Son of
Adam, I fell ill but you did not visit Me.' He will say, 'O
Lord, and how could I have visited You! You are the Lord
of the worlds!' He will say, 'Did you not know that My
servant so-and-so had fallen ill and you did not visit him?
Did you not know that if you had visited him you would
have found Me with him?'

'Son of Adam, I asked you for food but you did not
feed Me.' He will say, 'O Lord, how could I have fed You!
You are the Lord of the worlds!' He will say, 'Did you not
know that My servant so-and-so had asked you for food
and you did not feed him? Did you not know that if you
had fed him you would surely have found Me with him?'

'Son of Adam, I asked you to give Me drink but you did not give Me.' He will say, 'O Lord, how could I have given You drink! You are the Lord of the worlds!' He will say, 'My servant so-and-so had asked you to give him drink and you did not give him. Had you given him drink you would surely have found Me with him.' (*Muslim.*)

So, Allah regards the rights and duties that He has defined between His creation as His rights and duties. The Messenger of Allah has said: 'All creatures are Allah's family; and Allah loves most those who treat His family well and kindly.' (*Bayhaqi.*)

## THE REGISTERS OF DEEDS

In a *hadith* narrated by Sayyida Aisha, the Prophet said that all the deeds that we perform are written down in three registers:

- One register contains the deeds of those who have associated partners with Allah. Allah will not forgive those who commit *shirk* or polytheism. He forgives all sins except *shirk*.
- The second register contains those deeds that Allah will not forgive, unless they have been compensated for. These are the ones between fellow human beings.
- The third register contains the deeds about our personal duties to Allah. They are the deeds between man and his Creator like *Salat* and *Sawm*. Allah determines whether they are forgiven or not.

The second register of deeds is especially important for us to consider because there is no Divine pardon in cases where personal rights have been violated. Forgiveness can only come from the person concerned – either directly or when Allah makes it possible for that person to grant a pardon. The Prophet Muhammad said in this regard:

> Whoever is guilty of doing some wrong against a fellow human being, whether in regard to his honour or anything else, he should obtain his forgiveness before the Day of Judgement, when there will be no money to pay for it. If he has any good deeds to his credit, they will be taken away from him to the extent of his wrongdoing. And if he has no good deeds, the sins of the wronged-one will be taken and put on him. (*Bukhari.*)

### OBLIGATIONS TO YOUR FAMILY

Your first obligation after satisfying your personal needs is to your family: *O you who believe! Save yourself and your family from a fire whose fuel is men and stones.* [al-Tahrim 66: 6.]

Fulfilment of your responsibilities towards your family is certainly an onerous task which requires a considerable amount of effort and time on your part. This task can be made easier, more rewarding and indeed more satisfying if you are careful in following the guidelines set out by the Prophet in the selection of your marriage partners.

When choosing your prospective spouse, ensure that you check your *niyya* or intention. Remind yourself that in seeking to get married you are fulfilling an obligation [al-Nur 24: 32-33], and in so doing you are also following a very strong tradition of the Prophet. *Imam* Bukhari narrated that the Prophet strongly advised all young people who possess the means to get married, to do so. Marriage will in turn assist you in safeguarding your chastity and hopefully, increase your *iman* and commitment to Islam. The Prophet further commented on the benefits of a blessed marriage as follows: 'Whoever is granted a righteous wife by Allah, Allah has helped him in half of his faith. So let him fear Allah in the remaining half.' (*Tabarani.*) This exhortation, of course, applies equally to both men and women.

Your choice of spouse should be based foremost on the merit of *taqwa*. Take time to make the best choice, for this too, is an investment in your future and that of your 'future' children, *insha Allah*. Accordingly, the Messenger of God said:

> Do not marry women for their beauty, maybe their beauty will lead them to destruction; and do not marry them for their wealth, maybe their wealth will cause them to become haughty. But marry them for their *taqwa* (piety). A wide-nosed, clumsy slave-woman who possesses faith is better [than the above categories]. (*Ibn Majah.*)

Look for a partner who will bring comfort to your eyes, one who has a pure heart and one who will encourage you and participate in your *dawa* work [al-Rum 30: 21]. In this way, not only will you benefit from the *baraka* or blessing of Allah in your *dawa* efforts, but your home will also be filled with the *Nur* of Allah and become a source of inspiration for your efforts [al-Araf 7: 189]. For this reason, we are told in the Quran that the *Ibadur Rahman* or true Servants of the Most Gracious, make the *dua*:

> *Our Lord, grant us in our spouses and children comfort to our eyes.*
> *And make us exemplary to the God-fearing.* [al-Furqan 25: 74.]

Having chosen the most suitable spouse, remember that your responsibility to yourself and to your family has not ended. Rather, your obligations in this regard have just started. You must follow the Prophet and be the best *uswa* or example to your family. Sayyida Aisha, the Prophet's wife, narrated that he said: 'The best of you is he who is best to his family, and I am the best among you towards my family.' (*Tirmidhi.*)

Within the family, both husband and wife have different but equal roles to play. Both parties must complement each other in the fulfilment of their responsibilities: *They are garments for you while you are garments for them.* [al-Baqara 2: 187.]

To further deepen the love and to improve communication between members of your family – spouse, children, parents – you should aim to establish the following three activities in your home.

• Firstly, perform some of your daily *Salat* collectively with your family. The Prophet said that, 'when you have finished your [*Fard*] Prayer in the *masjid*, you should offer the rest of your Prayer at home for Allah will bless your home because of your Prayer.' (*Muslim.*)

• Secondly, establish an *usra* or family circle to study the Quran with your family. The Quran alludes to reading of the Quran in families and in homes in the following verse: *And remember that which is recited in your houses of the Revelations of God and the Wisdom.* [al-Ahzab 33: 34.] You should aim to hold these sessions at least twice weekly, if not more regularly. Remember that the first recipients of the Message of the Quran were the members of the Prophet's household. They were the ones he paid most attention to in the early phase of his mission in Makka. So, you also must ensure that you spend adequate 'quality' time in educating and training your family.

Thirdly, develop the habit of having meals with your family. This will also provide a golden opportunity to interact with everyone, discuss family matters and reflect upon issues of the day.

Finally, to ensure that your home is a place of comfort and relaxation, you need to manage the stress in your life by adopting a balanced approach to living. Some degree of stress is inevitable and good. It keeps you aware and responsive. However, too much stress can damage your health, your relationships, and your ability to work for the sake of Allah. If you are taking your daily work stress to your home, then you may be disrupting one of the most important sources of your well-being. You must continually evaluate yourself by sitting with your family and discussing your performance. Discuss the responses to the following points with your family:

- The time I spend at work or in studying does not prevent me from having good communication with my family.
- My family is aware of what I want to achieve in my job, my studies and my life.
- Most of my time at home is not spent in working or studying at the expense of interacting with my family.
- I adequately participate in family matters so that in future I will not be guilty of neglecting my family.
- My time is balanced among my family, *masjid*, personal obligations and among non-Muslims.
- My morality is the same at home as it is at school, work, the *masjid* and among non-Muslims.
- My family means more to me than worldly possessions and accomplishments.
- I keep an open mind when I consider how my decisions will affect my family.

- I am involved with all my family members and I try to share in their areas of interest.
- It is easy for me to relax when I leave my work or my studies. I appreciate the beauty that Allah has placed around me.[5]

## OBLIGATIONS TO YOUR CHILDREN

As a parent, you must treat your children with love and kindness. The Prophet Muhammad said, 'He does not belong to us, Muslims, who is not kind to our young and does not respect our old.' (*Tirmidhi.*) Indeed, if people were to observe this single *hadith* in their inter-personal relations, many of the evils and discords that plague society would be removed.

Each child has the right to a good name, good character, good training, a quality education, and to be married to a suitable and compatible spouse. The Prophet further emphasised, 'No father can give a better gift to his children than providing them with a good education.' (*Bayhaqi.*)

Within the family, both mother and father have important roles to play in the growth and development of their children. But, mothers have an even more important role because they are the real teachers. The love and attention they can provide, the father cannot match. The father, of course, has to contribute as much as he can in spending quality time with his children and being the best role model for them. But, the real training will come primarily from the mother's affection, compassion, example and teaching.

We must also treat all of our children with the full care and attention that they deserve, be they male or female. However, in contemporary times, and a similar situation existed in the time of the Prophet, parents seem to give preferential treatment to their sons. This is why the Prophet has told us that we have a special obligation to our female off-spring. Ibn Abbas, may Allah be pleased with him, narrated that he said:

> Anyone who looks after and brings up three daughters, or sisters, educates them well, treats them with compassion, until Allah makes them self-sufficient, Allah guarantees him Paradise.' A man asked. 'Suppose there are only two?' He said, 'Yes, two as well.' People said, 'And if there be only one?' He said, 'Yes, even if there is only one.' (*Sharh al-Sunna*.)

This is how the Prophet emphasised the rights and obligations towards our children with special regard towards our daughters. This is something we must consider carefully.

## OBLIGATIONS TO YOUR PARENTS

After your obligations to Allah, your parents have the greatest right over you. You should treat them with love, kindness and respect. *Your Lord has decreed that you shall serve none but Him, and do good to your parents. Should one or both of them reach old age with you, never say 'Ugh' to them, nor scold either of them; but speak to them kindly and respectfully.* [al-Isra 17: 23.]

After every Prayer you should make *dua* for their well-being. The Quran says, *spread over them the wings of humility and mercy and say, My Lord, have mercy upon them, as they raised me up when I was little.* [al-Isra 17: 24]

Even if your parents are non-Muslims and they insist on you participating in that which is unlawful, you still have an obligation to treat them with goodness and kindness. Remember that their cultural background may not make them easily receptive to your new faith. So, the best way you can present Islam to them is to become a loving, obedient and caring child. Your *uswa* or example to your parents should also reflect the message of the Quran and the conduct of the Prophet Muhammad. The Quran explains the attitude we must adopt as follows:

> *And We enjoined upon man goodness towards his parents: his mother bore him by bearing strain upon strain, and his weaning takes two years. Hence, be thankful to Me and to your parents. With Me is the end of all journeys. Yet, should they endeavour to force you to make gods beside Allah, of whom you have no knowledge, then do not obey them. But, even then keep them company in this world's life with customary good behaviour, but follow the faith of those who turn towards Me.* [Luqman 31: 14-15.]

*Hadith* literature is also filled with many accounts and guidelines concerning the manner in which we should treat our parents even if they are non-Muslims. In one account, Asma, may Allah be pleased with her, recorded the advice of the Prophet when she turned to him, being unsure about the manner in which she should treat her mother who was still a non-Muslim:

> The mother of Asma, the daughter of Abu Bakr, was still a polytheist when she came to visit Asma during the time of the Muslims' peace treaty with the Quraysh. Asma asked the Prophet, 'O Messenger of Allah, my mother has come to see me. Should I receive her and treat her with all

the affection that is her due?' He said, 'Yes, treat her with full affection.' (*Bukhari, Muslim.*)

## OBLIGATIONS TO YOUR FELLOW MUSLIMS

*Ukhuwwa,* brotherhood in Islam, is primarily an ideological bond that binds Muslims to each other. [al-Hujurat 49: 10.] The Prophet said: 'The strongest link of faith is to love someone in order to gain the pleasure of Allah and to hate someone for the sake of Allah.' (*Ahmad.*) This relationship with your brother or sister should be based on the following:

- *Sincere advice:* You should give *nasiha* or sincere advice and counsel and you should also wish your brother well. A *hadith* states that '[The essence of] *Din* or religion is *nasiha.*' (*Muslim.*) True *iman* cannot be attained 'until you love for your brother what you love for yourself.' (*Bukhari, Muslim.*) The Prophet also said: 'The Believer is a mirror to a Believer, and the Believer is a brother to a Believer. He removes his injuries from him and protects him in his absence.' (*Tirmidhi.*)
- *Self-sacrifice:* You should give preference to your brother's welfare over your personal needs. The Quran records the attitude of true Believers: *But* [they] *give preference over themselves, even though poverty was their* [own lot]. [al-Hashr 59: 9.]
- *Justice:* The Quran declares: *Allah commands adl or justice and ihsan or doing that which is best.* [al-Nahl 16: 90.] You must fulfil all your obligations – moral, economic, social, and political – to all Muslims with firm and resolute justice.
- *Doing that which is best:* If *adl* is considered the foundation of your relationship, then, *ihsan* is its perfection. *Ihsan* demands that you do even more good to your brother. Additionally, if

your brother does some wrong you must respond to him
and his actions in a positive manner. The Quran advises: *The
good deed and the evil deed cannot be equal. Repel* [the evil] *with
that, which is better. Then he, between whom and you there was
enmity,* [will become] *as though he was a close friend.* [al-Fussilat
41: 34.]

- *Mercy:* In the Quran, Allah has used the term *rahma* or mercy
to depict the relationship between Muslims: *Muhammad is the
Messenger of Allah; and those who are with him are strong against
unbelievers,* [but] *full of compassion [ruhama] among themselves.*
[al-Fath 48: 29.] The Prophet also taught us: 'He who shows
mercy, Allah will shower His mercy upon him. Be merciful
to the people of this world so that the One above will shower
mercy on you.' (*Abu Dawud.*) He also said: 'The Believers in
their mutual love, compassion and sympathy are like one
body: when one of its parts suffers from some illness, the rest
of the body shares its suffering with sleeplessness and fever.'
(*Bukhari, Muslim.*)

- *Forgiveness:* Your heart should be filled with forgiveness for
'anger destroys *iman* like poisonous medicine turns honey
into waste.' (*Bayhaqi.*) The Quran also states: *So, pass over*
[their faults] *and ask for* [Allah's] *forgiveness for them.* [Al Imran
3: 159.]

- *Patience and perseverance:* You must demonstrate *sabr* or
patience and perseverance with your brother. Strive to forgive
your brother wholeheartedly despite having the ability and
the means to take revenge. The Quran states: *But, indeed, if
any show patience and forgive, that would be an affair of great
resolution.* [al-Shura 42: 43.]

- *Reliance and appreciation:* Your brother must be able to count on you in times of need. You should share in the pain of his adversity and the pleasure of his prosperity.

There are also certain things that you should consider in order to preserve the relationship with your brother and to prevent its disintegration. These include:

- Respect for his rights. [al-Baqara 2: 229.]
- Respect for the value of his life. [al-Nisa 4: 93.]
- Being careful with your language ensuring that you do not use abusive language or words that will offend him. [al-Hujurat 49: 11.]
- Ensuring that you never backbite or slander him. [al-Hujurat 49: 12.]
- Ensuring that you never embarrass him, belittle him, cast suspicion on him, ridicule him or go in search simply to expose his faults. [al-Hujurat 49: 11.]
- Ensuring that you do not hurt or harm him in any way; and finally, never become jealous of him. [al-Falaq 113: 5]

You can also make the relationship with your brother stronger by:

- Maintaining his honour and prestige.
- Participating in his pain and sorrow.
- Offering criticism and sincere advice to him; meeting him regularly.
- Visiting him when he is ill and making *dua* for his speedy recovery.
- Meeting him with love and a cheerful disposition; greeting him with words of peace.
- Embracing and shaking his hand on meeting him.

- Calling him by the best of names.
- Inquiring about his personal matters and expressing your concern and offering your assistance.
- Offering him gifts to express your love and closeness.
- Expressing your gratitude to him regularly.
- Sharing a meal with him whenever possible.
- Making *dua* for him regularly.
- Responding to him with love and affection.
- Always striving to settle your disputes with him in an amicable manner; being willing to forgive him.

Finally, always keep before you the verse of the Quran:

*The Believers, men and women, are protectors of one another: they enjoin what is just and forbid what is evil: they observe regular Prayers, practise regular charity and obey Allah and His Messenger. On them will Allah pour His Mercy: for Allah is Exalted in power, Wise.* [al-Tawba 9: 71.]

### OBLIGATIONS OF EMPLOYERS AND EMPLOYEES

As an employer, you have an obligation to care for your staff; provide the most suitable working environment; and ensure that they are fully compensated punctually, for all their services rendered: 'Give the labourer his wages before his sweat dries.' (*Ibn Majah.*) The Prophet also said that one of the persons he shall be against on the Day of Judgement is the man who does not pay the right wages to his employees after their labours.

As an employee, you must perform your job with diligence and proficiency. 'Verily, Allah loves that when anyone of you

does a job he should perfect it.' (*Bayhaqi*.) The Quran also
declares: *Work, because Allah, the Prophet and the Believers will
witness your work.* [al-Tawba 9: 105.] Know that the best food is
that which comes from your own efforts: 'No one eats better
food than what he earns by the labour of his own hands.'
(*Bukhari*.)

OBLIGATIONS TO YOUR NEIGHBOURS

Neighbours have rights, be they Muslims or non-Muslims. The
Prophet of Allah said: 'He is not a true Believer who eats his fill
while his neighbour is hungry.' (*Bayhaqi*.)

Thus, the quality of your *Din* and fate in the *Akhira* will also
be determined by how well you fulfil your obligations towards
your neighbours. In a *hadith* narrated by Abu Hurayrah, may
Allah be pleased with him, a man said:

'O Messenger of Allah, such and such woman has a
reputation for engaging very much in Prayers, Fasting and
Almsgiving, but she hurts her neighbours with her tongue
quite often.' He said, 'She will go to Hell.' Then he said,
'O Messenger of Allah, such and such woman engages in
only a little Prayer, Fasting and Almsgiving and gives just
a few pieces of cheese in charity, but she does not hurt her
neighbours with her tongue.' He said, 'She will go to
Paradise.' (*Ahmad, Bayhaqi*.)

The Quran defines the neighbour in a very wide sense. [al-
Nisa 4: 36-37.] One class of neighbours is our relatives. Another
class are those who are not our relatives and the third class of

IN THE EARLY HOURS

neighbours are those who sit with us, even for a few minutes. This third class of neighbours is a very wide group and includes those who sit by your side. If you are travelling in a taxi, bus, train or aeroplane the person who is sitting by your side is your neighbour. If you are in the office, your co-worker is your neighbour. If you are at school, your classmate is your neighbour.

The Prophet gave a comprehensive account of our duties towards our neighbours when requested to do so by one of his Companions:

> If he asks for a loan, you should give him a loan; if he wants your help, you should help him; if he be sick, you should go to see him; if he be needy you should try to fulfil his need; if he gets good news, you should congratulate him; if any calamity befalls him, it is your duty to console him; if he dies, you should attend his funeral; you should not raise your walls to such a height that they obstruct the ventilation of your neighbour's house, even if he is willing; do not tantalise your neighbour with the smell of your delicious food unless you send a portion of it to him; if you bring fruit into your house then send some to your neighbour; otherwise, keep it hidden from your neighbour, and you should also be careful that your children do not take some out, else the children of your neighbour may feel disappointed. (*Taharani.*)

Among the rights of your neighbour is that his life, property and honour must be protected. Violation of any of them is *haram* or unlawful. His life is inviolable. To kill someone – be he Muslim or non-Muslim – is such a great crime that if someone commits first degree murder Allah says that person will live in *Jahannam* for ever and ever. Of course, if the death was accidental, one can pay compensation to the victim's family.

Remember that the life of a non-Muslim is as important as that of a Muslim. The Prophet Muhammad said that, 'One who kills a non-Muslim whose protection is pledged will never smell the fragrance of *Janna*, even though it reaches as far as 40 years distance.' (*Bukhari, Muslim.*)

So the life of the non-Muslim is also inviolable, as is his property and his honour. All must be respected and safeguarded. This is especially important for us to consider because we live in a multi-cultural and multi-religious society and, unfortunately, there are many misconceptions prevailing among Muslims about the extent of their obligations towards non-Muslims. The Prophet himself used to pay special attention to the needs of non-Muslims even when there was poverty, hardship and difficulties in the Muslim community.

## THE RIGHTS OF ANIMALS

Animals have rights, for all of Allah's creatures comprise His 'family'. Sahl ibn Amr narrated that once the Messenger of Allah, passed by a camel who was so emaciated that his belly seemed to have disappeared. He said, 'Fear Allah regarding the animals who cannot speak. Ride on them while they are healthy, and eat of them when they are healthy.' (*Abu Dawud.*)

A famous *hadith* says that 'a woman was punished and thrown into Hell-fire on account of her cat. She kept it tied up till it died of hunger: she neither gave it something to eat nor drink, nor let it go so that it could eat things on earth'. (*Bukhari, Muslim.*) The Prophet also said:

'Forgiveness was granted to a prostitute! She came upon a dog at the mouth of a well, which was panting and was about to die of thirst. She took off her leather sock, tied it with her headscarf and drew some water from the well for the dog. It was for this act of kindness that she was forgiven her sins.' When asked, 'Are we rewarded even for good we do to animals?' he replied, 'Reward is given for good done to any living creature.' (*Bukhari, Muslim.*)

If Allah commands us not to treat animals in this way, you can well imagine the extent of our obligations to human beings. The greater the benevolence exhibited by someone, the dearer that person is to Allah.

### SUMMARY

All creatures are Allah's family; and Allah loves most those who treat His family well and kindly. Our responsibility to others is especially important for us to consider for there is no Divine pardon in cases where personal rights have been violated.

Your primary obligation after satisfying your personal needs is towards your family. Indeed, after Allah, your parents have the greatest right over you. Fulfil your obligations towards your spouse and treat your children with love and kindness.

When it comes to the obligations to your fellow Muslims, know that the strongest link of faith is to love someone in order to gain the pleasure of Allah.

As an employer, know that you have an important responsibility towards your employees. Similarly, as an employee, you must perform your work with proficiency.

Your fate in the *Akhira* will also be determined by how well you fulfil your obligations to your neighbours be they Muslims or non-Muslims. The Prophet used to pay particular attention to the needs of non-Muslims even when there were difficulties in the Muslim community.

Animals have rights for all of Allah's creatures comprise His 'family': 'Fear Allah regarding the animals who cannot speak. Ride on them while they are healthy, and eat of them when they are healthy.'

May Allah enable us all to fulfil our obligations to the members of His family.

## CHAPTER SEVEN

# *Meeting Allah*

THE most important questions in life are those that deal with the meaning and purpose of man's existence. The Quran explains that the human being has been placed on this earth to utilise his enormous potential to conduct himself in a manner which will fulfil his purpose in life.

> *It is He who has created death and life that He may test which of you is best in deed.* [al-Mulk 67: 2.]

The Quran further explains that man's role on earth is to live as his Creator desires him to live: in surrender and worship to Him alone. This is not because Allah in any way needs his worship, but because man needs to worship only his Creator and none else so that his own nature is not perverted and corrupted, and so that he does not live in opposition to his intrinsic character. Only by so living will his earthly life be set on the right path and prosper, bringing him peace and happiness.

> *I have not created jinn and men except to serve Me. I desire of them no provision; neither do I desire that they should feed Me. Surely God is the All-Provider, the Possessor of Strength, the Eternal.* [al-Dhariyat 51: 56-58.]

Man, with no 'mentionable' history before birth, has been given *the faculties of hearing and seeing,* [al-Dahr 76: 2] *two eyes and a tongue, and a pair of lips,* [al-Balad 90: 8-9] as well as the capacity to reason and discern between right and wrong in using his freedom of will.

Given freedom of will, judgement is inevitable. The human being must give an account of his conduct and must face the consequences of how he lives his life. Obviously, to be judged fairly, this judgement must be made only after his earthly life has come to an end, and only by the One who gave this life, who knows everything, and who is All-Powerful and All-Just. Only then can he be judged fairly, and duly rewarded and punished, for everything – from his innermost thoughts to the consequences of his conduct that extend far and wide, and beyond his life for generations to come.

> *What, did you think that We created you in mere idle play, and that you would not be returned to Us? But, high exalted is God, the King, the True! There is no god but He, the Lord of the Noble Throne.* [al-Muminun 23: 115-116.]

A person's ultimate destiny, therefore, lies in the Life to Come, in the *Akhira.* Everyone will be judged there by due process of justice, fairly and equitably, mercifully and kindly. No one will be wronged or dealt with unjustly even by an atom's weight.

> *Surely God shall not wrong so much as an atom's weight.* [al-Nisa 4: 40.]

> *This is only what you had sent forth; you are being recompensed only for what you had done before.* [al-Kahf 18: 49.]

Thus, everything in our lives is being recorded. Even the smallest of incidents will be replayed before our eyes on the Day of Judgement. That Judgement will be final and one from which there will be no escape. Paradise will be the reward for excellence in doing good, while Hell-fire will be the penalty for those who were ungrateful and indulged in evil:

> The parable of the Paradise promised to those who are conscious of God [is that of a Garden] through which running waters flow: [but, unlike an earthly garden,] its fruits will be everlasting, and [so will be] its shade. Such will be the destiny of those who remain conscious of God – just as the destiny of those who deny the truth will be the fire. [al-Rad 13: 35.]

The delights and pleasures of the Hereafter, as well as the penalty for those who condemn themselves to darkness and the wrath of Allah, are described in such great detail in the Quran that almost one quarter of it is related to the *Akhira*. This is what the Prophet came to convey and this is what instils meaning and purpose to our lives.

### THE OBJECTIVE OF LIFE

When the lifestyle of one who is working solely for the material gains of this world is compared with that of a person who is striving for the everlasting rewards of the Hereafter, there is seemingly very little difference. In both cases, each person is seen to be striving to maintain a quality life. The Quran, however, states that the two parties are far from equal: *Is then the one who believes equal to the man who is a transgressor and wicked? Not equal are they.* [al-Sajda 32: 18.]

It is clear that the non-believer, limited to himself and feeding upon his own desires, cannot compare with the true Believer. The non-believer may find that all his worldly desires are fulfilled, but his accomplishments will only bring temporary satisfaction:

> *To him who desires only this fleeting life, We grant him only here and only as much as We please, only to whomever We will; but in the end We consign him to Hell.* [al-Isra 17: 18.]

The true Believer on the other hand, may achieve worldly gains but he realises that true contentment will only come when the ultimate reward of Paradise and the pleasure of his Lord is achieved.

> *Verily, that which is with Allah is best for you, if you but knew: all that which is with you is bound to end, whereas all that which is with Allah is everlasting.* [al-Nahl 16: 95-96.]

This understanding of life and its true objective is the secret of the believer's strength and support. This makes him the most powerful and resourceful person to walk upon the earth. The Quran continues in Sura al-Isra:

> *But, as for those who desire the life to come, and strive for it as it ought to be striven for, and are true Believers – they are the ones whose strivings find acceptance and reward.* [al-Isra 17: 19.]

Start, then, to prepare for the *Akhira* today! Why waste your time and energy on what will perish when you can use the same

to earn the delights and pleasures of the Life to Come?
Everything you have must be put forward as an investment for
that life, but you must keep in mind that the investment is not
the objective. All that Allah has bestowed on you – body, mind,
faculties and property – are valuables for investment, but the real
objective is to earn the pleasure of Allah and the rewards of *Janna*.

Remember that your personal destiny and, therefore, the end
of all your life's pursuits, lie in the *Akhira*, but the road to that
destiny lies in *Dunya*, in this world. Indeed the achievements
made during the time of the Prophet were the results of full
participation in this world – neither withdrawing nor retiring
from it – for the sake of the Life to Come. The Prophet and his
Companions planned for this world as though they were going
to stay here forever but equally they sought the rewards of the
Hereafter as though death was close at hand. It is this delicate
balance that you must strive to achieve in your approach to life.
The Prophet Muhammad said:

> This *Din* or way of life is easy. But if anyone overdoes it,
> it gets the better of him. So keep to the right course,
> approximate to perfection, rejoice, and ask for help in the
> mornings, the evenings, and some of the later part of the
> night. (*Bukhari*.)

## THE REALITY OF THE HEREAFTER

For those who sat and listened to the Prophet, the Hereafter
became almost a living reality to the extent that they could
almost visualise it with their own eyes. On some occasions,
during the Prophet's descriptions of the *Akhira*, they observed

him going forward as if to grasp something while on other occasions he would withdraw as if to save himself. When questioned about those unusual movements the Prophet explained that as he spoke, he saw the fruits of *Janna* in front of him. He reached out wanting to seize some so that he could show them. He said that, had he done so, it would have provided enough food for the entire world in all times to come. Similarly, when he withdrew, he saw the Hell-fire in front of him and wanted to save himself from it. It was this and other similar experiences witnessed by the *Sahaba* which were responsible for reforming their lives so completely that all their morals, manners, activities, goals in life – indeed, their entire purpose of existence – was determined by their awareness of their meeting with Allah. It is this reality and conviction in our ultimate fate – repeatedly emphasised in the Quran and in the life example of the Prophet – that we must continuously refer to for inspiration in conducting life's activities.

## THE CERTAINTY OF DEATH

Allah has created everything with a fixed life span. The Quran states: *It is not given to any soul to die save by God's permission, and at an appointed time.* [Al Imran 3: 145.] Indeed there is no certainty in life except death. *Every soul will taste death.* [Al Imran 3: 185.] Not only is death itself inescapable, but the place and the very day and hour of death have been forever fixed: *No person knows what he will earn tomorrow and no person knows in what land he will die.* [Luqman 31: 34.] *When the time arrives they cannot tarry a single moment nor can they go ahead.* [al-Nahl 16: 61.]

In death, we are compelled to return to God. In life, however, we can choose to draw closer to God voluntarily by living our lives according to His will. In this way, we have the opportunity to meet

Allah and gain His pleasure even before we leave this world.

Those who fail to use the bounties of Allah to earn His pleasure during this life, will forever regret their mistakes, for the cessation of life brings the cessation of opportunities for redemption and salvation, as the Quran warns:

> *When death comes to one of them, he says, 'My Lord, let me return, let me return to life, so that I may act righteously in whatever I have left behind.' Nay, it is but a meaningless word he utters; for, behind them now is the barrier of death until the day they shall be raised up. Then, when the Trumpet will be blown, no ties of kinship will remain between them that day, neither would anyone be able to take care of another. Then, they whose weight of good deeds is heavy in the balance will attain salvation. But, they whose weight is light in the balance, will have squandered their own lives. In Hell will they abide forever.* [al-Muminun 23: 99-103.]

## MAN'S FORGETFULNESS

Though death is certain, we tend to forget from time to time our meeting with our Lord. This forgetfulness, although part of human nature can make us stray from our true mission in life: *If anyone withdraws himself from Allah's remembrance, Most Gracious, We appoint for him an evil one to be his intimate companion.* [al-Zukhruf 43: 36.] Forgetfulness, however, can be overcome by remembering Allah in all of life's activities, as the Quran again declares: *Those who fear Allah, when a thought of evil from Shaytan assaults them, bring Allah to remembrance – whereupon, lo! They see aright.* [al-Araf 7: 201.] Additionally, we are urged in the Quran to make the following supplication:

*Our Lord, take us not to task if we forget or make mistakes. Our Lord, lay not upon us a burden like that which You laid on those before us.*

*Our Lord, make us not bear burdens which we have no strength to bear. Pardon us, and forgive us, and have mercy on us. You are our Lord Supreme: Help us against people who deny the truth.* [al-Baqara 2: 286.]

Know that to fear death from which there is no escape is *foolish*. Having no fear of what is going to happen after death, though it is within our power to change it in our favour, is *reckless*. Allah reminds us in the Quran, *Do not throw yourself into destruction with your own hands.* [al-Baqara 2: 195.] For, no effort to please Allah will be left unrewarded, while every effort made to seek the pleasures of this world will come to naught. Moreover, the Prophet reminded us that nothing will go with us to our graves except our deeds and that constant reminder of death will assist in keeping our indulgence in *Dunya* in perspective: 'Remember often the terminator of pleasures [i.e. death]'. (*Tirmidhi.*) He also advised that we should take time to attend *Janaza* or funeral prayers, as well as visit the graves of those who have made the transition into the Next-life, for these too will serve as reminders of our eventual fate: 'He who expects to meet God should visit the graves for they remind us of the Hereafter.' (*Muslim.*)

The Prophet also warned us that if we seek only the fulfilment of our selfish worldly desires, our lives may well become filled with frustration:

Whoever allows the world to become his biggest concern has nothing to do with Allah, and Allah will instil four qualities into his heart: anxiety which will never leave him, business which he will never be free from; poverty which he will never rid himself of, and hope which he will never fulfil. (*Tabarani*.)

Additionally, one of the worst punishments the Quran describes is reserved for those who remain forgetful of Allah. On the Day of Judgement Allah will not speak to them. He will not even look in their direction. In this world they will claim to belong to Allah but they are heedless of His commands. On the Day that matters most, there will be a wall between them and Allah. His mercy and His compassion will be overflowing, but not for them.

*Behold, those who barter away their bond with Allah and their pledges for a trifling gain – they shall not partake in the blessings of the life to come; and Allah will neither speak unto them nor will He cleanse them of their sins; and grievous suffering awaits them.* [Al Imran 3: 77.]

### SEEKING ALLAH'S MERCY

The abundance of Allah's *rahma* or mercy will not come without pure actions. Pure actions, however, when performed, will make you deserving of Allah's mercy. This, in turn, will enable you to earn the delights of *Janna* and His pleasure. The Quran proclaims: *Call on Him with fear and longing. Surely, Allah's mercy is ever near to the doers of good.* [al-Araf 7: 56.] The Messenger of God also said:

'No one will be saved [from the Hell-fire and admitted into Paradise] by his deeds alone.' When asked, 'Not even you, O Messenger of God!', he said, 'Yes, not even me, unless Allah covers me with His mercy. So, do good deeds properly, sincerely and moderately in the morning, in the afternoon and during part of the night. Always remember moderation and always abide by moderation. Thus, you will reach your destination.' (*Bukhari, Muslim.*)

Be reassured that Allah is not a vengeful God, ready to punish, but rather, one who is full of mercy and compassion. He, Himself has declared: *My mercy encompasses all things.* [al-Araf 7: 156.] Likewise, consider the manner in which our actions are recorded in His scale of justice, as explained by the Prophet:

Allah records the good deeds and the bad deeds thus: If anyone intends to do a good deed but does not actually do it, Allah writes it down with Him as a full good deed. If he intends it, and does it too, Allah writes it down with Him as ten to seven hundred times that good deed, or many times over. If anyone intends to do a bad deed but does not actually do it, Allah writes it down with Him as a full good deed. When he intends a bad deed and does it as well, only then Allah writes it down as one bad deed. (*Bukhari, Muslim.*)

Thus, as long as our actions are worthy and deserving of Allah's mercy, His mercy will not be denied to us. The Prophet has again explained:

There are one hundred parts of mercy. Allah has given only one part which is distributed among the *jinn*, humankind, animals and insects. It is because of this that they are kind to one another, show mercy to one another; it is because of it that a wild animal is kind to its young. But, Allah has kept ninety-nine parts of mercy with Him, which He will show to His servants on the Day of Resurrection. (*Bukhari, Muslim.*)

### SEEKING ALLAH'S FORGIVENESS

The decision to live our lives for the sake of Allah is no guarantee that we will not forget Allah and commit mistakes for 'all children of Adam are sinners, but best among sinners are those who constantly repent'. (*Tirmidhi.*) *Imam* Bukhari recorded that even the Prophet, though he was sinless, 'sought Allah's forgiveness 70 times a day'. We should therefore, constantly seek the forgiveness of Allah for every single sin, small or great. Allah says:

*Ask forgiveness from your Lord, then turn towards Him in repentance; He will loosen the sky over you in abundance, and He will add strength unto your strength.* [Hud 11: 52.]

Seeking continuous forgiveness of Allah will assist in ensuring that our hearts and souls remain pure and wholesome. The Prophet said in this regard:

When a Believer sins, a black spot appears on his heart. But if he repents and seeks Allah's forgiveness, his heart becomes cleansed and polished. However if he continues to commit more and more sins [without seeking forgiveness], the spot continues to spread and ultimately covers all of his heart. This is the rust which Allah mentions [in the Quran]: *What deeds they earn rust upon their hearts.* [al-Mutaffifin 83: 14.] (*Ahmad, Tirmidhi.*)

Whatever the magnitude of our misdeeds, Allah is always ready to respond with an even greater amount of pardon. Therefore, never despair of the mercy of Allah, in seeking His forgiveness, even for those sins committed repeatedly: *O My servants who have transgressed against themselves, despair not of Allah's mercy; for Allah forgives all sins, surely He is the All-Forgiving, the Mercy-Giving.* [al-Zumar 39: 53.] Thus, as long as there is hope there remains opportunity for redemption and salvation.

Be aware, though, that the best form of repentance involves a firm resolve to reform and do better. The Messenger of Allah said:

Remain conscious of Allah and fear Him wherever you are, and follow a bad deed with a good deed which will wipe it out, and behave well towards people. (*Tirmidhi.*)

SELF-EVALUATION

The Prophet emphasised the necessity of *Ihtisab* or self-evaluation at every opportunity: 'Everyone starts his day and is a vendor of his soul, either freeing it or bringing about its ruin.' (*Muslim.*) Umar ibn al-Khattab, may Allah be pleased with him, also said in this respect:

Judge yourself before you are judged, evaluate yourself before you are evaluated and be ready for the greatest investigation.

At every Prayer time, especially in the early hours of the morning, when you are alone and can feel your own heart beating – seek forgiveness from Allah. The time of *Salat al-Fajr*, before the start of each day, is an ideal occasion to take account of yourself and plan for the day ahead.

*Imam* Tirmidhi related that the Prophet said, on the Day of Judgement no child of Adam will move from the presence of God, unless he has answered the following five questions:

- In what pursuits and work did he spend his time?
- For what ends did he use his mental and physical energies?
- By what means did he earn his wealth?
- How did he spend his wealth?
- How far did he act according to what he knew was right?

These five points can serve as a useful self-analysis programme. They can assist in checking our moral motivations, God-consciousness and determination to work for the cause of Allah. This self-analysis programme, when implemented on a regular basis, will serve as an important measure of your readiness to meet with Allah.

### CONQUERING FEAR OF DEATH

The Day of Judgement, though it is to be feared, must also inspire in us a desire and eagerness to meet Allah. Sayyida Aisha reported that the Prophet said:

'Whoever loves to meet Allah, Allah loves to meet with him; and whoever dislikes the meeting with Allah, Allah also dislikes the meeting with him.'

I asked: 'O Prophet of God, is it because of the dislike of death, for all of us dislike death?'

He said: 'It is not so, but rather it is that when the Believer is given news of Allah's mercy, His approval and His Paradise, he likes to meet Allah and Allah likes to meet him; but when the unbeliever is given news of Allah's punishment and His displeasure, He dislikes to meet Allah and Allah dislikes to meet him.' (*Muslim.*)

Our eagerness and desire to meet Allah should therefore, be echoed in all our Prayers. The Prophet Muhammad used to supplicate repeatedly:

> O Allah, I ask You for a soothing life after death, and I ask You for the pleasure of looking upon Your Face and for the yearning to meet You, free from suffering distress or from trial that leads one astray. O Allah, adorn us with the ornament of faith and make us guides and rightly guided. (*Nasai.*)

This desire to meet Allah will calm our fear of death, which is only a natural instinct. Even the Prophet Musa, on whom be peace, out of fear ran away when he saw his staff turning into a serpent. [Ta Ha 20: 17-24.] Fear, though, can be conquered with *dhikr*, doing good and keeping ever before us, our meeting with the Lord and Master of the Day of Judgement.

> *Whoever hopes to meet his Lord. He should do good deeds and associate none other in the service of his Lord.* [al-Kahf 18: 110.]

## SUMMARY

Preparation to meet Allah must be the purpose and ultimate goal of our existence. It is the most critical decision and resolution we must make today. This will set the course and direction of our entire lives – to live according to the Quran, as shown by that most noble of exemplars, Muhammad, upon whom be peace.

The knowledge that Allah is pleased with us will be the climax of our mission in life. This will be attained when we find Him responding, God willing, to each of us in our hour of greatest need with the reassuring and welcoming words:

> *O soul at peace, return unto your Lord, well-pleased, well-pleasing! Enter among My servants! Enter My Paradise!* [al-Fajr 89: 27-30.]

# Notes

1. Al-Ghazali in *Ihya*. See *Inner Dimensions of Islamic Worship*, Islamic Foundation, Leicester, p. 29.

2. Cited by al-Ghazali in *Ihya Ulum al-Din*. See *Inner Dimensions of Islamic Worship*, Islamic Foundation, Leicester, p. 76.

3. Fathi Yakan, *Problems of the Dawa and the Daiya*, IIFSO, Kuwait, 1984, P. 71.

4. See Quran: 33: 4-5; 5: 67; 2: 151; 48: 28; 9: 33; 61: 9; 7: 157.

5. *Islamic Horizons*, p. 12, February 1985, Indianapolis.

# Further Reading

- *Way to the Quran* by Khurram Murad,
  The Islamic Foundation, Leicester.

- *Let Us be Muslims* by Sayyid Abul Ala Mawdudi,
  translated and edited by Khurram Murad,
  The Islamic Foundation, Leicester.

- *Sacrifice: The Making of a Muslim* by Khurram Murad,
  The Islamic Foundation, Leicester.

- *The Islamic Movement: Dynamics of Values, Power and Change*
  by Sayyid Abul Ala Mawdudi, translated and edited by
  Khurram Murad, The Islamic Foundation, Leicester.

- *Remembrance and Prayer: The Way of Prophet Muhammad* by
  Muhammad al-Ghazali, The Islamic Foundation, Leicester.

- *Inner Dimensions of Islamic Worship* by al-Ghazali, trans. by
  Muhtar Holland, The Islamic Foundation, Leicester.

- *Morals and Manners in Islam: A Guide to Islamic Adab* by
  Marwan Ibrahim al-Kaysi, The Islamic Foundation,
  Leicester.

- *Lasting Prayers* by Ahmad Zaki Hammad,
  Quranic Literary Society, Illinois.

- *To be a Muslim* by Fathi Yakan,
  American Trust Publications, Indianapolis.

- *The Islamic Movement: Problems and Perspectives* by
  Fathi Yakan, American Trust Publications, Indianapolis.

- *Freedom and Responsibility in the Quranic Perspective* by
  Hassan al-Anani, American Trust Publications, Indianapolis.

- *The Muslim Character* by Muhammad al-Ghazali,
  IIFSO, Kuwait.

- *Selected Prayers* by Jamal Badawi, Ta Ha Publishers, London.

- *Islam the Natural Way* by Abdul Wahid Hamid,
  MELS, London.

# Index of Quranic Verses

7: 31 *p36*
7: 42 *p74*
7: 56 *p139*
7: 189 *p115*
7: 201 *p137*

AL-ANFAL
8: 2 *p42*
8: 66 *p74*

AL-TAWBA
9: 24 *p105*
9: 71 *p124*
9: 103 *p95*
9: 105 *p125*
9: 111 *pp2, 7, 97*

YUNUS
10: 25 *p83*

HUD
11: 52 *p141*
11: 90 *p58*

YUSUF
12: 84 *p74*

AL-RAD
13: 28 *p55*
13: 35 *p133*

IBRAHIM
14: 7 *p60*
14: 18 *p60*
14: 22 *p8*

AL-HIJR
15: 56 *p78*

AL-NAHL
16: 17-19 *p58*
16: 61 *p136*
16: 78 *p28*
16: 90 *p121*
16: 95-96 *p134*

AL-ISRA
17: 18 *p134*
17: 19 *pp12, 134*
17: 23 *p119*
17: 24 *p119*
17: 32 *p81*
17: 78 *pp44, 54*
17: 110 *p37*

AL-KAHF
18: 27-28 *p52*
18: 49 *p132*
18: 110 *p144*

TA HA
20: 14 *p33*
20: 17-24 *p144*
20: 115 *p15*

AL-ANBIYA
21: 107 *p93*

AL-HAJJ
22: 46 *p24*
22: 78 *p69*

AL-MUMINUN
23: 99-103 *p137*
23: 115-116 *p132*

AL-NUR
24: 21 *p19*
24: 30 *p81*
24: 31 *p81*
24: 32-33 *p114*

AL-FURQAN
25: 64 *p38*
25: 67 *p107*
25: 70 *p17*
25: 74 *p115*

AL-SHUARA
26: 77-82 *p58*
26: 88-89 *p23*

AL-HASHR
59: 7 *p89*
59: 9 *pp106, 121*
59: 19 *p25*
59: 20 *p2*

AL-SAFF
61: 2-3 *p73*
61: 10 *p62*

AL-JUMUA
62: 9-10 *p26*

AL-MUNAFIQUN
63: 9-10 *p27*

AL-TALAQ
65: 3 *p68*
65: 7 *p74*

AL-TAHRIM
66: 6 *p114*

AL-MULK
67: 2 *p131*

AL-QALAM
68: 4 *p75*

AL-MA'ARIJ
70: 5 *p74*
70: 22-23 *p35*

AL-MUZZAMMIL
73: 6 *pix*
73: 20 *p95*

AL-MUDDATHTHIR
74: 2-3 *p69*

AL-DAHR
76: 2 *p132*
76: 8-9 *p97*

AL-NAZIAT
79: 40-41 *p19*
79: 41 *p2*

AL-MUTAFFIFIN
83: 14 *p142*

AL-ALA
87: 9-10 *p53*
87: 14-15 *p25*

AL-FAJR
89: 27-30 *p145*

AL-BALAD
90: 8-9 *p132*

AL-SHAMS
91: 9 *p2*

AL-LAYL
92: 4-10 *p97*
92: 5-7 *p13*
92: 18 *p95*

AL-DUHA
93: 6-10 *p60*

AL-TIN
95: 4-6 *p9*

AL-ALAQ
96: 1-5 *p69*
96: 19 *p37*

AL-ZALZALAH
99: 6-8 *p9*

AL-ASR
103: 3 *p53*

AL-MAUN
107: 1-7 *p72*
107: 4-6 *p35*

AL-FALAQ
113: 5 *p123*

How Do I
Help a Hurting
Friend?

# How Do I
# Help a Hurting
# Friend?

## Rod J. K. Wilson

**BakerBooks**
Grand Rapids, Michigan

Published by Baker Books
a division of Baker Publishing Group
P.O. Box 6287, Grand Rapids, MI 49516-6287
www.bakerbooks.com

Printed in the United States of America

Library of Congress Cataloging-in-Publication Data
Wilson, Rod.
    How do I help a hurting friend? / Rod J. K. Wilson.
        p.   cm.
    Includes bibliographical references.
    ISBN 10: 0-8010-6609-3 (pbk.)
    ISBN 978-0-8010-6609-2 (pbk.)
        1. Caring—Religious aspects—Christianity. 2. Helping behavior—Religious aspects—Christianity. 3. Friendship—Religious aspects—Christianity. I. Title.
    BV4647.S9W55 2006
    253—dc22                                                        2005036430

This book is dedicated to
the people in "The Support Group,"
who showed courage in being willing
to deal with real problems—

Kathy, Marilyn, Neil, Evi, Jim,
Cheryl, Ken, Brian, Linda, Sandy,
Vanessa, Bev,
and especially to the memories of
Kelly and Karen

# Contents

## Acknowledgments

The writing of a book is usually the end result of a series of connections and relationships that have been woven together. I am indebted to the following people for their contribution to this project.

The staff of Baker Publishing Group brought their usual thoroughness and thoughtfulness to the table.

My administrative assistant, Bev Bandstra, is a great help in all aspects of my work and also brings a careful editorial eye to the written page.

My friends who are involved in the care of others—Laraine Birnie, Brian Cunnington, Rudy Dirks, Paddy Ducklow, Paul Fletcher, Jay Gurnett, Peter Roebbelen, Cathy Sakiyama, Ken and Gail Stevenson, Don Symons, Glenn and Mary Taylor, and Nicholas Wilson—had something unique to offer at various stages of the writing.

For many years James and Heather Ann Penner have provided a safe place for me to be able to share my own hurts, and in that sense they know how to help a hurting friend.

Finally to my daughter Jess, who knows what it is to experience pain, and my wife, Bev, who has been my most loyal friend in the midst of both joy and sorrow—thank you!

# 1

# Please Understand Me

People have problems.
If you are a lay leader in a local church, sit on a church committee, attend a small group, form part of the youth leadership team, serve food in the kitchen, carry out any responsibility in the church, or simply hang around after the Sunday morning service, you have ample evidence to support this claim.

While this simple sentence has only three words, it reflects a complex reality in our broken world. We all struggle. We all do battle. We all have various things we have to face. Look around. Look within. People have problems.

What do people who are struggling with problems need? In our Western culture, where we have an answer for every question and a solution for every difficulty, we have a natural tendency to want to solve the problem immediately. When someone has a struggle with self-image, we want it to disappear. If a member of our small group comes from a dysfunctional family, we want them to get past it. The fellow deacon struggling with depression produces in us a desire for the quick fix.

When the quick fix does not come, this is the point at which most friends and family members struggle. Not only is the person experiencing the difficulty tired of their problem but others are growing weary of it as well.

When is it going to go away? When is the problem going to stop? Isn't there a solution out there somewhere? Can't these things be cured? A lot of us move from being tired of the difficulty into growing tired of the person. They become a nuisance, an irritant, someone to be avoided rather than embraced. This powerful message is often picked up by the other person: if you are not going to get better, I am not going to be there for you.

The ripple effects of this sad scenario are many. Relationships become damaged and the person with the problem has their difficulties compounded by interpersonal strain. The person who has withdrawn experiences a degree of guilt and remorse but is not sure what to do about it. They know impatience with others is not an ideal way to live but they believe they do not have any other options. In many situations the person with the problem leaves the church only to have the same pattern redevelop in a new community. People in the new community are drawn in, but after a significant period of time trying to help the person out of their difficulty, they eventually feel helpless and pull back. I wonder sometimes whether church hopping, or as I like to call it, the circulation of the saints in evangelical churches, is more about people with problems not getting what they need than anything that is related to the church and its programs.

So what do people with problems need? Among many other things, they need to be understood. _Don't give quick solutions. Listen._

The last five words in this simple sentence highlight a complex issue in human relationships. When presented with someone's problems our natural tendency is not to understand. Most of us respond by *evaluating*, *advising*, or *interpreting* before even beginning to understand.

Take eight-year-old Michael. Born to a cocaine-addicted mother, he was sent from foster home to foster home for the first six years of his life. For the past two years he has been in a stable environment and his adoptive parents have done their best to nurture and care for him, although he continues to be shy and insecure. Periodically, Michael's tendencies to explore come into tension with his parents' strong desire to have a neat and clean house. His father, in particular, is a neat freak and highly values a spotless floor in the front foyer of their house. Dad, who also likes the house to be quiet, struggles with how loudly Michael speaks when he is excited.

On this particular occasion Michael comes running up the driveway with a large frog that he has caught in the pond down the street. His face is beaming, reflecting his satisfaction in capturing this delightful creature. Given his age, his excitement, and, most importantly, his background, he is not concerned at all with the fact that he had secured the frog from a very muddy side of the pond. The door opens, Michael screams in a high-pitched voice for Mom and Dad to come and see what he caught, and the mud dribbles all over the front foyer.

What is the parental dilemma in this scenario? Michael has self-image problems. He finds it easy to put himself down, to not value what he has done, and to experience a general worthlessness as he goes through life. In this moment he is in a different space. He is pleased with himself, proud of what he has done and wants to share it enthusiastically with people he cares about. The test for Mom and particularly for Dad is clear. They have two choices as they evaluate: If they want to understand Michael and listen to him in the fullest sense possible, they will recognize the priority of a child who feels significant and expresses his accomplishment with enthusiasm even though he has created a floor that needs to be cleaned. In contrast, they could evaluate the situation, put a priority on the importance of a clean floor, and create an environment where Michael feels devalued and is punished for being enthusiastic.

While evaluating is typical for many of us, the most natural response to the problems of others is advising. Arnold is a workaholic in the classic sense of the word. He leaves for work very early every morning, rarely gets home for supper, and spends a substantial portion of most weekends at his desk. Holidays are not part of his thinking, so while his wife and children will force him to get away now and again, he is in constant contact with work and seems to never be quite relaxed. Underneath his apparently successful exterior is an uptight, insecure person whose sense of identity is wrapped up in performance and behavior. In other words, he needs to be doing in order to feel that he is all right.

Friends of Arnold and his wife decide that what he needs is a proper vacation. The reason that he is so burned-out and fatigued is that he has not taken enough time off. They give him a gift of a long weekend away at a lakeside resort. "This will do you good," they tell him. "It will help you slow down and make you feel better again. We have found ourselves recharged after going there for a long weekend."

No one could question the sincerity of their intent, but in their desire to advise they have really not understood Arnold. A weekend away would be like a small bandage on a large open wound. Until he deals with the inner dynamics that are driving the workaholism, he will continue to experience the symptoms of burnout.

Apart from evaluating and advising, we also have a natural tendency to interpret. Charis has really struggled in her five-year-old marriage. Her husband, Gerrit, out of his own sense of pain, has a high need to control both situations and people. When there is ambiguity in any situation he quickly moves to eliminate it and bring the "right" perspective to bear. Charis is often embarrassed in social situations at church when she gives an opinion or an idea and Gerrit quickly jumps in to correct her. Typically this takes some time and she feels like a child as he functions in a parental role. She also has the intuitive sense that their interaction embarrasses others, as they are not sure how to react when Gerrit is in this mode.

For most of the five years, Charis has been trying to deal with Gerrit's control but has not been sure what to do about it. She is reluctant to tell friends or family because she does not want them to have a bad impression of her husband. She is fearful of counseling, so has not resorted to that route either. Finally, one day, she decides to tell her good friend Elizabeth. Elizabeth divorced Cam a few years ago after he engaged in serial extramarital affairs and showed no indication of change.

Charis was only a few moments into the conversation when Elizabeth moved to the edge of her chair and exclaimed, "Tell me no more. You don't need to live a life like that. This is exactly what happened with Cam."

Clearly Charis will not come out of that interaction with a sense of being understood, heard, and listened to. Elizabeth has interpreted the marriage through the grid of her own experience and has not stopped to really hear Charis's experience, not even to hear that there has been no infidelity.

These vignettes do not teach us that evaluating, advising, and interpreting are always wrong and inappropriate. In all problems there is a place for these kinds of interventions—if they are well timed. But the most important thing is for us to recognize that what people need most is understanding. While understanding always provides the foundation for other kinds of help, it is important in and of itself. Understanding is a wonderful gift to give others.

Ask twenty people to tell you who has had the most influence in their lives. After they have given you a list of names, ask them to list the qualities those people possessed. In the vast majority of cases you will find the notable absence of the phrases "gives good advice" or "always provides great solutions to my problems," and the frequent presence of phrases such as "is a good listener" or "really understands." A similar kind of analysis can be done within a family system. Think of all the members of your family. Whom do you feel the closest to? More than likely it will be the person who has skills in understanding, sensitivity, and listening, not someone who has all the answers to every problem you present.

We all want to be understood. We want to be around people who show genuine humility, who empty themselves of their own concerns, and who give us their full attention. We are drawn to people who suspend their own needs to control and dominate and who display openness to our story. We seek relationships with people who really want to tune into the meaning of another's experience and are willing to express that meaning back to us. And of course, such a posture invites us to look inside ourselves and recognize that we need to be that kind of person.

There are two major ways we can develop an ability to understand others. One way is to work on our listening skills. By learning how to pay careful attention—sorting the details, and sifting through the relevant and the irrelevant information—we begin to receive what others are saying. We then seek to communicate that understanding back to them so they can rework it, shape it, and through the dialogue have a deeper sense of self-understanding. Listening is hard work because we are not just processing what others are communicating; we are seeking to pay attention not only to the meaning embedded in their words but also to what they are not saying. In doing so we are not engaging in a process of evaluation but in a process that seeks to accept and value the other.

Listening skills are not easily taught and they are difficult to learn, but many fine books and courses address this important area.

The other skill set for tuning in to others consists of expanding our understanding of the nature of problems that people are experiencing. This takes us beyond the skills of listening to a broader view of the problem itself. Take the medical practitioner. If she is doing her job well she will have picked up good interview skills, a facility for asking appropriate questions, and an overall demeanor that communicates a desire to understand. Many of us actually select our doctor and dentist based on these types of criteria. Is she personable? Does she listen well? Can I ask her questions? Does she seem to understand?

But that is only half the story. While I want my doctor to have good interpersonal skills and be personable, I also want him to understand medical problems. If he asks the right questions in the right way and allows me to open up but does not know much about physiology and anatomy, I will probably go elsewhere for treatment. Good process always needs to be combined with good content. That is the major thrust of this book. While the process skills of good listening are addressed through many other venues, the skill of understanding the content of people's problems is not addressed to the same degree. This book is an attempt to right that balance.

But why pursue the understanding of others' problems? What would motivate us to engage in such an enterprise? In his practical chapter on the use of the tongue, James points out a fundamental problem in the human condition:

> With it we bless the Lord and Father, and with it we curse those who are made in the likeness of God. From the same mouth come blessing and cursing. My brothers and sisters, this ought not to be so.
>
> James 3:9–10

What is the nature of the inconsistency in this passage? On a superficial level, it would appear to revolve around the fact that we both praise and curse, two contradictory responses. But the last phrase in verse 9 forces us to look at the inconsistency in a more substantive manner. When we praise God and curse people, we are praising and cursing the same object. Because people are made in God's likeness, we are saying something profound about God when we do not show respect to people. This is the realization that needs to drive us. Our fundamental respect for the person created in God's image can fuel our desire to understand others. The inseparable link between the Creator and the creature puts relational dynamics in the right context.

> For it was you who formed my inward parts;
>> you knit me together in my mother's womb.
> I praise you, for I am fearfully and wonderfully made.
>> Wonderful are your works;
> that I know very well.
>> My frame was not hidden from you,
> when I was being made in secret,
>> intricately woven in the depths of the earth.
> Your eyes beheld my unformed substance.
> In your book were written
>> all the days that were formed for me,
>> when none of them as yet existed.

Psalm 139:13–16

While the psalmist is speaking with God about himself, these truths apply to our understanding of others as well. The presence of God at conception, during the formation of the body, and in the living of one's life is a testament to his power and omniscience. An awareness that others were created by God and were knit together in their mother's womb is an occasion for praise and wonder. No doubt there will be times when we will grow tired of someone and they will become a nuisance, an irritant, someone to be avoided rather than embraced. However, when we are constantly reoriented to the belief that all persons are created in the image of God and because of that have dignity, value, and worth, our motivation to care for them will be rooted in undeniable spiritual realities. It is in that spirit and with that impetus that we spend time trying to understand others.

Unfortunately, many people in church communities have minimal information on which to call when confronted with the various problems people experience. They do not understand the nature of self-image or the stages of grief. They cannot distinguish between people who are having a bad day and those who are depressed. They give superficial answers to those struggling with burnout, and they tell those from dysfunctional families to get on with their lives and stop dwelling on the past. If you are involved in a church community at all, you are going to end up talking to individuals who are struggling. Simply hanging around after the Sunday morning service is often enough to provide a context where people can share what they are going through. These contacts will occur incidentally, accidentally, and often without any preplanning. The question is whether hurting people will have the experience of being understood. Not just will they be listened to, but even more, will they feel understood?

Those in lay leadership roles are usually well intentioned and skilled in some other field, so they are placed in a position that requires involvement with people. In some cases, although not all, they have the process skills we discussed earlier and are able to listen well, express empathy, and make others feel at ease. Usually they have spiritual sensitivity and interest and a desire to follow God in all that they do. Their commitment to be an elder, a deacon, a committee or ministry leader reflects that sensibility. But in most cases they move into pastoral situations without much in-depth understanding of the nature of the problem. Sadly, this lack of competence is sometimes paired with a lack of self-awareness, a dangerous combination when it comes to pastoral ministry, even at a lay level. There is nothing more dangerous than a church leader who does not know that he or she does not know. Unconscious incompetence is a serious ailment.

In over twenty-five years of counseling, teaching, and pastoral ministry, I have tried to pay careful attention to the kinds of problems that people have. It is hard to categorize problems because they are fluid and not easily defined. In addition, problems are usually so intertwined that you cannot easily isolate them. In many people's lives, the tapestry is made up of various strands coming from diverse directions. So to list all the problems that the average church person or lay leader is going to bump up against would require a lengthy book.

I have chosen to illustrate the major contention of this book—that people need to be understood—by unpacking five problem areas: self-image, grief, depression, burnout, and dysfunctional families. If you are involved in a local church, as an active member or a lay leader, it is inevitable you will cross paths with someone who is struggling with one or more of these challenges.

In supplying this finite list of five, I am not suggesting that there are not other problems that could be delineated. Rather, I am proposing that the average Christian is going to have to respond to people who struggle in one or more of these areas. It is my hope that looking at these five areas in more detail will not only lead you to a greater appreciation for the priority and importance of understanding others in the complexity of their lives, but also that you will be able to apply some of the principles outlined here to other problem areas.

I have five goals for this book.

1. To provide a succinct description of each of these five problems in language that the typical Christian can understand. While there are many technical books written on each of these subjects, most of them are not accessible to the average person who has little or no experience in psychiatry, psychology, or other social sciences. Many of these books, even those that are oriented within a Christian context, present the problem in a theoretical framework, which makes it difficult for the typical church person to use the material in a helpful way.

2. To provide a blending of biblical, theological, and spiritual thinking about each of these problems. As Christians, we need to be able to think about each of these problems with our faith in the foreground. Some readers will find this emphasis too brief, while others will not value the Christian tone of this book. It is not my intent to bring an in-depth biblical or theological formulation to each of these problems. I will, however, try to present them in ways that reflect the experience of those who are struggling, because this is where true understanding commences.

3. To provide a short description of what it is like to experience this particular problem. Rather than thinking about problems in a distant, clinical manner, we need to think through what it is like for people to actually live through this particular difficulty. As I have written each of these sections, I have tried to visualize real people that I have met and talked to. I have also tried to stress that most problems have a physical, relational, emotional, action, cognitive, historical, environmental, and spiritual component (note the "PREACHES" acrostic) to them. As a result, I present problems as multifaceted in both their origin and resolution.

4. To provide a practical list of ways that co-pilgrims can help those who are struggling. These lists are not given as pragmatic prescriptions to help you solve the problem as much as to provide some tangible guides to lead you to a deeper level of understanding and interaction. In the spirit of the book, which stresses understanding, each of these sections is intended to provide areas to reflect on and implement with wisdom and discernment as God works through you.

5. To provide a reflection on the importance of blending professional intervention with the body of Christ taking its caring and understanding role seriously. It is dangerous to use an either/or paradigm when it comes to dealing with people's problems. Rather than proposing that people either go to a ministry of the church for assistance, or they go for professional help, a both/and paradigm is more effective. In this way we are responsible both for understanding the individual and encouraging referral when the person needs the help of a professional.

Just as God did not promise to solve and cure all of our problems but to provide his presence and peace, so we too have the privilege to be present to those created in God's image so they will experience a deeper measure of shalom. We cannot provide the final cure, but our genuine care will give them a deeper sense of being understood—a great gift in this culture. And when all is said and done, I suspect that care is more important than cure anyway.

# Self-Image

## What is self-image?

Sitting across from me in my office was an attractive and competent woman speaking words that made no sense to me. "I feel so ugly and I feel like I can't do anything." Ugly? Not just from a male perspective, but simply as a fellow human being, there was no way she was ugly. If this was ugly, then most of us were in a sorry physical state. And can't do anything? Her accomplishments far surpassed those of most people I knew, and I was incredulous that she would summarize what she had done so negatively.

In the presence of those claims most of us impulsively rush to one or more of the following statements:

"You need to be more positive."

"Trust me. You are not ugly."

"I know many people who have not done half of what you have done."

"I can't believe you are saying these things."

"But you have so many things going for you."

"Stop talking that way. You are making no sense."

"How can you talk that way? God loves you and values you as his child."

What do you think will happen to this woman's view of herself as a result of these statements? Do you think she will become more positive and trust the perception of the person who is listening? Will she come to understand, in that moment of time, that she has many things going for her and needs to stop believing what she said? Will the statement that God loves her and values her suddenly transform her perspective so that she sees herself as attractive and worthwhile? I think you can figure out the answer: no.

Why will she resist the input she has received from an outsider's viewpoint? Because the definition of self-image has not been fully understood by the other. What is self-image?

Me looking at me.

My father was an engineer and my younger brother, after showing early interest in that kind of profession, also pursued the field of engineering as a career. As a result, I was the only male in my family who had no interest in math and sciences and no interest in that kind of career. While no one in my family ever sat down and said "you are not math and sciences oriented" or "you are not mechanical" or "you are not into technical pursuits," I slowly picked up the message that when it came to these areas of endeavor I was not up to par. If the plumbing required repairs or the lawn mower needed to be fixed, I would watch my brother or father get involved while I stayed on the sidelines. And while I never had the sense either of them were intentionally putting me on the margins, I felt that was my place. After many years of receiving this message I eventually saw myself as technically challenged.

Three years after my wife and I were married, we moved into an older house. It required some work and I remember the trauma of undertaking some of these projects. Prior to commencing the task I was anxious, and when I was engaged I was telling myself that I would not be successful.

My wife, Bev, would often stand by, encouraging and coaching, and when the job was over she would tell me that it looked good and I should be proud of it. My response? I would argue with her! I would point out problems or areas where things could have been done better and make sure she saw the components of the job that were far from well done.

Why would I argue with a compliment? Because it contradicted my self-image. Me looking at me. In the realm of the technical and the mechanical, I had come to see myself as "less than" my brother and my father. When I did undertake these kinds of tasks, it was important to me to see the world in a way that fit with my view of myself. I did not think I was good in technical arenas, therefore I was not. When Bev would challenge, encourage, and praise me, I would dismiss "her looking at me" and let "me looking at me" take priority.

My technical prowess, or lack thereof, has not created significant psychological or family difficulties for me, but this scenario illustrates the definition of self-image. By definition, my self-image is exactly that—it is my own personal view of myself. It is not your view of me. It is not the perspective that people in general hold. Nor, interestingly, is it God's view of me. It is my view of me. In fact, it may be one of the most personal things about ourselves. That is why we cling to it so tenaciously.

But where does it come from? When we understand the history of our self-image we will be able to bring greater sensitivity to those who are struggling in this area. Self-image is not something we are born with. A newborn does not arrive with a sense of self, perceived from their perspective. Reacting instinctively to the physical side of life, the new baby experiences heat, cold, wetness, dryness, hunger, and thirst. A sense of identity is not present at this stage of life. The baby cries when hungry, sleeps when tired, and does the other thing when the need arises! In this process there is no self-analysis, introspection, or self-evaluation. Literally, there is no image of oneself.

As the bodily process matures, a general sense of identity develops. Older babies start to develop an ability to distinguish between "out there" and "right here." During this stage they will play with their hands and feet and touch various parts of their body as they begin to collect information on who they are. Soon they learn their name and they begin to realize that there is a "self" that is separate from the rest of the world. They have a space and a place in the universe.

As the baby moves into childhood, there is greater interaction with others. Parents and significant others speak to the child and mutual dialogue goes on. Language develops and the child learns labels and categories and before long has a repertoire of terms they can apply to themselves and to others. The child develops language from the outside world, both through listening and direct imitation. Soon parents are hearing their phrases parroted back to them, at times bringing a sense of joy and satisfaction and at other times, remorse and guilt.

This is a stage that some have called "the looking glass self." In essence, what I hear others say about me I begin to say to myself. The terms that others use to describe me become the terms I utilize to describe myself. As I look in the mirror, offered by others, I see myself through their eyes. In other words, I begin to incorporate into my self-image the image others have of me. For many of us this process continued through childhood and well into adolescence. Messages from those around us were deeply embedded in our thinking and we began to own them in the fullest sense of the word. In many ways our self-image was a mirror of what others presented to us. We came to believe what we were told.

As the self-image becomes entrenched, we look for ways to confirm what we believe about ourselves. So the university student who has a poor self-image that says "I am not a good student" is not sure what to do when he gets an A on a final exam. There is an inconsistency between his self-perception and the grade—something has to give. Given the strong negative message that is well-rooted in the student's history, the chances of this new and positive information being worked into his thinking are slim. More than likely the student will conclude, "This was an easy course," so he can continue with the same self-image regarding academic abilities. In many cases, a person with a very low self-image in academic areas will not even pursue university. They have already concluded that they not only will not do well, but also cannot do well.

Typically this process can be captured in a threefold cycle:

1. I was "taught" through words, actions, and silence how to feel about myself in particular areas from my parents, significant others, and life circumstances.
2. I have become a good student of this teaching, so I tend to see myself in terms of my self-perception and to act in a way that is consistent with this perception.
3. When I have an encounter with a person or circumstance that contradicts my self-image, I will experience inconsistency, but will tend to fall back on my historical self-perception rather than let the new information change my perspective.

When it comes to areas like technical prowess or academic excellence, the psychological implications and damage may or may not be extensive. But take the case of someone who grows up in a home where they are told they are no good, will never amount to anything, are a good-for-nothing. If those kinds of messages become ingrained into the self-image and the person begins to feel that way about themselves and act consistently with that view, the emotional damage could be quite significant.

**How do we understand self-image from a biblical perspective?**

There are many ways biblical wisdom can help inform our understanding of self-image. For our purposes here, we will look at five.

*1. Focus on accuracy when it comes to self-image.*

The focus on the self in much of psychological literature has brought a number of terms into use. When we utilize the term *self-image* we are focusing on the individual's view of himself or herself. Some popular psychological literature uses the term *self-esteem*, indicating that we need to esteem, value, and appreciate ourselves. While some aspects of this emphasis are needed, the term *self-image* is more fundamental. To refer to self-image is simply to indicate that all humans, beyond the infant stage, have a view of themselves and that this perspective can be quite influential throughout our lives. It says nothing about whether the image of oneself is positive or negative.

When Paul writes to the Romans about the foundational nature of love and spiritual gifts, he introduces the section with an interesting statement:

> For by the grace given to me I say to everyone among you not to think of yourself more highly than you ought to think, but to think with sober judgment, each according to the measure of faith that God has assigned.
>
> Romans 12:3

I grew up in a church environment where the first part of this verse was drilled into us, not just in words but in subtle forms of communication. The great sin was to be puffed up, to be proud, to think too highly of yourself. It was considered problematic to encourage people because that might give them a "swelled head." And of course the unbiblical antidote to that "problem" was to put yourself down and think very little of yourself. This was important for everyone but especially for women, who were trained to see themselves negatively. That environment produced many people with very poor self-images who were led to believe that this was not only biblical, but also God's desire. However, as is often the case with our view of Scripture, we need to read the whole passage to understand the complete teaching on how we are to view ourselves.

Paul is about to discuss the importance of spiritual gifts, which are received in faith through God's grace. He will be arguing that all of us form part of one body and that within that body there are different gifts. Notice that the gifts are exactly that—expressions of God's grace rather than indications of our own competence or abilities. When you fully grasp the significance of a gift, you become absorbed with the giver rather than the receiver.

To prepare for this emphasis, Paul indicates that the Christian needs to not view herself too highly but with "sober judgment." One translation of this phrase is "accurately." In other words, when we look at ourselves and our gifts we should not have an inflated view of ourselves, but rather one that accurately reflects reality. If my gift is teaching, I should simply accept this as a bestowment given by God, rooted in his grace, and not something that I should either be arrogant about or deny. To have the gift of teaching and then act proudly is as dangerous a tendency as having the gift of teaching and pretending I do not. When it comes to the instruction of Romans 12:3, the message about self-image is direct—view yourself accurately.

### 2. View yourself in light of your own responsibility rather than in comparison to others.

The sensitive balance between how I view myself and others is carefully unpacked by Paul in Galatians.

My friends, if anyone is detected in a transgression, you who have received the Spirit should restore such a one in a spirit of gentleness. Take care that you yourselves are not tempted. Bear one another's burdens, and in this way you will fulfill the law of Christ. For if those who are nothing think they are something, they deceive themselves. All must test their own work; then that work, rather than their neighbor's work, will become a cause for pride. For all must carry their own loads.

Galatians 6:1–5

Some of the Galatian Christians were slipping into difficulty because false teachers were luring people into sin. Paul encourages other Christians to get involved by engaging in sensitive restoration while being careful not to get tripped up by the same difficulties. When people are struggling with sin, they are carrying a heavy burden, and it is the clear responsibility of the rest of the body to share that load. When they share the load, people are not only supportive and helpful to the person who is experiencing weariness, they are also fulfilling a higher mandate, namely, following the explicit teaching and example of Christ himself.

There are cases, though, where we distance ourselves from people who are struggling. We withdraw into smugness and self-sufficiency and believe that the restoration of others is somehow not our responsibility. In essence, we think that we are "something"—someone who would not get themselves in such a mess or fall into such difficulty. Paul's argument here is direct. If you think you are something when you are nothing, you deceive yourself. In other words, if you claim no responsibility for the gentle encouragement of one who is carrying a burden, your knowledge of the law of Christ is woefully inaccurate. Or, if you imply that you would never fall into the same sin, your self-assessment is woefully inaccurate.

In addition, we need to avoid the natural tendency to assess ourselves in light of others and determine what we are like using them as the standard. The testing of our own actions takes place in light of ultimate standards, like the law of Christ. When we meet those standards we can engage in honest self-reflection that rejoices and takes pride in what we have done. In essence, we can take pride in ourselves knowing that we have met God's desires and have not simply engaged in comparison with others. When we do this, we can fully understand what it means to "carry [our] own loads." We need to submit personally to final accountability before God, to live in a way that honors his standards.

So as we look at ourselves, we should see passion for following the law of Christ by ministering to others, honesty that allows us to see ourselves for what we are, and humility that prevents us from comparing ourselves with others and not carrying our own burden.

### 3. Understand the correct approach to the die-to-self teaching.

One of the most powerful truths of the gospel is contained in the words of Galatians 2:19–20:

> I have been crucified with Christ; and it is no longer I who live, but it is Christ who lives in me. And the life I now live in the flesh I live by faith in the Son of God, who loved me and gave himself for me.

One rendering of this passage produces a view of self that is not only negative and repulsive, but also confusing. The inaccurate argument proceeds as follows. When Christ died you died as well. You are now dead. You are nothing. You have no sense of self because it is gone. If self rears its head at all (even though it is dead!) you are to continually die to self. I have talked with many Christians who are bewildered with what this means in day-to-day living and have many questions as a result. Who is the self? Who has died? How come self is still there if it is dead? What does Galatians 2:20 really teach?

Within the confines and purposes of this book, we are not going to elucidate all the fine points around the die-to-self theology. However, it is important to respond to the questions raised above, beginning with the clear teaching of Romans 6:1–14. In that passage a number of truths are abundantly clear:

   a. Christians have died to the life of sin.
   b. Just as Christ died, so we die as well.
   c. Just as Christ was raised from the dead, we too are raised.
   d. Our sinful identity died, in fact was crucified, with Christ.
   e. In dying, our sinful identity no longer controls us.
   f. In living, our life is lived with God as the focus.
   g. The practical reality of this process is worked out all the time.
   h. We are striving to live in such a way that sin is no longer our master.

Without a clear understanding of Romans 6, we run the risk of misinterpreting Galatians 2:20. Who is the self referred to in the latter passage? It is our sinful identity, the essence of who we are without Christ. Who has died because of the work of Christ on the cross? That same sinful identity and essence. The "I" that has been crucified with Christ and the "I" that no longer lives is another way of talking about what Romans 6 calls the sinful self, the self that is oriented primarily and fundamentally toward sin. It is not my personality, who I am, my skills, gifts, abilities, and proclivities.

Let's put this discussion in practical terms. Gayle is a bubbly, friendly, warm, and engaging young person. She does not know Christ as personal Savior but is appreciated, liked, and affirmed by all her friends. After an invitation from a Christian friend, she gets involved in an Alpha group and before long makes a personal commitment to Jesus as Lord and Savior. The question is—who has been crucified as a result of her conversion? Does the bubbly, friendly, warm, and engaging Gayle die? Does her personality die as a result of conversion? Obviously not. Conversion does not wipe out genetic and environmental history and create a completely new personality. That is not what dies at salvation. What dies is the sinful self, the core of Gayle that is oriented toward sin and focused away from God—the side of her that is an enemy of God and is hostile toward God. That is what dies because of the work of the cross. And what comes to life, in a way that parallels the resurrection of Christ, is the life that is oriented toward God and has him as the focus.

Scripture does not lead us to conclude that the self is repulsive and negative. The life that is oriented to sin is crucified with Christ, but neither the personality nor the entire essence of the person is wiped out. Because of the sin of our first parents, the image of God has been tarnished but not wiped out completely. The work of Christ does not produce a good-for-nothing but a fallen something.

### 4. Understand the true nature of pride and humility.

Many evangelicals have grown up in contexts where there is a profound misunderstanding about the true nature of pride and humility. Pride is seen as speaking positively about yourself, and humility is seen as a negative self-assessment. I remember as a kid going to the door at the back of the church to shake the preacher's hand. At times I would say something like "I appreciated that message. Thank you." Often the response would be something like, "Don't thank me. I am not a good speaker or communicator. That was not me but the Holy Spirit speaking through his Word." Early in my Christian experience, I thought that was the height of humility. In the presence of a compliment, this godly man was putting himself down and redirecting my attention to the work of

God. But I puzzled over the phrase "that was not me" because it was him. I saw his lips moving!

Prior to biblical times, the word *humility* was understood as "groveling in the dust." The lower you got and the more you engaged in self-denigration, the more humble you were. But the biblical record elevated the word to a higher level. Humility was no longer about negative self-preoccupation but rather about service that put the other first and put self in perspective. The great statement about Jesus in Philippians 2:7–8 is an excellent summation of this teaching: "And being found in human form, he humbled himself and became obedient to the point of death—even death on a cross."

Jesus's ministry was not characterized by self-put-downs. He was not absorbed with how inadequate he was or how terrible he was. His focus was on serving others and, in many ways, his sense of self was not a primary but a secondary emphasis. He really did fulfill what Paul asked the Philippians to do when he said, "In humility regard others as better than yourselves" (2:3). In Jesus's case, this was expressed not by talking about himself negatively, but by giving to others and serving others to the point where he was willing to die for them on a cross. His sacrifice epitomized humility.

In his book *The Screwtape Letters*, C. S. Lewis describes humility as "self forgetfulness" and interestingly argues that "God's whole effort therefore will be to get man's mind off the subject of his own value altogether."[1] In many ways that is what humility is about. When someone comes to the preacher at the door and says "thank you," the appropriate response might be something like "You're welcome—thanks for the encouragement. I hope God uses this passage in all of our lives." Simply acknowledging the encouragement is not the same as being self-preoccupied. We have all had the experience of telling someone how much we appreciated what they did and listening to them spend the next five minutes putting themselves down. While their response appears humble, in that they are groveling and telling you how awful they are, they are in fact self-preoccupied and by the biblical standard are demonstrating pride.

I have found the short injunction in 1 Timothy 3:6 interesting in this regard. The church is told that an overseer "must not be a recent convert, or he may be puffed up with conceit and fall into the condemnation of the devil." One could argue that conceit for a new church leader might be expressed in bragging, an excessive sense of power and influence, or a belief that he has "made it." But conceit may also be clothed in the garb of absorption with one's faults, failures, and shortcomings—of self-preoccupation. Anything that drives us in toward ourselves, and makes us oblivious to the needs of others around us, moves us into pride and away from humility. By this standard, we need to carefully monitor our self-image.

### 5. Unpack "love your neighbor as yourself" carefully.

The idea that we need to love ourselves has subtly crept into Christian circles through a misunderstanding of the "greatest commandment." When asked to provide the most important commandment, Jesus replied,

> "Hear, O Israel: the Lord our God, the Lord is one; you shall love the Lord your God with all your heart, and with all your soul, and with all your mind, and with all your strength." The second is this, "You shall love your neighbor as yourself." There is no other commandment greater than these.
>
> Mark 12:29–31

It is clear from these words that love involves two commandments. We need to love God and love others. From other passages in Scripture we know that love is not an experiential feeling that resides in my stomach but a behavioral response rooted in my commitment to God. Our love for God and for others is demonstrated in acts of kindness that flow out of a commitment of character. When Jesus commands us to love our enemies (Matt. 5:44), he is not inviting us to experience warmth and serenity at an emotional level. Rather, he focuses on the orientation of humble service. We pray for our enemies, give to them, and meet their needs, and in so doing, fulfill the law of Christ.

Nowhere in the Mark 12 passage does it state or imply that love for oneself is a necessary and important component of the commandment. We are not commanded to love ourselves in order to provide a foundation for us to love others and love God. In fact, there is an assumption that our doing, serving, and giving to others occurs to the same degree we do likewise for ourselves. When we wake up in the morning to wash, dress ourselves, eat breakfast, and generally tend to our personal needs we are exhibiting, in a biblical sense, a love for ourselves that needs to be reflected in our response to others. This is why Paul could use the same paradigm to argue that husbands need to love their wives

> as they do their own bodies. He who loves his wife loves himself. For no one ever hates his own body, but he nourishes and tenderly cares for it, just as Christ does for the church.
>
> Ephesians 5:28–29

Paul is not implying that husbands need to have warm and sentimental feelings toward their own bodies in order to truly love their wives. Rather, he is suggesting that the behavioral care we provide for ourselves needs to be reflected in our attitudes to others. In fact, it is assumed that this self-care, or self-love, is in existence for all of us.

**What is it like to experience your self-image?**

In some ways this sounds like a strange question. How does a person experience a self-image? Depending on the kind of self-image we have, the experience can be very positive or quite negative. When I was in elementary school, I ended up doing a lot of public speaking. Some of my earliest memories of school are of standing up in front of my class, and in some cases the whole school, to give an oral presentation. I do not remember whether I performed well or poorly, only that I was involved extensively. When I entered high school I was thinking about being a teacher, largely because of those early experiences. Early on, my self-image had a component that said, "You are an up-front person." It is not surprising that much of my life has been centered around public speaking in various contexts. I have lived my life in a way that is consistent with my self-image.

Most of us, however, also have historical experiences that provide content for our self-image that stimulates negative outcomes. Earl was brought up in a Christian home where criticism was a regular part of the family conversation. His father gravitated from hostile, discouraging comments to a silence that always had a negative feel to it. Early in school, Earl learned that bad marks were symptomatic of his stupidity, because that was the word that his dad used. He has vivid recollections of sitting in the den on the big sofa hearing his dad bellow, "If you were not so stupid you would be able to get better marks than these."

His mother, out of her own dysfunctional background, always linked love, acceptance, and care with good behavior. If Earl did things right and behaved well, he experienced her affirmation and love. But if he was out of line, he knew he was falling far short of the standard and her love would be withheld. There were periods when he was in high school when his mother would not speak to him for days on end because he had done something that displeased her.

The church where the family attended was highly committed to a traditional evangelistic-style message every Sunday. Even though Earl had accepted Christ as a youngster, he went through church, week after week, hearing preaching about how bad people were, how far short they had fallen, and how real hell was for those who had not accepted Christ. In a conceptual sense, he understood that this preaching did not apply to him, but in many ways it reminded him of the message he received at home—you are falling short and do not measure up. Every Sunday he felt like he was not a Christian.

Earl developed a way to cope with all these negative messages. He became the classic people pleaser. In relationships, he would spend part of his time trying to figure out what other people wanted and then the rest of the time trying to make them happy. His own needs, desires, and interests became secondary, and he was focused solely on pleasing people. Those who observed Earl superficially saw him as a fine example of Christian service and humility, but in the process they missed what was really going on.

His self-image was having a powerful influence. Deep inside, he believed that he was no good. He could not meet the standard set by parents, God, and others. The only way he could atone for these "sins" was to make others happy. So his life's pursuit was to overwork and overextend himself so that others were happy with him. It appeared that he was concerned for others, but the sad reality was that his excessive work was compensating for a deep lack he experienced on the inside. In many ways his doing for others was not about others at all; it was really to make himself feel good. Even his relationship with God had a similar quality. He would try to please God not because he loved God and felt a desire to serve and worship him, but because he was fearful of wrath and judgment. All Earl's Christian service was about guilt and obligation, not love and desire.

These simple stories illustrate some principles that need to be understood about self-image.

### *1. Self-image does not always relate to the facts or to reality.*

Notice that my memories of public speaking are not concerned with whether I did well or not. I have a self-image that says "I do public speaking," but the issue of performance is obscured. On the positive side, one could say that is helpful. I am not deterred by past negative experiences or blocked by poor performances. On the other hand, there is a danger. What if my self-image is not accurate in the fullest sense? What if I see myself as a public speaker but most people think I am poor at it? What if my self-image is so locked in that I cannot see the facts for what they are?

A similar analysis could be brought to Earl's situation. He feels like he is no good, always falling short, never making the grade. In essence, he has become a student of his early "schooling." He has adopted what he was told by others and he is acting as if it were true. Why does he have to overwork all the time? Because he is no good and if he does not work hard, he will not be accepted. But is that reality? Is everyone out there like his father? Does God really believe that we have to atone for our own sins? Is grace really something you have to work for? Clearly Earl's self-image is not tied to the facts or to the reality of the world, but it still persists and remains influential.

### 2. The self-talk of self-image is not easily accessible to others.

You cannot determine someone's self-image by observing them from the outside. Many of us display behaviors that camouflage what we really think about ourselves. When Earl is working hard for others, those who observe him may see a successful, hardworking person who wants to help others; they do not see that he is compensating for deficits that are rooted in his past. Similarly, someone listening to me speak publicly will not know that my historical experiences are having a large influence in my current activities.

Negative self-talk comes in various forms. Some of the following self-statements may be operative for someone you know. While these statements are not verbalized and may only operate in a subconscious way, they nonetheless have a profound effect on the individual's personal experience.

If I don't meet my high standards I will end up as a second-rate person.

People will think less of me if I make a mistake.

If I try hard enough I should be able to excel at anything.

I should never display weakness.

Any time I do not please others, I am a failure.

If I fail at something, it means that I am not a good person.

If I fail, I deserve to be punished.

Acceptance must be earned.

### 3. Self-image issues often spill over into relationships.

Jessy has struggled with her self-image for years. She feels like she can never make the grade. Her constant feelings of guilt and obligation make her weary of all she is doing to keep others happy. She is involved on a committee at church that is responsible for welcoming newcomers. Part way through the last meeting, the chair of the group indicated that Jessy and her welcoming partner might want to start coming a little earlier on Sunday because visitors were arriving earlier than most people thought they would. Her suggestion was given gently and kindly and had the well-being of the visitors as the only motivation.

Jessy was livid. She went home after the meeting angry and upset, and dumped it all over her roommate, who tried to help her work through what had happened. The more they talked, the more Jessy's anger turned to sadness and depression and, before long, she was crying. She began to talk about feeling no good and wondered whether she should even be involved in ministry at the church.

What was happening to Jessy? From the events of the meeting, nothing particularly traumatic occurred. The woman who was chairing gave her some feedback. That is all it was—plain and simple feedback. There was no ill will, no bad intent, and even the tone in which it was communicated was fine. But Jessy was devastated to the point that she questioned her involvement in the newcomers ministry. Why?

Clearly Jessy's self-image was playing a huge role in this situation. On the surface it looked like an interpersonal problem that required resolution, but in reality, it was not about Jessy's communication with the woman but her communication with herself. Because of some historical experiences that had influenced her significantly, she was plagued by two of the self-statements from the list above:

Any time I do not please others, I am a failure.
If I fail at something, it means that I am not a good person.

She interpreted the feedback at the meeting as an indication that she was not pleasing the other person and, by implication, that made her a failure. And to be a failure meant that she was not a good person. Viewed through a logical grid the connections between these various thoughts are loose at best, but Jessy's experience is deep and significant. Her self-image dynamics were having a significant effect on interpersonal relationships. And if she were to go and confront the other woman, it is quite possible that the situation would get worse interpersonally, unless she was willing to take responsibility for her own self-talk.

**So how can I minister to those who are having problems with self-image?**

*Recognize the cultural messages that impact self-image.*

We are strongly shaped by the cultural messages that come our way in various forms every day. The self-image of both genders is affected in different ways, so it is important to stay attuned to those messages so we can truly understand and minister to those who may be impacted negatively.

Women are subjected to media and advertising messages that put an emphasis on the size and shape of their bodies. In a North American culture where women function as sex objects for men, it is very easy for a woman to become absorbed with what she looks like. Her self-image will be heavily influenced by this focus. The impact of this on younger girls is particularly significant. Girls in late childhood and early adolescence are exposed to caricatures of the perfect body that can lead to negative self-messages and eventually to behaviors that are counterproductive. The prevalence of eating disorders among adolescent girls is at least partially due to self-images being affected by cultural messages about the ideal body.

Although there is a cultural shift occurring in this generation, men are still subjected to messages that indicate doing and performing are crucial to their well-being. Men who do well in their job are perceived as successful people who are worth a lot. The response of many men during midlife, job loss, and retirement indicates that their self-image is intimately tied up with doing well at work. Many men in these times of transition find emptiness inside. They discover that their identity does not feel secure because performance has been taken out of their life.

Friends can often talk about matters of cultural influence, and this can help the person who is battling self-image issues put some of their struggles in a context. The woman who finds out she is negatively influenced by cultural messages about appearance is not going to suddenly stop feeling the way she does, and the man who is obsessed with the link between performance and identity is not going to shift his thinking overnight; however, fresh understanding will move them along in the journey.

### Acknowledge the power of history and respond accordingly.

Self-image is formed in the crucible of early experiences. As a result, it is resistant to simplistic interventions. If someone thinks they are ugly and that self-statement can be traced to early influences by significant others, they are not going to feel beautiful because you tell them "but you are gorgeous." It is therefore advisable to stay away from challenges and arguments that are an attempt to talk people out of their view of themselves.

The danger of the above advice is that it could easily lead us to give up and say there is no hope for the person with a problematic self-image. If they are resistant to simplistic interventions, we might as well sit back and say nothing. However, we need to recognize that just as the concept of self was formed in a context that was both spoken and unspoken, so the shift into a healthier, more accurate self-image will also need a context that is spoken and unspoken.

I have seen people, for instance, who have been shy and withdrawn because they have learned to say to themselves "I am shy and withdrawn." They learned that self-perception early in life and functioned consistently with it for years. When these labels were challenged gently and they were placed in a community where their opinions and feelings were sought out, they eventually became less shy and less withdrawn. They were able to begin to see themselves as someone with opinions and insights. In the right context, change occurred. However, the change was not prompted by simple words spoken into a vacuum. When a community is motivated by a desire to relate to people for who they are, rather than who they think they are, a context for change is created.

The same is true in individual friendships. If the person you are relating to in the context of your small group experiences acceptance and affirmation from you, their historical tapes will receive a little nudge, a gentle rebuke, a compassionate confrontation. Again, this will not radically alter their view of themselves immediately, but it will begin the recording of a new tape.

One final note on the influence of history. Many people will give someone who is struggling a book or tape to help them deal with their difficulties. Well-meaning family members, upon learning of the plight of the individual, believe that if they read this book or listen to that tape, they will be helped immeasurably. While books and tapes, along with sermons and lectures, have their place, we need to recognize that all books are read and all tapes are heard with the full engagement of active self-talk. I have given many good and helpful books to people only to find that they did not like it, did not agree with it, or did not find it helpful. Why? Because their self-talk drowned out the message from the book, tape, or sermon, so the talk from outside made little impact. One way to rectify this problem is to read a book or listen to a tape together so you can engage in dialogue with the self-talk of the person.

### Deal with children sensitively.

Because the labels that become part of our self-image are inculcated early in life, it is important for all of us who have contact with children to influence them in ways that will facilitate the development of accurate self-images. A number of points need to be remembered:

1. Work on your own self-image. Because labels are often passed down through the generations, we need to be sure our own inner work is continually being done well. Our self-talk needs constant

assessment, modification, and refinement, not just for our own well-being, but also for that of the children around us.

2. Discipline behavior while affirming the child. In the context of discipline, many of us find ourselves saying very hostile and cruel things to our children. While behavior needs to be addressed—that was a bad thing you did—the person still needs to be valued—I still love you in spite of what you did.

3. Handle incompetence properly. Children will fail and make mistakes, so we need to balance the push for ambition with realistic goals. We always want to ask, "What kind of self-statements do I want this child to use in the future when they fail?"

4. Challenge inaccurate labels. When we listen for the self-talk of a child, we will hear how they really feel about themselves. If the labels are inaccurate it is wise to gently and firmly challenge the label. Just as we want children to learn to speak to others well, we also want them to speak to themselves well.

5. Remember that overindulgence and overprotection can create poor self-images. I have heard many people say, "I don't understand why I am so down on myself. I came from a very strong family." Sometimes parents in strong families take over for children and, in the process of overprotecting them, teach the child that they are incapable and cannot do things for themselves.

6. Remember that children, in particular, grapple with three large self-image questions as they live their lives—How do I look (appearance)? How am I doing (performance)? and How important am I (status)? Rather than just focusing on the behavior of children, a typical obsession of adults, it is important to listen for these three questions, because they play a significant role in the functioning of children.

*Pay attention to the unique self-image issues faced by seniors.*

Because self-image is so intertwined with identity and performance, it plays itself out in different ways through the various seasons of life. For seniors who are going through retirement, the cessation of workplace performance can have a detrimental impact on their sense of self. If work has been important to their well-being and self-acceptance, retirement can precipitate feelings of inadequacy, especially in a culture where one gets the sense that "younger is better."

A similar dynamic can go on for seniors who have found their sense of self in raising children. In these cases "being good" means being a good parent, and the success of parenting is assessed by how well the adult children turn out. So in the event of the divorce of one of their children, an older parent can experience failure or inadequacy, and feel like they must have done something wrong.

Again, the understanding response is not to work on changing this inner dialogue instantly, but to gently help the senior find a sense of well-being in who they are, rather than what they have done.

### *Focus on accuracy and priority rather than feeling good.*

It is very easy to tell others that they should always feel positively about themselves. But we should keep in mind the biblical mandate, which is not necessarily about feeling good, but about accuracy of self-perception and a lack of self-obsession. Take Mike, who is eighteen. He has been playing baseball all his life and has lived in a fantasy world that one day he will be a professional. He played with a fairly decent team during his last year of high school, so he believes that he will be selected by one of the major colleges and will receive a significant scholarship. The time for being accepted comes and goes and no one even expresses interest in him. Mike is devastated and starts to beat himself up emotionally.

What is the right response in this situation? To focus on bolstering Mike's self-image by saying things like "You really are a major league ballplayer," "They made a mistake; you really are good," "Don't worry about it; you may have another chance" runs risks because the accuracy of those statements is in question. If he really is major league material, why did no one want him? If he is that good, why did they make a mistake? What guarantee is there that he will have another chance? A more sensitive and appropriate response may be to focus on accuracy. Maybe his view of himself has not been accurate and needs to shift. On the other hand, maybe he needs to define himself in other ways that do not include baseball. Maybe the content of his self-image has some problems and baseball needs to have a different priority.

Obviously, moving Mike to think about the accuracy of his self-image and the priority of baseball in it is not done insensitively or without careful understanding of Mike and what he is like. However, it may need to be done, given the discrepancy between his self-image and the circumstances he finds himself in.

### Give people alternatives to their self-talk.

As we listen for self-talk in others, we will inevitably hear labels that are inaccurate or inappropriate. It is not appropriate to challenge the self-talk directly and claim it is wrong. What we need to do is provide alternatives. Depending on your relationship with the person, you might get them to list their self-talk in a particular sphere of life.

I can't do it.
I never could do anything right.
I will never be able to change.

This could be followed by helping the person cross-examine each of their self-statements.

What does *can't* mean? Where is the evidence that you can't? Is this an issue of ability or willingness?
Is that an accurate statement? List some things you have done well. Is there one incident that leads you to this conclusion?
Why are you saying never? What does change mean for you? Are you setting realistic goals?

This process of coaching can lead a person to make some strides in a specific area. More importantly, the individual may learn to do his or her own internal cross-examination in the future.

*Refer if the self-image is becoming personally debilitating or is negatively impacting other relationships.*

Because we all have problems and at times go through self-image struggles, it would be inappropriate to say that everyone who has difficulties in this area should go for professional help. However, in my experience there are two criteria to utilize before making a referral. First, is the person becoming debilitated as a result of their self-image? Some people have such powerfully negative self-talk that it renders them ineffective in all sorts of ways. I have known people who have lived lives of paranoia and fear, not because of what was going on in their external circumstances, but because their self-image had such a counterproductive hold on them. In those cases the support of a friend or family member will not be sufficient to resolve the problem.

Referral should also occur when the self-image difficulties are spilling over regularly into relationships. The situation with Jessy, cited earlier, happens all the time in Christian communities. Someone in the body has a very poor self-image and rather than dealing with it directly, they allow it to unduly influence their relationships with others. They regularly find themselves overly sensitive and taking a long time to recover from hurt. Someone will send them a note or make a phone call and it will lead them to want to resign from their position. Because they are not open to feedback or challenge, they hide behind walls of defensiveness, irritability, and justification. In these cases as well, appropriate help is not going to occur solely with the intervention of a friend.

**Summary**

Self-image is simply me looking at me, and is rooted in the messages I have received from others. Most of us tend to live consistent with our self-image and funnel our current experiences through that grid. Christians need to have clarity on five aspects of self-image:

1.  Focus on accuracy when it comes to self-image.

2. View yourself in light of your own responsibility rather than in comparison to others.
3. Understand the correct approach to the die-to-self teaching.
4. Understand the true nature of pride and humility.
5. Unpack "love your neighbor as yourself" carefully.

To better understand people's experiences, we need to know:

1. Self-image does not always relate to the facts or to reality.
2. The self-talk of self-image is not easily accessible to others.
3. Self-image issues often spill over into relationships.

When ministering to those who are having problems with self-image:

Recognize the cultural messages that impact self-image.

Acknowledge the power of history and respond accordingly.

Deal with children sensitively.

Pay attention to the unique self-image issues faced by seniors.

Focus on accuracy and priority rather than good feeling.

Give people alternatives to their self-talk.

Refer if the self-image is becoming personally debilitating or is negatively impacting other relationships.

# 3

# Grief

**What is grief?**

Andrew is distracted in church this morning. He was the victim of company downsizing on Friday and is still trying to process the shock. Although Melissa has been waiting for the divorce papers for the past three months, she is experiencing an incredible range of emotions today. The papers came through this past week and she does not know whether to be happy or sad. This is the first Sunday in this church for Sarah and Jeremy. They have just moved from some distance and are in the process of settling in. While they are enjoying the service, they feel tentative and numb. Margaret has been away from church for a number of weeks. Her husband of forty-six years passed away recently after a long and painful battle with cancer. She cries quietly, remembering the way it was when Sam sat beside her in the pew.

One experience characterizes Andrew, Melissa, Sarah, Jeremy, and Margaret. Grief.

What is grief? Grief is the experience we go through when something or someone is taken away from us. It is a sense of loss, although not necessarily the loss of something positive. And it is a loss that is personal and individual. What one person experiences as a loss will be quite different from what someone else does.

So grief, a word most often associated with death, may come about through many circumstances of life. In losing his job, Andrew is experiencing a sense of loss. He had worked at that company for ten years and is experiencing the emptiness of having employment taken away from him. That is not to say that his employment was enjoyable and satisfying all the time. In fact, he struggled a lot at work and often talked about looking for something else.

Melissa was in a very abusive marriage, and when her husband left her for another woman, she was devastated. It has been three years since he left, but a year ago he informed her that he was marrying someone else and would be serving her divorce papers. She had hoped that the marriage could be salvaged in spite of his pronouncement. When the papers arrived, her sense of loss was deep. Not only had she lost her husband and her marriage, but now she had also lost her sense of hope that reconciliation was possible. On a deeper level she had to give up and lose her childhood fantasy that she would marry, have children, and in the words of many fairy tales, live happily ever after.

Our understanding of those experiencing grief is deepened when we realize that grief cannot be measured against an objective standard. Sarah and Jeremy are tentative and numb as they sit in a new church for the first time. What have they lost? We do not know the answer to that question unless we know their story. Imagine that Sarah and Jeremy both lost jobs as a result of poor end-of-year evaluations, and when they could not find anything else, decided to move. Or what if they were a younger couple, looking for a sense of adventure and novelty and therefore made a major geographical shift? Possibly they were caring for aged and infirm parents and when they passed away, Jeremy and Sarah felt the freedom to move. Can you see the different senses of loss that would occur? Their feelings of being tentative and numb would be qualitatively different in each different scenario.

Recognizing the personal and individual nature of grief makes us better listeners and helps us avoid trite and simplistic analyses. Think of all the things you have heard people say after someone has lost a spouse after many years of marriage.

"But they had so many years together."

"Many people do not have their spouse that long."

"Think of all the people who never had a partner."

"It is good that he was taken. He was so ill."

If loss is personal and individual, then my understanding of Margaret needs to be informed, not by my theoretical speculation, but by my understanding of her. After losing her life partner of forty-six years, her sense of loss is profound. As she sits, quietly crying in the pew, what is going through her mind? What specific losses is she experiencing as a result of his death? Maybe Margaret would have been happy to attend to him for many more years in spite of the fact he was so unwell. Maybe she is experiencing the loss of being a caregiver. Maybe. We don't really know until we listen.

When we expand the definition of loss beyond the most obvious loss, namely death, we are able to deepen our understanding of many experiences. In fact, one might refer to this list as "little deaths."

Job change or loss

Separation/divorce

Leaving home

Growing up

Graduation

Infertility

Leaving the hospital

Losing a contest/game

Moving

Changing churches

Promotion

Retirement

Surgery

**Is grief an appropriate Christian response?**

Grief, like many human experiences, requires us to be attentive and sensitive to the experience of another. If we never get outside our own personal ideas about why things happen and why people are feeling what they are feeling, we will misunderstand those in grief in profound ways. One of the best places to see this illustrated is the funeral home. In that context, we inadvertently reveal our ability or lack of ability to understand.

Margaret is standing beside a coffin. In that coffin is Sam, her husband. When you stop and let those two sentences sink in, you realize a little of her experience. A coffin is for a dead person. A person who does not engage in conversation. A person who does not hug. A person who does not sit across the table from you at dinner. A person who does not go on holidays. A person who does not laugh and cry. A person who does not challenge and argue. A person who does not have sex. A person who does not buy Christmas and birthday presents. A person who does not recommend books. A person who does not go to movies. A person who does not plant the flowers in spring. And this person, this person who "does not" is not just any person. This is Sam.

They first met fifty-one years ago when their families were on holidays at a small bed and breakfast in New England. Margaret, then fifteen, was reluctant to go on that particular holiday with her parents. She was at that stage where peers had more significance in her life, so being with Mom and Dad for a week was not her idea of a good time. Seventeen-year-old Sam saw the time away with his parents as a great opportunity to golf with his dad. They had played some of the courses in the area before, so he came on the trip with anticipation.

The two families came down for breakfast at the same time on the second day. Sam and Margaret were quiet as their parents chatted about the area, but they were intrigued with each other. Part of it was the excitement of being away from home and having someone your own age around, but there was more to it than that. Down at the beach later in the day the families connected again, and before long Sam and Margaret were swimming together and enjoying each other's company. As the week wore on they became inseparable, and Sam's interest in golf was gone. Margaret was his sole focus. Five summers later, Sam and Margaret were married.

But now Sam is in a coffin and Margaret is standing beside him.

The colloquial phrase used in these scenarios is "pay your respects." Ideally, this means a process of esteeming, honoring, and valuing both the person who has died, as well as those who remain.

"He looks so good."

"It is good God has taken him from you, Margaret. He was suffering so much."

"You had more years with him than I thought you would."

"I hope you can get on with your life now. These past few years of caring for Sam have been exhausting for you."

"I think God may have taken Sam to bring your son back to church."

"Isn't it good to know we will all be united in heaven?"

"All things work together for good, Margaret. I am sure that God has a purpose in all this."

Ignore the intent of each of these comments. When it comes to caring for friends, most people have good intent. They genuinely try to express sensitivity to the person going through loss. Instead, focus on the impact these comments might have on Margaret. Not one of the comments addresses her sense of loss or her experience of grief. They range from a superficial analysis of how Sam looks (why do we talk about what dead people look like?), to injunctions to get on with her life, to sloppy theology indicating that God took Sam either for a particular reason, like the restoration of their son, or for some nebulous purpose that no one can explain.

Why does this happen more often than not? Many Christians either do not understand grief or else have come to the erroneous conclusion that it is unbiblical or un-Christian. To correct this serious inadequacy we need to deal with at least some of the biblical material.

### 1. Grief in response to death

After his brothers sold Joseph to the Midianite merchants, they returned to their father, Jacob, and told him that Joseph had been devoured by a ferocious animal.

> Then Jacob tore his garments, and put sackcloth on his loins, and mourned for his son many days. All his sons and all his daughters sought to comfort him; but he refused to be comforted, and said, "No, I shall go down to Sheol to my son, mourning." Thus his father bewailed him.
>
> Genesis 37:34–35

The man of God knew that his dead son would be with Jehovah and that he was "better off." However, the eternal well-being of the son did not address the human experience of the father. The mourning and weeping were appropriate responses in light of the death of a son that he loved.

Although Moses was one hundred and twenty years of age when he died and had lived a full and significant life, that did not prevent his followers from expressing their deep sense of loss. "The Israelites wept for Moses in the plains of Moab thirty days; then the period of mourning for Moses was ended" (Deut. 34:8). There is no question that Middle Eastern culture has different social norms when it comes to grief and loss, but the reality that grief was acknowledged and allowed cannot be ignored.

While not much is stated in the passage, it is interesting to note Jesus's response on hearing about the death of John the Baptist: "Now when Jesus heard this, he withdrew from there in a boat to a deserted place by himself" (Matt. 14:13).

It is also noteworthy that the shortest verse in the English Bible is a poignant summation of Jesus's response to the death of Lazarus: "Jesus began to weep" (John 11:35). It is all the more significant given that Jesus knew that he would be raising Lazarus from the dead.

### 2. Grief in response to infertility

My wife and I have had a long struggle with infertility. From the diagnosis stage—a jolting time that was out of the blue—up until midlife, we have battled a deep sense of loss. Not only is there the obvious loss of not having a biological child of our own, there is also the loss of childhood fantasies and dreams. Both of us grew up thinking about having children and assumed that we would. And then, because of the nature of the menstrual cycle, there is a sense in which every month is a "little loss." While we have rejoiced in the Lord's provision of our adopted daughter, Jessica, adoption does not answer all the losses that are embedded in the experience of infertility.

The first chapter of 1 Samuel describes the pain experienced by Hannah, who "was deeply distressed and prayed to the LORD, and wept bitterly" (1:10). While the chapter ends with the birth of Samuel, Scripture is careful to enunciate the grief that Hannah went through with infertility.

### 3. Grief in response to anticipated loss

The child that resulted from the unfaithfulness of David and Bathsheba became ill. In anticipation of what might happen and the losses that could occur,

> David therefore pleaded with God for the child; David fasted, and went in and lay all night on the ground. The elders of his house stood beside him, urging him to rise from the ground; but he would not, nor did he eat food with them.
>
> 2 Samuel 12:16–17

The experience of Hezekiah is similar as he becomes ill and anticipates his death: "In the noontide of my days I must depart; I am consigned to the gates of Sheol for the rest of my years" (Isa. 38:10).

The ultimate experience of grief in response to anticipated loss is Jesus's experience in the Garden of Gethsemane.

> I am deeply grieved, even to death; remain here, and stay awake with me . . . My Father, if it is possible, let this cup pass from me; yet not what I want but what you want.
>
> Matthew 26:38–39

### 4. Grief in response to the rebellion of people

After God's pleasure with his creation of the world and people, Genesis 6:6–7 is a shocking reminder of God's capacity to experience grief in response to the rebellion of his children.

> And the LORD was sorry that he had made humankind on the earth, and it grieved him to his heart. So the LORD said, "I will blot out from the earth the human beings I have created—people together with animals and creeping things and birds of the air, for I am sorry that I have made them."

God's sense of loss must have been profound when he realized how far his children had wandered. "When Israel was a child, I loved him, and out of Egypt I called my son. The more I called them, the more they went from me" (Hos. 11:1–2).

Jesus expresses a similar sentiment.

> As he came near and saw the city, he wept over it, saying, "If you, even you, had only recognized on this day the things that make for peace! But now they are hidden from your eyes."
>
> Luke 19:41–42

These few references indicate that grief and loss are part of the biblical record. And while they are not prescriptive passages, that is, they don't tell us that we must grieve, they do illustrate that grief is a typical human experience. Not surprisingly these passages reflect the fact that we are image bearers of a God who also experiences grief.

How can we frame grief and loss from a Christian perspective? Paul addresses this in 1 Thessalonians 4:13:

> But we do not want you to be uninformed, brothers and sisters, about those who have died, so that you may not grieve as others do who have no hope.

Paul assumes that Christians and non-Christians experience grief. He does not advise Christians to avoid grief because they have faith. Faith and grief are not in opposition to one another. Paul's focus is not the presence or absence of grief, but the quality of it. The key distinction between Christian and non-Christian grief is the presence of hope. If there is hope—a confidence in the future—in the midst of grief, we will respond differently than we would if hope was absent. We know what that difference is: the addition of hope to grief serves to eliminate the influence of despair.

Paul's personal response to the thought of his friend Epaphroditus's death illustrates this point well.

He was indeed so ill that he nearly died. But God had mercy on him, and not only on him but on me also, so that I would not have one sorrow after another.

Philippians 2:27

Although he knew that Christians would go to be with the Lord at death, and he had a sense of hope about God's work in the world, Paul was sorrowful that his friend was sick. He also recognized that he was spared additional sorrow when Epaphroditus got better. Grief was very much a part of Paul's experience as a Christian.

**What is the experience of grief like?**

*1. It is comprehensive.*

By its very nature, grief is comprehensive: all aspects of the individual are impacted by the experience. While we may be somewhat removed from the situation, those who are close to it may go through some or all of the following symptoms.

- Physical
  stomach/chest discomfort

lack of energy

disruption of sleep, appetite, and sexual interest

- Relational

    distancing from people

    depersonalizing of others

    withdrawal from social initiation

- Emotional

    sad, angry, shocked, numb

    anxious and fearful

    feeling lonely and isolated

- Action

    unmotivated to do things

    lack of energy when doing things

    slower movements

- Cognitive

    forgetful

    lack of attention and preoccupation

    disbelief

- Historical

    more significant grief if more perception of loss in history

    more disruptive if loss is more recent

    will want to recount the details of the loss

- Environmental

    perceive the world as distant

    struggle reaching out to external world

    present world less important than world beyond grave

- Spiritual

    major questions about life and death

    doubt about what happens after death

    struggle with role God may or may not have played in loss

### 2. It requires the managing of feelings.

Because the experience of grief is so emotionally powerful, people who have trouble managing, accepting, and dealing with their feelings will often struggle to express their grief. In the mistaken belief that life is oriented around "keeping feelings out of it," they bury the pain of the loss and try to "get on with their life." While they may experience the loss at a deep level, they are unable and at times unwilling to express it. The result is that the work of grief is difficult to undertake.

Men, in particular, seem to struggle with this more than women, although neither gender is immune to this problem. Out of a desire to be "strong" or "together," many men act as if nothing has happened when a loss occurs, or they cover it up with bravado or humor. At times, this strategy can become enmeshed with Christian thinking and can even appear very spiritual. A man who is actually denying his inner pain can look like he has it together by citing Scripture passages and theological truths. However, the pain will show itself in other more indirect ways, such as nagging physical difficulties like headaches, gastrointestinal problems, and weight gain or loss, as well as in irritability, impatience, and difficulties relating to others.

It is important to remember that people who struggle with managing their feelings also need to be understood. For reasons that are not always obvious, they may not understand what they are experiencing themselves, so their reticence in being open about their feelings may have more to do with ignorance of their inner life than an unwillingness to share. I was told a true story about a woman trying to get a man to talk about how he felt when a particular thing happened to him. In exasperation he exclaimed, "I wasn't hungry, I wasn't tired, and I wasn't thirsty. What do you mean, how was I feeling?" In situations like this the person will not experience the weight of the grief until another loss occurs in their life. Often it takes a succession of losses before people who have trouble managing their emotions are able to come to grips with what they are experiencing.

### 3. It is tied to the person's history of losses.

We cannot understand an individual's response to loss until we know what preceded it. In the case of Margaret, we know that she lost her husband of many years. That is a significant loss, but it can be exacerbated or lessened depending on what preceded it. Let's say, for instance, that Margaret had aged parents who were still alive and she had never been through the death of a loved one prior to Sam's passing. Her sense of shock will be greater, largely because she has not had other experiences to help shape her understanding of loss and what it means to her.

A couple who has struggled with infertility will experience a much deeper sense of loss when the one pregnancy that does succeed results in a stillbirth. Typically, their grief will be more intense than the couple that has already had two children and then has a stillborn child.

A church that has an eighty-year history, with a number of different pastors coming and going during that time, will experience the departure of a pastor in a much different way than a church that is only twenty and has had only one pastor. Both communities of faith will experience loss, but the younger church will find it more difficult.

A friend of mine had experienced a lot of loss in his life. He had struggled keeping jobs and relationships and found himself single into midlife. After balking at going for help for some time, he finally agreed to receive counseling. After a few months of connecting with the counselor and establishing a good rapport, the counselor became ill quite suddenly and died. My friend's sense of loss was considerably greater than other counselees because of his history of losses.

### 4. It is best understood through stages.

One of the things we know about grief and loss is that there is no neat linear pattern to it. It is not easy to predict how Andrew will respond to the downsizing or how Melissa will react to the divorce or how the move will go for Sarah and Jeremy. We do know, however, that there are various stages that people go through when they are dealing with loss.

A simple way of viewing grief is to describe it as a fourfold process:

1.  Shock (I can't believe it!)
2.  Reality (This is what happened!)
3.  Reaction (Here is how I am feeling!)
4.  Recovery (I am moving on with my life!)

One of my childhood friends died of a brain tumor in his early forties. From the time John was diagnosed until a number of months after his death, I went back and forth through these four stages. I regularly used the phrase "I can't believe it" to describe my experience. It was incomprehensible to me that someone I knew as strong and able would waste away and die in his early forties. To anyone who wanted to listen, I would repeat "John stories," both from the past and from the present, many times repeating what happened over and over again. I would also share the various feelings that I was experiencing. Sometimes I felt peaceful, at other times angry, frustrated, and depressed. In the midst of it all, I felt a deep sense of my own mortality. It took probably a year before John's death was not in the center of my world and I was able to move on. It was not that I forgot John or ignored the reality of his death, but I was able to put his death in better perspective over time.

My experience with these stages illustrates a number of things about the hard work of grief:

1.  Grief takes time. Significant losses take a minimum of one or two years to process well. It cannot and should not be rushed.
2.  The stages are not linear. The move from shock through reality to reaction and recovery is not sequential. It is possible to move back and forth through the stages many times and be surprised at what you are experiencing.
3.  Each stage has its own length. Intuitively, most of us want to move to recovery quickly and get on with our lives. However, depending on the circumstances, each stage needs its own time to do its work.

Some of us need to stay in shock and reality for quite a while before
we can embrace reaction and recovery.

4. Each one of us will be different. There is no set pattern for how
   people should process loss. We need to respect that each of us,
   even in response to the same loss, may process it very differently.

**So how can I minister to those who are having problems with grief?**

*Identify losses as "little deaths."*

When we comprehend the power of loss and the grief that goes with it,
we will be able to help others frame the experience they are going through.
The individual in your small group who has just lost a job, the woman
who just went through a divorce, the couple struggling with infertility,
the family who just went bankrupt, are all in situations that may raise
grief responses. In some cases they will be aware that they are more tired,
more removed from people, unmotivated or forgetful, but they will not
be labeling it as grief in response to loss. In these kinds of situations, I
have found that the question, "This seems like a death, doesn't it?" often
brings tears to the surface as the person gets in touch with the depth of
their loss. This kind of understanding will help the person move through
the stages of grief.

*Recognize that different stages bring different opportunities.*

When our responses are based on the foundation of care and understanding, we can reach out to people and be of help. When people are
in shock:

- Be there. There is nothing more valuable than someone by your
  side when you are struggling with the shock of loss. You cannot
  minimize the significance of your physical presence when someone
  is going through bereavement.
- Avoid giving advice. Shock, by definition, implies disorientation
  and lack of direction. Even if your advice is good, it will not be ap-

propriate at this stage. Recognize that our tendency to advise comes not from our desire to reach out to the person going through grief, but from our own need to do something in the midst of a situation that seems so much out of our control.

- Offer practical help. There are many practical things (e.g., meals prepared, errands run, driving people to appointments, insurance and business arrangements, phone calls, etc.) that need to be done when a loss occurs. This is especially true within the first week after a death. There are a vast number of areas that need attention and concentration, and the person going through grief will benefit from practical help.

When people are coping with reality:

- Be a good listener. One of the things that happens when people are experiencing grief is that they will tell you the same story over and over again. Not only will there be details about the death itself, but also stories about their life with the person. Listen each time as if it was the first time.
- Be patient. Grief is emotionally disruptive and it makes most of us say and do irrational things. It is easy to tire of people who are irrational, but remember that your character is best revealed in wearying circumstances.
- Avoid moralizing. When people are coping with the details of their story, they do not want to hear the moral of the story. This is not to discount the accuracy or validity of the moral or the spiritual lesson you may see in the situation, but rather to recognize the importance of timing.

When people are in reaction:

- Recognize that they are filled with varied feelings. People will work through their grief more effectively if they do not just experience emotions but also express them.

- Avoid judging their feelings. One of the best ways to shut down the expression of feeling is to assess it. This is particularly true with anger, one of the emotions that seems to be negated most often. Allow people the freedom to simply experience the vast range of feelings that are a natural part of grief.
- Help the grieving person examine what they are feeling. Good interaction will allow the grieving person to understand what they are experiencing. Because their feelings are all over the map, careful listening and processing will bring clarity. Allow people the opportunity to name the emotions they are feeling, to talk about them and unpack them without any sense that they are wrong and inappropriate.

When people are moving toward recovery:

- Encourage them. This stage, done well, will allow them to move into the rest of their lives in a healthier manner. Encouragement in this stage does not deny what has happened or ignore the significance of the loss, but it helps the person to see the present in light of the future.
- Aid them with decision-making. People need help when they are reorienting their lives. They will be making important decisions about where to live, what relationships to be involved in, what lifestyle they wish to choose, etc.
- Address their guilt. Many individuals feel they are doing something wrong when they start moving on with their lives. Somehow it feels disrespectful to "leave the deceased behind" and embrace the future. Appropriate reassurance can be helpful in this stage.

### Be there at various points in the process.

When people experience a loss, the natural tendency is to be there when the loss actually occurs. When someone is fired, it is easy to have them over for supper the next week. When someone dies, it is obvious that going to the funeral home is the appropriate thing to do. When your teenage daughter loses a volleyball tournament, it can help to talk to her that night. While these are appropriate responses, it ignores the reality that losses do not stop after they have happened.

It has been over twenty years since my wife, Bev, and I received our infertility diagnosis. At that stage the sense of loss was profound and we moved back and forth between shock and reality. Over those twenty years we have experienced the loss in different ways. Now that we are in our fifties and biology is going to close the door completely, the sense of loss is more final and complete. People who are sensitive to issues of grief around infertility would be very valuable to us in our own processing of the loss. Our loss did not end twenty years ago. In many ways it only began then.

The same is true for death. Funerals are so poorly timed in terms of loss. Very few grieving friends and family are out of the shock stage by the time the funeral arrives. And yet our words of comfort at the funeral home and in funeral homilies often indicate that the survivors are in the recovery stage, ready to get on with their lives. Well-meaning visitors will look at the faces and demeanor of the family and conclude, "She is doing well." Nothing could be further from the truth. She has had so many people around her since her husband died that she has no idea how she feels.

These realities emphasize the importance of being there during the whole process of loss. Weeks, months, and years after losses, speak to the person about it, drop them a note, or make a call. The fear that raising the loss with the person will upset them is a misplaced fear. In the first place, "upset" is not bad; and in most cases, people will be glad to know that you are remembering them. This is particularly true at special events. If my friend John's two children get married, there will be happiness at the wedding but also a sense of loss. Most children and wives assume that Dad will be there when the children are married. Undoubtedly, John will be missed.

I have found that this basic practice is often ignored because "I didn't want to bother you" or "I knew others would be calling you" or "I'm sure you have had a lot of people connecting with you." It is better to connect and demonstrate care at various points after the initial loss than speculate about what others are doing.

### Use biblical material and resources sensitively.

In a powerful book that describes his own grief over the death of his wife, C. S. Lewis says:

> Talk to me about the truth of religion and I'll listen gladly. Talk to me about the duty of religion and I'll listen submissively. But don't come talking to me about the consolations of religion or I shall suspect that you don't understand.[1]

It is a self-evident, but often forgotten, fact—quoting Scripture does not always reflect wisdom and discernment. That the devil himself quoted Scripture is the most blatant demonstration of this reality. But there are many other examples in all of our lives when we resort to quoting biblical material and offering theological insights while showing a profound lack of sensitivity.

When people are in the midst of grief, particularly the early stages, they do not need biblical exegesis or systematic theology. What they need is the presence of Christ and the work of the Holy Spirit demonstrated through our presence. Isn't it interesting that, in Scripture, often what God promises, when we are in the turmoil of our problems, is not answers or solutions but his presence? In the same way, we can bring a little word here or there from Scripture into the lives of people who are experiencing deep loss, but mostly what we can offer is quietly being there.

The writer of the Hebrews captures this idea well in 13:5: "Keep your lives free from the love of money, and be content with what you have; for [God] has said, 'I will never leave you or forsake you.'" Because many of the Christians of that time got entangled with excessive passion for money and lost their contentment, it was easy to live a life of angst and anxiety, wishing and wanting for more. The biblical writer does not provide a list of steps so those who are in trouble can work their way out of it. Rather, we are reminded of a profound truth found in Deuteronomy 31:6, one that focuses on the presence of God as an antidote to worry and discontent. To tell a grieving person that God will never leave them or forsake them and to demonstrate that you will also incarnate the same truth as much as possible, does not solve their grief as much as provide a presence.

A major temptation in this area relates to the tendency to give a theological explanation as to why the loss occurred. We live in a culture that is obsessed with "why," and our tendency to want to answer the why question seems to increase in situations where the loss is great. I remember talking to a woman in counseling whose teenage son had passed away in tragic circumstances. He had been in the process of preparing for a life of missionary service when his life was prematurely snuffed out. She was not only battling the grief of having lost a child so young in life, but was also confronting her view of God after a well-meaning Christian friend told her that the reason her son was taken was because God knew that he was not going to turn out well and he was sparing the family that pain! Can you imagine the impact of such words spoken into a situation already characterized by unspeakable grief?

Rabbi Harold S. Kushner describes a conversation between a pastor and a mother after the death of her young son:

> "I know that this is a painful time for you. But I know that you will get through it all right, because God never sends us more of a burden than we can bear. God only let this happen to you because He knows that you are strong enough to handle it." [Her response?] "If only I was a weaker person, Robbie would still be alive."[2]

Another version of the why obsession relates to an after-the-fact explanation. Rather than saying God took the person because of something that he or she was going to do, we say that God took them so that someone would become a Christian either at the funeral or just after. While I, with the angels, rejoice when someone comes into the kingdom, this has always struck me as a strange view of God. He picks someone out, decides they are going to die, and the whole purpose is to get someone else into the kingdom? We may say these things in a well-meaning way but all they do is compound the problem of grief by adding theological confusion to the mix.

### *Let people express their pain in their own way.*

Many of our church communities have an antiseptic quality to them. They give the impression that pain is not acceptable; moreover, the structure of the church is set up to be sure that feelings of any sort are kept down. For people experiencing grief, this is a tragic situation. When the people of God do not allow you to experience human responses, where are you going to go?

We all express pain uniquely. Some will cry quietly, while others will sob uncontrollably and others will never cry. Some people readily verbalize what they are feeling, while others like to keep things in. Some want to "do something" when they are hurting, while others would prefer to sit down with a friend over coffee.

Determine the unique style of the grieving person before you commence a helping role. Relate to them with a style that fits them, not one that best fits you. This, in effect, gives them permission to respond in their own way. Such permission-giving will forge a strong relationship where you will be able to truly hear and understand.

### *Recognize the unique circumstances of suicide.*

All that has been said about grief applies to those who are left behind after a suicide, but there are some unique components that need to be understood. One relates to theological concerns, the other to issues of responsibility.

Thomas Aquinas, the Catholic theologian, argued that all sin must be confessed in order to be forgiven. This teaching has led many Roman Catholics to see suicide as the unpardonable sin. By definition, one cannot confess the sin of suicide. Evangelicals need to bring a different grid to bear on this situation. If what Christ has done on the cross is able to atone for my sin, that includes all my sin, past, present, and future. Even if we were to think of suicide as a sin, an assumption in itself, it would be forgiven based on what Christ has done. Family members and friends may need this careful reassurance after a suicide.

The other issue relates to responsibility. I have had two friends commit suicide. One I knew quite well all the way through high school and university, and the other for only a year when I was older. When Phil and Kelly died, many of us who knew them experienced a degree of guilt and self-blame. Did we miss something? Was there anything we could have done? Could we have prevented the suicide? Did we do something wrong? In response to our own grief over the suicide, we needed people around us who would understand.

We needed to be heard. Those are genuine questions when someone close to you commits suicide. We also needed someone to help us sift through appropriate and inappropriate guilt and self-blame. While one person is never responsible for the suicide of another, there may be some circumstances when more could have or should have been done. Lastly, we needed people who would help us understand the multiple causes behind all behavior, but especially suicide.

There are always fundamental causes, factors lurking in the person's past, that provide a broad historical context for their suicide. Usually there are contributing causes, more immediate factors that set the stage. Finally, there are precipitating factors, an incident or event that preceded the suicide. As we help people deal with their sense of responsibility and guilt because of the suicide, it can be helpful to tease out the separation of these three levels of cause. Often the person was not around for the early formative years, was not a party to the contributing causes that set the stage for the suicide, nor did they do anything to precipitate the event. While this will not eliminate all guilt and self-blame, this simple formulation can help people separate out where their responsibility lies.

### *Handle children like they are children.*

It is difficult enough to deal with the grief of adults, but it is even more complicated to deal with the grief of children. However, there are some simple principles that will help in our interaction with children, whether they are experiencing death or "little deaths."

1.  Be honest and admit to the reality of the situation. When we pretend with children we do them a disservice. So to tell a young child who lost a grandmother that "she is happy now" is to add confusion. The child's reasoning will go something like this—Why is she happy if she has left us? A more appropriate line might be "We know Grandma is in heaven so she is happy to be with Jesus, but we are still here and we miss her."

2.  Treat death as a normal part of life rather than something that should lead to fear and denial. I once dealt with a woman whose mother told her, after her father's death, that "we are not going to talk about him again." Any questions or concerns she had could not be addressed. Not surprisingly, she ignored death and did not incorporate it into a full view of life. In families where the death of a family member is not talked about, damage is done to both the children and the adults.

3.  Be sensitive to each child's personality and allow them to talk about the person who has died. Like adults, children will process death in unique ways, but most of them will want to talk about the person. One feature of this conversation will be an endless list of questions. All of them do not have to be answered but can be affirmed as legitimate and acceptable.

4.  Prior to late childhood, children tend to be more concrete thinkers. This means that accepting Jesus into your heart, for an eight-year-old, means exactly that—Jesus now resides in your chest. By the same token, a child who is told that someone is alive in heaven will probably wonder why they are not coming back. Most adult theology has a degree of abstractness to it, but in the presence of younger children we will need to take into account their concrete thinking.

5.  Children do not have the verbal skills or self-understanding to express all of their feelings. Many of them will "behave" their feel-

ings rather than "express" them. After a loved one dies, a child's behavior may deteriorate. Adults should recognize that this is a grief response, not just a case of simple misbehavior.

### Explore the special dynamics in the death of a parent.

Many of us have a childlike sense that our parents will live forever. Since they have been around for our whole life, we have a subtle belief that this will continue indefinitely. This is probably more the case for those of us who are baby boomers who grew up in a time of optimism and unlimited possibilities. The death of a parent is a reminder that life is not perfect and disruption is part of its fabric. In this sense, the death of a parent may also be the death of a dream of the way life is, or at least the way we hoped it would be. With the mobility of the culture and the career changes experienced by so many, parents have often become the one constant in life.

When both parents pass on, many children have to come to grips with the fact that they are nobody's child and there is no one standing between them and the grave. There will be various responses to such a state. Some will grasp this new sense of future with courage and fortitude and others will struggle with the fact that, under normal circumstances, they will be the next to pass on.

There is some evidence that a significant number of people will change careers after the death of a parent, and that some will leave a marriage—if the original motivation for marriage was to escape from a dysfunctional parent-child relationship. Somehow the passing of a parent opens up new horizons when the sense of obligation to the parent is gone. By the same token, those involved in a strong and stable marriage may experience renewed commitment as a result of the parental death.

A similar dynamic occurs with siblings. If the parent was the glue that held the family together, their death can bring a separation between siblings. If there was strength in the sibling relationship already, the death can enhance closeness. Shared conversations about parental loss can create a new bond.

All of these variables emphasize, again, the importance of really tuning in to the experience of others. There is no one standard response to losing a parent. Some will experience deep grief because they have not only lost a parent, but also their prime confidante and close friend. For others, the parent made little significant impact during life so their death is a continuation of the child's experience. And then there are situations where the child experienced profound neglect and abuse when the parent was alive. Parental death in this situation may bring anger, frustration, and unresolved conflict to the surface.

### Remember that death does not bring an end to relational difficulties.

I have talked with many people who think that their difficulties with a friend, parent, spouse, or child will end when that person dies. But after the death, they find that the reality of human relationships and the power of history and memory are such that death does not bring an end to the relationship. If people are experiencing anger or a lack of resolution with someone before they die, it is highly likely that this will continue after their death. The same principle occurs in the "little death" of divorce. One of the shocks experienced by many couples after divorce is that they do not feel completely resolved about the tensions that produced the difficulties. Being aware of this reality will help us deal with people in a more sensitive way.

### Anticipate change in family dynamics after a death.

It can be helpful to let people know that the passing of a family member completely changes the relational dynamics within the family. Prior to the death the family had a certain style of functioning, but after the death all the relationships change. When one individual is taken out of the family system everyone relates differently. If the deceased provided the life and buoyancy when the family got together, that now needs to be replaced. If the deceased was the problem person in the family, the family will now need a new focus of attention. If the deceased person was leaned on by certain family members, those family members may be forced to change their loyalty.

If someone had a long-term illness prior to their death, they became the focus of the family as other members took on a caregiving role. The individual's health and well-being were the prime topic of conversation when the family was together and any unresolved conflict and tensions got buried. After the death, the family no longer has the patient to provide focus and is forced back into its pre-illness state. Individual family members who only function well when they are giving care have to adopt a new strategy for relating in the family; in addition, the predeath conflicts may resurface.

These principles also apply when divorce hits a family. This "little death" forces the family to function differently because the relationships within the family are changed significantly. The spouse who is now outside the family has to relate differently to each member of the family. It is much like a death, but the person is still alive, with all the complications that this brings.

**Summary**

Grief is the personal and individual experience we go through when something or someone is taken away from us. Christians need to have clarity on the biblical perspective of grief in response to:

1. Death
2. Infertility
3. Anticipated loss
4. The rebellion of people

In understanding people's experience, we need to know that grief:

1. is comprehensive;
2. requires the managing of feelings;
3. is tied to the person's history of losses;
4. is best understood through stages.

When ministering to those who are having problems with grief:

Identify losses as "little deaths."

Recognize that different stages bring different opportunities.

Be there at various points in the process.

Use biblical material and resources sensitively.

Let people express their pain in their own way.

Recognize the unique circumstances of suicide.

Handle children like they are children.

Explore the special dynamics in the death of a parent.

Remember that death does not bring an end to relational difficulties.

Anticipate change in family dynamics after a death.

# 4

# Depression

## What is depression?

Sarah has been a missionary in Africa for ten years. She is respected by her colleagues in the mission as well as by the nationals. Committed to evangelism and church planting, she utilizes her gifts well in teaching, encouragement, and pastoral care. Both in administrative meetings and in actual field involvement, she is revered as a fine example of what a missionary should be. Most of her colleagues would say that, periodically, a critical attitude comes out, with a hint of anger, but generally she seems to connect well with others. Unknown to them, though, Sarah battles a deep sadness almost every day, especially in the morning. Getting out of bed is very hard because she has no motivation and no interest in doing anything. She manages to get through the day but "manages" is the operative word.

Jacques is a successful businessman who has moved up the ranks in a multinational corporation to hold a position of considerable power and influence. He is quiet and described by many of his friends as introverted. In church meetings, he looks sullen, although no one would ever describe him as sad. He never goes to emotional extremes on either

73

end of the continuum. No one has ever seem him really down or upset, nor have they seen him extremely happy and up. Any input he gives at the church is appreciated and valued but it lacks a spark. He seems really flat a lot of the time.

Gillian is in the psychiatric ward being treated for depression. For the months prior to being hospitalized, she had been feeling increasingly down and sad. Paired with this was a feeling of being worthless and a deep sense of exhaustion and fatigue. She was having trouble sleeping and had lost a fair amount of weight. And to top it all off she enjoyed nothing. Even things like tennis and movies, which used to give her a sense of buoyancy, made no impact. The black hole of hopelessness was so deep that she had been thinking about suicide, even though she did not think that she would actually do anything.

Wilhelm had left school early to pursue his dream of being a stand-up comedian. In the early days he did not get many jobs and ended up in dingy bars in small towns telling jokes to very few people. But the last two years have seen a big turnaround. He is in high demand and was even one of the lead acts in an event that had many of the top-name comedians on hand. When you are around him he retains his "stand-up" style. He is funny, up, optimistic, and energetic. People feed off him and love his manic side. What they do not see is the quiet life of substance abuse and promiscuity behind the scenes that help him deal with inner pain rooted in his childhood. He functions on little sleep, has severely fluctuating moods, and often goes on spending binges where he experiences significant euphoria.

Most people observing these four individuals would conclude that Gillian, the hospitalized person, is the one who is struggling with depression. The successful missionary, the quiet businessman, and the funny comedian do not appear to be sad, so obviously they are not depressed. However, these four vignettes illustrate one of the most powerful aspects of depression. It is multifaceted and is often hidden behind masks that do not reveal its true character. The fact is that Sarah, Jacques, and Wilhelm are also battling depression, a fact that may not be obvious to their friends or even to themselves.

Like many difficulties, depression not only has many faces but many different dynamics lurking behind it. When you walk into a room it is not always easy to pick out who is depressed, but it is even more difficult to observe the factors that have precipitated it. This is often the case with the role of anger in depression.

Take the case of Bill, who had been let go from his position after having worked at a company for fifteen years. He had started in the company as a shipping clerk but had moved up the ladder, and in recent years, was functioning as the vice-president of marketing. His dismissal was explained officially as being due to downsizing, but he had a sneaking suspicion that a new executive vice-president had played a significant role. Bill picked up, almost from the beginning, that the new executive did not appreciate him; Bill had some reason to suspect that he was involved in the decision.

For the first few weeks after he left the company, Bill was in shock, but he had bouts of enthusiasm and energy as he contemplated what he might do next. The severance package was generous, so there was no pressure to make a quick decision about anything else. But by week four he was starting to feel flat and irritable. He was not very motivated to do anything in the morning and his sleep was increasingly disturbed. At the beginning of this stage, he explained what was happening as being due to the fact that he was tired, but eventually his wife pointed out to him that it seemed like it was more than simple tiredness. With her prodding he admitted that he was feeling flat since being let go. He had nowhere to go in the morning and did not feel like he was making a contribution anywhere.

While Bill and his wife are unaware of the dynamics, we see here a case of someone who is experiencing depression that can be traced ultimately to unresolved anger. What is anger? Anger is an emotional experience that occurs when an expectation has been blocked. In other words, when I want something to happen or assume that it will happen and it does not, I experience anger. The depth and extent of the anger will be directly related to my values and priorities. If something is extremely important to me and I have expectations around that value, the violation of the expectation will create significant anger. On the other hand, if something happens that does not meet my expectations but it is in an area that does not matter that much to me, my anger will be minimal.

Bill is not a die-hard football fan, but when his team plays, he expects and hopes that they will win. When they lose he experiences frustration, but it lasts for an hour after the game and then it is gone completely. However, when you lose your job and you think it is due to some behind-the-scenes politics created by a new employee, the stakes are much higher. Bill expected that his service of fifteen years secured for him a predictable future with the company. But more than that, he thought he would be treated well by those above him. He thought the time and energy he expended over these many years would count for something. And he was only nine years from retirement. Why does he have to go out and look for work now?

But where does he express that anger? How does he deal with it? He would feel awkward marching back into the office and confronting his boss. It would be even more uncomfortable to go in and express his anger to the new executive. He does not even have solid evidence that he did something wrong. So the anger sits there, deep inside, eating away at him. And what happens to anger that percolates? It gets turned inward and becomes depression. The energy that is contained in the anger has nowhere to be released so it "attacks" the person experiencing it. In this case, Bill's depression is, in fact, anger turned inward. The real resolution will not come from focusing just on the depression, but also on the dynamics around the anger—dynamics that are not always easy to access either for the person experiencing them or, more importantly, for those friends and family members who are trying to be of help.

So what then is depression? Let's start first with what depression is not. It is not a down day, or a fleeting feeling of sadness or melancholy. Most of us have these kinds of experiences and are able to move on from them. They are not debilitating and do not have an adverse effect on our daily functioning. In being able to bounce back after a bad day or snap out of a sad experience, we are illustrating the exact opposite of depression. When someone is depressed they are exactly that—moving in a direction that is not high but low. People who are just having a down day are able to move to a higher level of energy and interest. Depressed people are not able to do this.

If you read the literature on clinical depression—the term most typically used to describe this problem—there are usually eight symptoms that are used diagnostically to determine if a person is depressed. The key is not to see these symptoms in isolation, but to understand them in a broader context of what is going on in the person's life. It is also important to remember that these symptoms need to be present with regularity and consistency, and a number of them need to be happening concurrently. One of the symptoms for a short period of time is not problematic or deserving of the diagnosis, but a significant number of the eight symptoms for an extended period of time would suggest that a competent professional should investigate for depression.

Significant change in appetite, sexual drive, and weight

Significant change in sleep pattern

Loss of energy and excessive fatigue

Feelings of worthlessness, self-reproach, and excessive guilt

Difficulty concentrating, remembering, and making decisions

Loss of motivation and enjoyment of regular tasks

General slowing down of all motor tasks

Suicidal tendencies

Without getting into great technical detail (given the purpose of this book), it is important to recognize that some people who have problems with depression also struggle with a manic component as well. Within the psychiatric community, the diagnostic term *bipolar disorder* is used to describe those people who have many of the symptoms described above, as well as some or all of the following symptoms, again concentrated over an extended period of time:

Significant elation and expansion of mood

Irritability with impulsive anger

Hyperactive, talkative, and highly distractible

Bad judgment leading to difficulties socially or at work

Inflated self-esteem

Involvement in risky activities that can bring painful circumstances

Diminished need for sleep

## How do we understand depression from a Christian perspective?

### 1. Anecdotal evidence

Those of us who have been involved in clinical work know that depression is not something that is confined to the non-Christian world. Some of the finest pastors, Christian leaders, preachers, teachers, and counselors I have known, to say nothing of godly homemakers, dedicated lay people, and motivated churchgoers, struggle with depression. On a given Sunday in any church, you can be quite confident that there are a significant number of people in the room that are, or have been, battling depression. Anecdotal evidence would suggest that spirituality and depression are not in opposition to one another.

### 2. Examples from history

We also have examples from history. Charles Haddon Spurgeon, recognized by many as one of the finest preachers over the past two hundred years, struggled with depression that lasted for months at a time. At one particular point, after the church where he was serving was burned down, he went into a severe depression. Similar stories have been reported about such Christian notables as Martin Luther, John Bunyan, and William Cowper. Their experiences would seem to illustrate that spiritual depth and commitment are no guarantee of protection from depression.

### 3. The story of Elijah

One could also look at the pages of Scripture to see some biblical characters going through depressive-like symptoms. Note the experience of Elijah in 1 Kings 19, after a spiritual triumph over the prophets of Baal. One would assume that after such a powerful experience with God, Elijah would be high and energetic, but at the beginning of the chapter he receives a message from Jezebel, who threatens him. Elijah is afraid, runs away, and goes out into the desert.

He went a day's journey into the wilderness and sat down under a solitary broom tree. He asked that he might die: "'It is enough; now, O Lord, take away my life, for I am no better than my ancestors.' Then he lay down under the broom tree and fell asleep" (1 Kings 19:4–5).

It would appear that Elijah's unique triumph over God's enemies did not guarantee him a life that was free of depressive symptoms.

### 4. Lament psalms

Many of the lament psalms list qualities of depression that grip the writer. Most noteworthy in this regard is Psalm 88. Notice the openness that the psalmist has about his pain, the fact that his calling on God did not make life easier, and the rather depressing end to the psalm even though the writer is imploring God to be of help. The black hole of depression is presented in tandem with a desire to know God and acknowledge his salvation.

> O LORD, God of my salvation,
>     when, at night, I cry out in your presence,
> let my prayer come before you;
>     incline your ear to my cry.

> For my soul is full of troubles,
>     and my life draws near to Sheol.
> I am counted among those who go down to the Pit;
>     I am like those who have no help,
> like those forsaken among the dead,

like the slain that lie in the grave,
like those whom you remember no more,
    for they are cut off from your hand.
You have put me in the depths of the Pit,
    in the regions dark and deep.
Your wrath lies heavy upon me,
    and you overwhelm me with all your waves. *Selah*

You have caused my companions to shun me;
    you have made me a thing of horror to them.
I am shut in so that I cannot escape;
    my eye grows dim through sorrow.
Every day I call on you, O LORD;
    I spread out my hands to you.
Do you work wonders for the dead?
    Do the shades rise up to praise you? *Selah*
Is your steadfast love declared in the grave,
    or your faithfulness in Abaddon?
Are your wonders known in the darkness,
    or your saving help in the land of forgetfulness?

But I, O LORD, cry out to you;
    in the morning my prayer comes before you.
O LORD, why do you cast me off?
    Why do you hide your face from me?
Wretched and close to death from my youth up,
    I suffer your terrors; I am desperate.
Your wrath has swept over me;
    your dread assaults destroy me.
They surround me like a flood all day long;
    from all sides they close in on me.
You have caused friend and neighbor to shun me;
    my companions are in darkness.

Similar analyses could be done of the books of Job, Jeremiah, and 2
Corinthians, writings that seem to pair spiritual aspiration with personal
experiences that are characterized by depressive symptoms. So to argue

that spiritual people do not get depressed and, by implication, that depressed people are not spiritual is to reflect an approach to biblical history that is superficial at best and insensitive at worst.

### 5. Internalized anger and spiritual problems

There are times when the underlying dynamics behind depression involve spiritual problems that need to be resolved. This is particularly true in the case of anger that is turned inward. The clearest statement on this issue is found in Ephesians 4:26–27: "Be angry but do not sin; do not let the sun go down on your anger, and do not make room for the devil."

The first sentence makes a distinction between being angry and sinning. On the one hand you can be angry, while on the other you can sin or not sin in that state. The meaning of this becomes much clearer when we understand that Paul uses the Greek word *orge*. In your *orge*, an anger that is characterized by a settled inner attitude, do not sin. In other words, this anger, which has the potential for revenge and personal animosity, can turn into sin. It is not the feeling of anger that is the problem here—it is what you do with it. The sin is linked more with personal animosity and vengeance rather than anger.

A different word for anger is employed in the second phrase. The anger that is linked with the sun going down is *parorgismos*. It is not that you need to resolve all conflicts before bed, but that you need to guard against nurturing your *orge*. Letting your *orge* fester may turn it into *parorgismos*, an anger characterized by irritation and exasperation, eventually leading to feelings of bitterness, cynicism, and depressive-like symptoms.

The final phrase in these two verses—"and do not make room for the devil"—can almost seem like an afterthought unrelated to what preceded it. However, these three phrases are very much intertwined. If anger moves into sin through a nurturing process which creates irritation and exasperation with resultant bitterness and depressive-like symptoms, we are giving the devil an inroad into our lives. In contemporary evangelical thinking, there is a significant amount of discussion about the role of the demonic. In this context, the biblical record links the demonic with how we manage our anger.

These two verses provide the touchstone for all the biblical material on anger. They show us that to conclude anger is wrong and sinful is only partially accurate. Depending on the situation that provokes it and the disposition of the person experiencing it, anger may be righteous or it may be sinful. But in the context of a discussion of spirituality and depression it is important to note that people like Bill, who are struggling with anger turned inward, run the risk of cultivating that anger over time and moving to a place where the devil can do his work. To not fight that battle and to succumb to the negative effects of brooding anger and depression is to engage in an unhealthy spiritual process.

**What is the experience of depression like?**

*1. It is comprehensive.*

Maybe more than any other difficulty that people experience, depression has an impact on almost every area of functioning. Individuals may experience some or all of the following symptoms:

- Physical
  reduced or increased appetite and sexual interest
  sleep problems and particular difficulty getting up in the morning
  lack of interest in any physical activities
- Relational
  withdrawal from others
  desire to escape often to the point of considering suicide
  oversensitive toward others and often critical
- Emotional
  sad and hopeless
  despair and profound apathy
  lurking anger and frustration

- Action

  general decrease in activity but a danger of overworking

  little activity done for fun, enjoyment, or pleasure

  lack of motivation for any responsibilities

- Cognitive

  all thinking seems to end up in a black hole

  negative view of self, the world, and the future

  disorientation and memory loss

- Historical

  sometimes depression is present in family background

  can be a lack of nurturing relationships in past

  often have tried many potential solutions

- Environmental

  world around is not seen to be friendly or inviting

  people and circumstances are seen negatively

  inner world is more powerful and influential than outer
  world

- Spiritual

  major questions about life and death

  struggle with God's ability or willingness to help

  church community seems distant

### 2. It is linked with multiple causes.

One of the problems with the term *depression* is that there are so many manifestations and expressions that no two depressed people may be experiencing the same thing. Furthermore, the causes of depression are just as multifaceted. For these reasons, if for no other, lay people need to bring careful and thoughtful understanding and, in all cases, encourage the involvement of a professional.

It is never wise to assume a single cause without having fully tuned in to the person's experience. There are at least ten different reasons why depression may afflict a person. In some cases, a number of these factors work in tandem to intensify the depression.

1. Insufficient rest. Mild forms of depression characterize people, like students, who go through prolonged periods without sufficient sleep.
2. Diet and exercise. A consistently poor diet with no exercise will create a physiological flatness that will eventually manifest some depressive symptoms.
3. Drug reactions. At times drug reactions can produce various forms of depression.
4. Repressed anger. People who have been through severe trauma, like sexual abuse, and have been unable to express their anger outwardly will sometimes turn it inward and become depressed.
5. Biochemical factors. The increased research on brain chemistry has clearly demonstrated that some depressions can be linked primarily with biochemical factors rather than psychological factors.
6. Endocrine dysfunction. Due to physiological factors, difficulties related to the thyroid, pituitary, or adrenal glands may cause depression, as may the premenstrual, postpartum, or premenopausal stages of life for women.
7. Faulty thinking. Quite apart from circumstances that are going on in life, erroneous thinking can produce depressive symptoms.
8. Success. An emotional valley that leads to depression can follow the elevation of mood that comes with success and completion.
9. Loss. Depending on the individual's history, loss or the perception of loss can trigger depression.
10. Faulty behavior. When their behavior violates social, moral, or legal standards, some people will react to this violation with depressive symptoms.

### 3. It often has faulty thinking associated with it.

While the experience of depression is largely emotional, aspects of the thinking process are affected as well. These faulty thoughts are often rooted in history and family dynamics, as well as forged through life experiences. There are at least five faulty thinking processes that frequently plague people who struggle with depression.

#### Conclusion without evidence

A depressed woman who does not value herself or anyone else can easily read the entire church as "unfriendly, uncaring, and uninterested in anyone but themselves." The reality is that her analysis reflects her psychological state more than it does the nature of the church but she, nonetheless, holds to this conclusion without any substantive evidence.

#### Conclusion based on one element

The man who has struggled with low-grade depression for many years will select one thing his wife has done wrong and conclude that she does not care about him, all the while ignoring the fact she has done an incredible number of things for him that reflect deep commitment. When confronted with many elements in a situation, the depressed person with faulty thinking will select one and build a case around it.

#### Conclusion about identity based on performance

The parent who concludes, "I am a terrible parent and should never have had kids," after getting angry with her son who is getting ready for school, is overgeneralizing and making an inference that will contribute to depressive feelings. Healthy thinking allows for the separation of what I do (performance) from who I am (identity).

#### Conclusion that makes the bad worse and the good questionable

People who struggle with depression will often make a catastrophe out of negative events and minimize those that are positive. They will describe an uncomfortable situation in rich detail while trivializing a positive experience, particularly one that might show the depressed person in a good light.

### Conclusion that is all-or-nothing

All-or-nothing thinking, especially in combination with some of the other faulty thinking processes, can easily lead to depressive symptoms. On a vacation, a depressed person with all-or-nothing thinking will tend to see the time away as either wonderful or awful, with a strong leaning toward the latter reaction.

### 4. It can be masked by the presence of an addiction.

All addictions involve bondage to a substance or activity that is the center of life because it promises an elevation in mood (I will *feel* better) and well-being (I will *be* better). This desire for an elevation in mood will send some depressed people into an addictive cycle. A great variety of substances or activities could be selected for this purpose. The list may include:

Alcohol

Caffeine

Drugs (over-the-counter and street)

Food

Gambling

Pornography

Sex

Work

Generally, you can assume that the depressed person who is addicted will display the following signs:

1.  Consistent use of the substance/activity so the elevation of mood occurs.

2. Difficulty in stopping even though they may have good intentions and plans.
3. Denial that there is a problem.
4. Even though mood may be elevated, the consequences of the addiction are negative and may be seen in family, physical, legal, vocational, and relational areas.
5. May be an increased tolerance of the substance or activity so that more is needed to achieve the desired elevation in mood.

One of the major problems with layering an addiction on top of depression is that it masks the real mood and creates another set of difficulties that need to be dealt with. And because addictions often involve secrecy and privacy, the depressed person suffers in silence without any sense of accountability to a community or individual. Ironically, this can intensify the sense of isolation they are already experiencing.

**So how can I minister to those who are having problems with depression?**

*Avoid solutions that ask people to simply make choices.*

All of us have three components to our psychological system: thinking/cognitive, feeling/emotive, and willing/volition. It is important to understand that the depressed person's problems reside in all three but because of flat feelings and faulty thinking, it is not easy to make decisions. Motivation and energy for life are a struggle, so it is hard for the depressed person to make choices to engage in particular behaviors.

In light of that understanding, reflect on the following lines:

"All you have to do is just . . ."

"Why don't you just . . ."

"If you would just . . ."

"If you were just to . . ."

Any piece of advice that has the word "just" in it is usually problematic. Each of these lines presupposes that a simple choice will move people out of depression. But if it were that simple, no one would be depressed. As sensitive helpers we need to recognize the importance of providing solutions that do not reside primarily in the will.

### Show compassion by committing to pray and be there.

It is very difficult for most depressed people to share their story with friends or family. Although changes are occurring, a stigma against depression still permeates our culture and creates a reluctance to open up. I have known many people who have taken the risk and shared their depression journey only to find that others don't want to hear it. In some cases, the story has been shared once and never raised by the other person again, leading the depressed person to feel that they should not have shared in the first place. This builds on the sense of alienation and isolation many depressed people have already, particularly if the nonresponse has come from a parent, sibling, spouse, or close friend. One always hopes that those who are supposed to be close will be there when the story is not positive, when the feelings are not exuberant, and when life is not looking good.

At times this poor response reflects a genuine lack of care and compassion. Some friends and family members show their true colors when they are exposed to something like depression. In a sense, their lack of loyalty is best revealed when life is most tough for the other person. However, at other times a lack of response stems from ignorance and a lack of understanding. Some people simply do not understand depression and because they are in unfamiliar territory, their natural propensity is to run in the opposite direction. Finally, there are times when the depression of others raises fear inside us. Undoubtedly the story of another impacts our own story and we experience fear when we hear others open up. Frequently they are putting into words some of our own unspoken feelings and perspectives. This is particularly true within families. When one family member admits to a struggle, it automatically forces parents, siblings, or spouses to reflect on their own vulnerability.

Christians need to remain open to hearing about depression in others. When the story is out, it needs to be met with compassion and sensitivity, along with a commitment to pray. Most importantly, we need to avoid running away from the story. When people finally risk being open with us about their depression, the most devastating thing that can occur is for us to withdraw. We need to be present, and prayerful, so the individual experiences the mediation of God's presence through his body—also known as you and me.

### *Make a thoughtful referral.*

Because of the multifaceted nature of depression, and because there is often a physiological and biochemical component, it is important that friends and family demonstrate care by having humility about their own abilities to help. One of the dangers in Christian circles is that we can bring a spiritual paradigm to bear on the depressed person and forget the fact that other dimensions are playing a significant role. I have seen too many situations where genuinely depressed people experience back-slapping and simplistically applied injunctions when what they need is competent professional help.

Referrals for people who are depressed need to blend the spiritual, medical, and psychological. Because psychiatrists and physicians have medical training, they are equipped to deal with issues around biochemistry, physiology, medication, and, if needed, hospitalization. Counselors, therapists, and psychologists can be helpful on the psychological and spiritual sides, but it is important that a medical consultation be part of this process. To only deal with the psychological or spiritual component of depression is to potentially miss a key factor. And, of course, the corollary is also true. To stress the medical to the exclusion of the psychological and spiritual is also problematic.

Because of the nature of the difficulty, depressed people struggle with motivation and energy. Simply telling them to go for help is not going to guarantee that this will happen. They will require support, coaching, and in some cases making an initial connection with the professional and driving the depressed person to the office. Helpers need to be careful not to take over and control the situation, but if such a response is in the best interests of the depressed person, it is a wise course of action.

Finally, if the depressed person is talking about suicide and even has a vague plan outlined it is important to connect with a professional. Ideally it is best to do this in consultation with the individual but, in some cases, it is necessary to break confidentiality. I have found that the most effective way to handle these situations is to initially appeal to the individual:

> "I am concerned that you are as down as you are and that you are talking about suicide. I think we need to connect with a professional so we can get you the kind of help that you need right now. Who would you like me to call?"

If the person is resistant to participating in the process of securing help, they can be gently forced.

> "I know you are feeling really uncomfortable right now and don't want to bother anyone but I want to drive you to the hospital. You need to get help before things get a lot worse. Let's go to the car."

In rare circumstances where the person is a threat to themselves or to others and they are unwilling to go on their own or let you take them, call the police. In most jurisdictions they will respond well and will take the person to the hospital. Obviously, this is a last resort, but at times, one needs to weigh the value of a person's sense of dignity against the value of their life.

### Bring hope into the situation.

One of the qualities that characterizes people who are depressed is that they feel hopeless. It is important to understand that this is not a statement of whether they are in fact hopeless. In response to people who feel hopeless, others will often seek to cheer them up with phrases like:

"But you have so much going for you."
"But there is hope."
"Life is not really that hopeless."
"Look at all the good things that are happening in your life."
"So-and-so has it much worse than you do."

We can be very confident that depressed people who feel hopeless will not start to feel hopeful as a result of these statements. Because a negative view of self, the world, and the future is at the core of the experience of depression, superficially positive statements do not easily penetrate to that core.

Having said that, hope can come in different forms. Our presence in the life of a depressed person gives them some sense of hope. Intuitively they know that we could give up on them and treat them as hopeless, but by hanging in with them we exude even minimal hope. When you are sharing the journey with a depressed person it is hard work, so to stay with them and not withdraw is a strong statement. As we talk with a depressed person it is important to stay confident and not catch their depressive mood. This does not require a "happy bear" demeanor, but a quiet confidence that we have trust in them, the world, and the future.

Because hope is such a foundational truth for the Christian, it is important for all helpers to remember the simple truth expressed in the old hymn, "My hope is built on nothing less than Jesus' blood and righteousness." When you are intimately involved with a depressed person, your own sense of grounding can be thrown off. It is important for our own well-being to constantly return to the foundation of hope. This does not mean we need to turn our understanding of biblical hope into injunctions that are dropped on the depressed person insensitively. It does mean that we will be centered in our own life, and that this will not only protect us in the midst of the other's depression, but our confidence may also influence others in quiet, indirect, and subtle ways.

*Promote a holistic approach to life.*

Because depression is comprehensive in its effect, it is important that we care for people by promoting health in various areas of life. This is especially important for evangelicals, who have a tendency to overspiritualize problems and ignore the medical and psychological sides of life. The fact remains that while some people may experience mild depression because they have not read their Bible, prayed, or attended church, the vast majority of depressed people have difficulties in other areas of life. Their depression cannot be linked solely with some spiritual deficit.

The first three components of the PREACHES acrostic—physical, relational, and emotional—are important when it comes to dealing with depression. I almost always encourage depressed people to get a physical as soon as possible. This allows for the elimination of potential explanations, but sometimes it reveals a physiological or biochemical component that requires medical intervention. Careful attention to diet and exercise will not solve depression, but it will certainly help. Because of motivational and energy difficulties, depressed people will not readily change their diet or begin to exercise, but they can be helped to make small modifications in these areas.

Because withdrawal from others is part of the depressive package, struggling individuals find it easiest to not pursue relationships. However, limited time with a few people can provide some social connection, which will bring a little vitality back into the system. Those people need to be wisely chosen, lest they be the kind of people who will intensify the depression.

The sad, hopeless, and despairing quality of depression means there is little emotional stimulation for the person going through these difficulties. In my experience, many depressed people have lived lives that are sensually deprived. They have paid little attention to the five senses (touching, tasting, seeing, hearing, smelling) and this has created a flatness of emotion and a lack of buoyancy. Again, not in an extreme or insensitive manner, depressed people can be encouraged to pay careful attention to one or more of the five senses. As these five "containers" of sensual experience fill up, there is a slight lightening of the emotional load.

While these gentle and consistent interventions in the physical, relational, and emotional sides of life will not solve the depression, they make a contribution to lessening its intensity.

### Stimulate realistic thinking and be an educator.

Out of a deep desire to help a depressed person, friends will often overdo their advice giving and not be as attuned to understanding. This may be more true with depression than any other of the difficulties that people experience. Because we all go through down times and periods of feeling less than our best, we readily assume that clinical depression is very similar. Somehow we feel the need to encourage people to be positive, get going, and become involved in something so the depression will lift.

What we need to offer friends who are struggling with depression is realism and education. Helping our friends understand the nature of depression is very freeing for them. Rather than expending energy and effort trying all sorts of simple solutions, they will be able to relax a little, having some understanding of what they are going through. To let them know that they may have some biochemical abnormalities is more compassionate than continually saying the problem is that you are lazy and need to do more. To help your friend recognize that depression after the birth of a child does not necessarily reflect her dislike of the child but may be related to physiological factors, takes the pressure off and does not compound the depression with false guilt. In each of these scenarios, a healthy dose of realism given in an educative spirit provides a compassionate environment for people to work through their depression.

### Do not function as an expert on medication.

Research in the past twenty years has confirmed that, no matter what the initial trigger might be, one of the major factors in depression is the imbalance of a brain chemical called serotonin. If correct amounts are not present, our thought processes, memory, sleep, and eating are all influenced. Newer antidepressant medications called SSRIs (selective serotonin reuptake inhibitors) help to adjust the levels of serotonin in the brain and relieve the symptoms of depression.

Over and over again I hear well-meaning Christians talking about the need for people to stop taking their antidepressant medication. This advice often stems from a belief that taking medication reflects a lack of trust in the Lord. In many senses, this is comparable to telling a diabetic to stop taking their insulin or advising someone with extreme respiratory problems to shut off their oxygen. Instead, we can see antidepressant medication in the same light as the insulin and oxygen: a gift from God, provided to sustain life and well-being. Again, we return to the topic of understanding. Without clear understanding we cannot provide helpful solutions. If a practitioner has made a professional judgment about antidepressant medication, it is not the responsibility of the lay person to render an amateur judgment based on a lack of understanding of brain chemistry.

As we support depressed people who are on medication, we need to be conscious of the physiological response that occurs when people go on antidepressant medication. Because this type of medication normally needs to reach a particular level in the body, it can take anywhere from four to six weeks for those levels to be achieved. Antidepressant medication does not start working the day you take it. In the early days of taking the medication, people will often report that it is not working or they think they should be off it because it has made no difference in their emotional state. Depressed people need to be patient and let the medication take its effect. Most physicians will want to see the person every couple of weeks to help stabilize the medication and to note any side effects.

In the early stages of taking a new medication, depending on the particular type, depressed people will also often describe symptoms like sleep disturbance, dry mouth, decreased/increased sexual interest, change in appetite, and irritability, all of which may decrease or cease after a number of months. Sometimes, similar side effects may occur when medication is being cut back or cut out completely. If disruptive symptoms either at the beginning or end of treatment persist, it would be wise to encourage the person to go back to the practitioner who prescribed it.

One of the frustrating side effects for a number of people on anti-depressant medication is decreased sexual function and interest. This does not characterize everyone on medication and it is not consistent across medications. However, when it does happen it is hard to deal with because these individuals have already experienced a flattening of sexual interest because of the depression. So when the medication adds further problems, it can be hard to cope with. As a friend or family member it is unlikely that you will be getting into the details of this particular side effect, but it can be reassuring to tell the person that this can happen with some medications. It can also be helpful to help them not overinterpret this problem. Some people who have lost sexual interest because of the medication inaccurately assume that they no longer love their spouse or no longer have interest in them. All couples have to work out the dynamics of sex and love in the relationship, but it would be unfair if a lack of sexual desire that stemmed from medication was overinterpreted.

In the spirit of this entire section, it is unwise for the depressed individual or their friends to decide to stop a course of antidepressant medication. Most physicians and psychiatrists will prescribe medication of this type for a minimum of eighteen to twenty-four months. In some cases, medication can be stopped after two years, but when the depression is clearly resistant to other forms of help, medication may be lifelong. In these cases, people, particularly Christians, often feel guilty. They may tell themselves, "If I was strong enough, or spiritual enough, I would not need this kind of help." These people need to be reminded sensitively that chemotherapy for cancer, penicillin for sinus infections, and aspirin for headaches do not reflect spiritual weakness in the individual receiving the help, but show courage and wisdom in that they are willing to give up control and submit to the expertise of someone else.

### Work sensitively with a depressed person who also has an addiction.

Cally struggled with depression most of her life but found that alcohol not only helped her dull the pain of the depression, but also gave her a heightened sense of joy and enthusiasm. In fact, when she was drinking, she was often at her best. As a friend you become aware of Cally's dual problem. What is the best way to respond?

The first step in dealing with someone who is addicted is to have them accept that they have a problem. Accept does not mean like, appreciate, or value. To accept her addiction, Cally needs to come to the place where she acknowledges that her alcohol intake is excessive both in quantity and in frequency. This may mean speaking very specifically to her. Rather than, "You are drinking too much," she may need to hear, "Do you know you hit your daughter quite hard when you were drinking last night?"

One aspect of acceptance is the identification of the negative impact the addiction is having on other areas of life. This may require you to have friends and family members give Cally feedback so she becomes fully aware of what others are seeing. This will not get rid of the denial completely, but if enough people speak to her directly about the nature of the problem, there is a heightened likelihood that she will come to accept responsibility for getting help.

Most addicted people, particularly those who are also struggling with depression, need help that is both supportive and insightful, as well as individual and communal. Breaking out of an addictive cycle on your own is not easy, so support is crucial. But support on its own is not enough. The addict who is using a substance or activity to dull the pain of depression needs to take a good look at the depression. What is causing it? What is its origin? How does the addiction help elevate the mood? What are the alternatives to the addiction? Most of these questions cannot be answered without the insightful help of a professional. But that is not to deny the importance of communal support and help. Part of the success of the Alcoholics Anonymous program is its emphasis on the power of the community to bring support and help. However, in my experience, the ideal support for the addict is a combination of an AA type of group, along with individual counseling from a trained counselor, and the thoughtful support of friends and family members.

*Support those who live with a depressed person.*

Living with a depressed person is very difficult. Everyday life can be unpredictable. Some days they may have energy and interest and then, almost without warning, they will be irritable, edgy, and flat. It is hard to plan life when someone is in a depressed state. The simple decision to go out with friends next Friday night can create a lot of tension. You know you have to let people know ahead of time that you will be there, but you are never quite sure whether the person struggling with depression will make it. And then if they do make it, you are not quite sure whether they will get through the night from an emotional perspective. They may be there physically, but the "black hole" may return, leading to detachment and a lack of interest.

Coping with this kind of person in the presence of children is particularly difficult. What do you tell them? How do you explain to an eight-year-old that Mom or Dad is depressed? The child is aware that the parent's spunk and spark is gone, but they are not capable of understanding the intricacies of depression. How does the nondepressed spouse handle this dilemma? They already carry much of the emotional burden in the house because of the depressed person's state, but they now end up parenting solo too.

At times, family members need to receive education about depression as well. There is nothing more devastating for a depressed family member than to receive no support from those who are supposedly close. Spouses of depressed individuals, along with children and any others that are immediately impacted, need to be contacted and nurtured. But in order to provide that kind of support, understanding is needed. What is depression? What is the person's experience? How can they be helped? A friend committed to understanding will provide a supportive educative role with family members.

**Summary**

Characterized by a cluster of symptoms that revolve around a loss of energy and motivation, depression is usually accompanied by significant changes in appetite, sexual drive, weight, and sleep. Depression is described as bipolar if the regular symptoms are combined with significant elation and expansion of mood, and are accompanied by irritability, hyperactivity, bad judgment, inflated self-esteem, and involvement in risky activities.

We understand depression from a Christian perspective through the following:

1. Anecdotal evidence
2. Examples from history
3. The story of Elijah
4. Lament psalms
5. Internalized anger and spiritual problems

In understanding people's experience, we need to know the following about depression:

1. It is comprehensive.
2. It is linked with multiple causes.
3. It often has faulty thinking associated with it.
4. It can be masked by the presence of an addiction.

When ministering to those who are having problems with depression:

Avoid solutions that ask people simply to make choices.

Show compassion by committing to pray and be there.

Make a thoughtful referral.

Bring hope into the situation.

Promote a holistic approach to life.

Stimulate realistic thinking and be an educator.

Do not function as an expert on medication.

Work sensitively with a depressed person who also has an addiction.

Support those who live with a depressed person.

# Burnout

## What is burnout?

In contemporary culture, the most frequent answer to the question "How are you doing?" is undoubtedly some combination of "I'm really busy/exhausted/swamped/overly committed/wiped." In fact, it has been a long time since I talked to someone who said they were not busy. At first blush this makes sense. Life does seem more chaotic, demands do seem greater, and the culture does seem more frantic. Does that mean everyone is burned-out? The answer to that question depends on how we understand the relationship between work and stress.

When I go "to work" in the morning, what is it I am going to? Essentially, I am involved in an enterprise that involves the exertion of effort, energy, and time with a view to accomplishing a specified task. Note that this exertion has nothing to do with the nature of my job. All work involves the expending of effort, energy, and time. It is also unrelated to whether I work outside the home or not. Those who work at home regularly engage in a process of exertion, and they will often end their day feeling like they have given effort, energy, and time to many tasks. And lastly, work in its technical sense is unrelated to pay. Volunteers in various settings work very hard but do not receive a stipend for that work.

The Canadian endocrinologist Hans Selye was one of the pioneers in the field of stress. For Selye, stress is the response of the body to any demand made upon it by a stressor. If I have an hour and a half commute to work each day, have a co-worker who is very taxing, and am employed in a volatile industry that has minimal predictability, I can be assured that my body is experiencing demands. The first stressor, the commute, can easily generate irritability and fatigue. Difficult co-workers are the kind of stressors that impact us emotionally and physically. An unpredictable workplace can be a stressor that impacts relationships and sleep. What is the cumulative effect of these three stressors? Demands are made on my body. Or in more colloquial language, I experience stress.

Selye is careful to point out that we have limited adaption energy—we are not able to adapt to all the stress that comes our way. Depletion occurs with repeated stress, and over the long term, aging results. Because stress impacts the body, the process of depletion often shows itself physically and physiologically. Thus it is no surprise that many seniors who have "worked" their whole life will experience a level of physical exhaustion and an appearance that reflect the toll of lifelong stress.

If we utilize Selye's definition, all work has a stressful component. It makes demands on the body and depletion is inevitable. When does it become excessive and problematic? When do we burn out? Two definitions will help us unpack these questions.

Tedium is the emotional drain that comes from any chronic pressure, while burnout is the emotional drain that results from intense and prolonged involvement with people.

When I was in high school I worked in a dairy. I considered myself quite fortunate in the summer of 1969 to be paid ninety dollars a week for summer employment. Because most seventeen-year-olds could not hope to make that kind of money, I was the envy of my friends. The first job assignment in the dairy was to stand part of the way down a conveyor belt that was transporting large glass jugs on their way to the bottle washer. Trucks had brought in these jugs from stores and individuals, and they were going to be washed and then filled with milk. My task was simple. I was to take each jug, look inside it, and take out any dirt, refuse, or bottle caps that may have found their way to the bottom. If I did not do this, that bottle would not be clean, and when the milk was added to it later on in the process, contamination would be a significant problem. I was exhausted when the day was over. Or, more accurately, I experienced tedium. Even though I was expending effort, energy, and time on my own and was not involved in a volatile industry, I experienced an emotional drain from the chronic pressure of having to do a boring job well.

My undergraduate thesis was on self-image in schizophrenics, which meant that I spent a considerable amount of time interviewing inpatients who had that diagnostic designation. With minimal training and experience, I found the experience daunting and my contact with the patients intense. Even though the task was research oriented, I came to care for these individuals and sought to connect with them in more personal ways. I remember walking away from the psychiatric hospital exhausted. It was not tedium from chronic pressure but the intense involvement with people that wiped me out emotionally and physically. I was ill equipped to care properly for this group of people, with the result that collecting data for an undergraduate thesis became overwhelming. I experienced burnout.

There are many symptoms of burnout, but if the following are present for a significant period of time there is a high likelihood that the individual is struggling to recover from a period that was characterized by intense involvement with people:

Withdrawal from people
Inability to relax and to sleep
Tension and anxiety
Constant fatigue
Persistent physical illness
Psychosomatic complaints
Depression

In the first year of my graduate program in clinical-counseling psychology, I found myself reacting to the experience at the psychiatric hospital in unhealthy ways. I overworked in all my courses, spent long hours in the internship setting where I was doing counseling, and tried to complete my master's thesis in a year. In essence, I coped with the burnout of the previous year by working harder, longer, and more intensely. I gave myself fully to my studies and it became the core, not just of my day, but also of my identity. I became my work. It controlled me and I ceased to control it. Work was the master. I was the slave. I had moved beyond the tedium of high school and the burnout of the psychiatric hospital to a workaholic state. What is a workaholic? Someone who gives himself or herself to the habitual and constant practice of work without any self-control. I recall with some pain the day in May when my girlfriend picked me up outside the university because I could not walk. My workaholism had done me in completely.

Let's review the terms to this point. Work is not bad. It is the exertion of effort, energy, and time to accomplish a particular task. Work is also unrelated to whether my primary workplace is inside or outside the home, or whether I receive any stipend for what I do. A key part of work is the presence of stress. By definition, work is a stressor that makes demands on the body. When work stress of any sort is chronic, we call it tedium. When the stress can be directly linked with intense involvement with people, burnout is a more accurate phrase. And when the individual works through the stress, tedium, and burnout to the point where work is master, workaholism sets in and identity becomes wrapped up exclusively in performance.

**Is there a biblical perspective on burnout?**

If one were to carry out a superficial investigation of Scripture, it would be easy to conclude that there is nothing about burnout in the Bible. However, a more careful analysis will reveal a number of themes that relate to the topic of work and, by implication, burnout.

## 1. Work and God

It is significant that the presentation of God at the beginning of Genesis is of one who is working. In fact, the first six days of creation are described as days of work. Divine persons expended effort, energy, and time to accomplish a particular task. However, this was not wearisome, tiring work, but the creative and enlivening expression of the Creator. God created heaven and earth with light, water, sky, vegetation, animals, and people. And all of it was and is a testimony to his essence.

> The heavens are telling the glory of God;
> and the firmament proclaims his handiwork.
> Day to day pours forth speech,
> and night to night declares knowledge.
> There is no speech, nor are there words;
> their voice is not heard;
> yet their voice goes out through all the earth,
> and their words to the end of the world.
>
> Psalm 19:1–4

And it did not stop there. God did not work at the beginning of time and then take an eternal break. The psalmist captures it so well in Psalm 121:1–4. The maker of heaven and earth did not cease from his labor when the earth was formed. He continues to be the helper for all humanity.

> I lift up my eyes to the hills—
> from where will my help come?
> My help comes from the LORD,
> who made heaven and earth.
> He will not let your foot be moved;
> he who keeps you will not slumber.
> He who keeps Israel
> will neither slumber nor sleep.

God is not just Creator, because "in him all things hold together" (Col. 1:17). Not surprisingly, when Jesus comes, he comments, "My Father is still working, and I also am working" (John 5:17).

It follows, then, that if God is at work and we are created in his image, we will be people who are committed to work. In our understanding that the "earth is the LORD's and all that is in it, the world, and those who live in it" (Ps. 24:1), we mirror God's work in the world by being participants with him in this creative enterprise.

### 2. Work and sabbath

Scripture is very clear in Genesis 2:2–3:

And on the seventh day God finished the work that he had done, and he rested on the seventh day from all the work that he had done. So God blessed the seventh day and hallowed it, because on it God rested from all the work that he had done in creation.

When rest (shabbat) is commanded as an integral part of the life of God's people, the pattern God established in the beginning is formative.

Remember the sabbath day, and keep it holy. Six days you shall labor and do all your work. But the seventh day is a sabbath to the LORD your God; you shall not do any work—you, your son or your daughter, your male or female slave, your livestock, or the alien resident in your towns. For in six days the LORD made heaven and earth, the sea, and all that is in them, but rested the seventh day; therefore the LORD blessed the sabbath day and consecrated it.

Exodus 20:8–11

This teaching continues when the sabbath is presented as a sign of the covenant between God and his people in Exodus 31:12–18, and when it is positioned as a reminder of the deliverance from Egypt in Deuteronomy 5:12–15.

What is significant is that work and rest are not positioned as polar opposites where one is pursued and the other ignored. A tapestry of work and rest is blended together in these early books of the Bible. Even God, who, since he is omnipotent, presumably was not tired after his work, saw fit to blend shabbat with production. A time of refreshment, re-creation, rejuvenation, rhythm, restoration, and remembering washed over into the days of production, accomplishment, creation, performance, and doing. It is not surprising then that the writer of Hebrews chooses to call our salvation a "sabbath rest" (4:9), signifying our rest from our own work. Clearly, God built a shabbat structure into his economy and, by his example, encourages us to avoid work without rhythm.

### 3. Work and satisfaction

It is hard to visualize the scene precisely, but the words are powerful nonetheless—"God saw everything that he had made, and indeed, it was very good" (Gen. 1:31). Clearly, God experienced satisfaction with and enjoyment of all that he had done. As his image-bearers, we are afforded a similar opportunity.

> I know that there is nothing better for them than to be happy and enjoy themselves as long as they live; moreover, it is God's gift that all should eat and drink and take pleasure in all their toil. . . . Likewise all to whom God gives wealth and possessions and whom he enables to enjoy them, and to accept their lot and find enjoyment in their toil—this is the gift of God. For they will scarcely brood over the days of their lives, because God keeps them occupied with the joy of their hearts.
>
> Ecclesiastes 3:12–13; 5:19–20

But clearly this does not always happen. We do not always experience joy and satisfaction with what we have done and often the process of getting there is painful. And then we experience tedium and burnout. Obviously these experiences are not consistent with being happy in one's work. Why is this?

Cursed is the ground because of you; in toil you shall eat of it all the days of your life; thorns and thistles it shall bring forth for you; and you shall eat the plants of the field. By the sweat of your face you shall eat bread until you return to the ground, for out of it you were taken; you are dust, and to dust you shall return.

Genesis 3:17–19

Since we first met God hard at work in the Bible, clearly work did not come from the fall, but the perspective that humanity had toward work was radically altered because of the fall. What was once joyous and pleasant because of its intimate connectedness with God is now burdensome and wearying. What was once fulfilling is now frustrating. And what once had a God-glorifying purpose is now a reflection of the curse of sin. The writer of Ecclesiastes describes this God-less view of work in poignant terms.

Then I saw that all toil and all skill in work come from one person's envy of another. . . . The lover of money will not be satisfied with money; nor the lover of wealth, with gain.

4:4; 5:10

Once humanity is alienated from God and his work in the world, work becomes tainted and sullied. And like every other aspect of life that has been impacted by sin, redemption is required. The negative side of work that is revealed through burnout, tedium, and workaholism needs to be brought back under the divine perspective. Once under God's perspective, satisfaction in one's work can replace the drivenness of a life that does not have God's creative buoyancy at the core.

### 4. Work and employment

Given the opening scene in Scripture where work is presented as valuable and as an expression of divine persons, it is not surprising that humans engage in specific forms of employment that become part of the biblical record. Among many examples that could be cited, consider the following:

| | |
|---|---|
| Baker | Genesis 40:1 |
| Barber | Ezekiel 5:1 |
| Boat builder | 1 Kings 9:26 |
| Carpenter | 2 Samuel 5:11 |
| Cook | 1 Samuel 8:13 |
| Gardener | John 20:15 |
| Perfumer | Exodus 30:35 |
| Seamstress | Ezekiel 13:18 |
| Stonemason | 2 Samuel 5:1 |
| Tax collector | Matthew 9:9 |
| Tentmaker | Acts 18:3 |

Similarly, Jesus illustrates key themes in his teaching by making reference to particular forms of work. In Matthew 20:1–16, the kingdom of heaven is elucidated with a vivid description of a landowner who hired people to work in his vineyard, while the parable of the sower in Mark 4:1–9 not only talks about the influence of God's Word, but even unpacks it by using a work image that would be familiar to his listeners in that agricultural context. Luke 12:13–21 explains being rich toward God with a compelling story about a rich landowner who embarked on a significant building program, while truth is described by a simple image of shepherds and sheep in John 10:1–21.

**What is the experience of burnout like?**

### 1. Excessive concern with quantity of work and time, mixed with a depersonalizing of others and denial

People who are on the road to burnout tend to be obsessed with time, tiredness, and the quantity of work. They will often list the number of meetings they attended, the number of people seen, the number of emails received on a daily basis, and the number of interruptions that have happened that day. They will recount the number of hours worked yesterday, this week, and the last month. They will tell you how long it has been since they have had a day off, a weekend away, or a vacation.

If you keep asking how much the person is doing or why they are doing it, they'll rattle off excuses to the point of denying there is a problem.

"This is a busy time of the week/month/year."

"If I just get through this phase I will be all right."

"We are really just starting up this new division so it makes sense."

"If I had better people working for me, life would be easier."

"I'm not that busy."

"I know lots of people who are busier than I am."

"I would rather burn out than rust out."

If you listen to their attitudes toward the people at work, you will often hear depersonalizing going on. "The customers" becomes "those jerks in L.A." or "the unhappy lot in the UK" or "them." They do not treat people like people, but see them as objects with appropriate labels. Their general feeling toward others: frustrated, cynical, short-tempered, irritable. They are chronically disappointed with and sarcastic about others. They cannot feel for others, or sense what others are going through. The people at work are not human beings with personal identities. They are threats and challenges. They are the enemy.

### 2. Generalized weariness

At the core of all burnout is creeping exhaustion. Going back to the PREACHES acrostic, this exhaustion hits heavily in the physical, emotional, and cognitive areas. Low energy and constant weariness often make the burned-out person more accident prone and more susceptible to nagging physical problems and ailments. Ironically, in spite of all the hard work, sleep is difficult. Their nights are often restless, filled with dreams and nightmares. The burned-out person almost never wakes up feeling refreshed and revitalized.

This weariness impacts more than the body. Because of the emotional depletion in burnout, the burned-out person has very little inner reserve. In fact, intense feelings of hopelessness, helplessness, sadness, anxiety, and depression are hard to keep out. Relationships become places of further depletion. They feel like friends and family are another demand, so they do not seek out loved ones for nourishment and replenishment. It is very typical for the burned-out person to come home from a social engagement exhausted from the experience.

This combination of symptoms leads to the development of negative attitudes toward self, work, and life in general. Although fully absorbed by work and completely dedicated to it, the burned-out person feels deep dissatisfaction with it. It is rare for them to finish a day feeling like the job has been done well. Their self-statements become harsh, critical, and self-demeaning. In many ways, the burned-out person is a successful failure—they look good to others who observe the externals but feel inferior and incompetent. And as this negative cognitive pattern unfolds, it is easy to take things out on their friends and family, who become the recipients of unfair and excessive demands.

### 3. More intensity in people-related fields

By definition, those who are employed in human services professions have a higher incidence of burnout. Nurses, doctors, counselors, pastors, and others who are in roles that involve helping others often enter this vocation with a strong desire to reach out to others and be of help. This early idealism bumps up against the realities of these professions. The people they are reaching out to don't stay in the hospital or the clinic; they move on with their lives. The people being helped are not always appreciative and grateful and, not infrequently, they can be uncooperative and unresponsive to care. It is no wonder that some of the literature is now referring to burnout as "compassion fatigue." One can become very exhausted caring for others.

Early in my training, I spent a year working with juvenile delinquents. I came into that role with high motivation and interest, and a genuine desire to make a difference. I did not have a grandiose sense of self or an inappropriate understanding of the field, but I did have a fair degree of youthful enthusiasm. It was not long before I was confronted with a number of juveniles who had no interest in improving their lot in life, families who seemed unsupportive of the mental health system, and a bureaucracy that did not always seem set up to accomplish human service goals. At the end of that year, I concluded that I could never work full-time with this group of people, in spite of the fact I had an excellent supervisor. In some sense I was burned-out, not simply because of my personal dynamics, but also because of the nature of the juvenile population and the social service system.

### 4. Influenced by individual and communal variables

Burnout becomes more complex in the intersection between personal and communal variables. Personal variables reflect an individual's background, personality, values, motives, and experiences. For example, I came into my role with high motivation and interest and a genuine desire to make a difference. Communal variables are related to the nature of the group I was helping, their families, and the bureaucracy of the system. So why was I burned-out?

Most people who are burned-out will resort to one or other pole on the continuum of blame. Some will self-blame, seeing their problem as related to some sort of weakness or liability lurking inside them. People who take the self-blame route tend to take various courses of action like quitting the job, going for counseling, or feeling guilty. Others will blame the organization, which could lead them to a desire to change the system. The question "What is wrong with me?" is replaced with a more outer-focused approach: "What can I do to make things better around here?"

When we listen to someone who is on the way to burnout, we need to be aware of where they are on this continuum. If they are blaming themselves but they are making an accurate assessment, then leaving the job or going for help are appropriate strategies. Doing so will enhance their self-understanding and better prepare them for a subsequent role. On the other hand, if they see the major problem as being "the system," and they are working on making things better, one of two things can result. If the system is open to correction and change, then good may result. But if there is unwillingness within the community to approach things differently, the burned-out person may find that their problems deepen and their symptoms increase.

In most situations, the cause of the burnout is not the individual or the community, but a combination of both. Let me illustrate with my own experience. I have worked in many communities and have found that one variable plays a key role in where I am with burnout—communication. By this I mean both the degree to which communication is clear and open and the degree to which the revealing and concealing of information is well understood. The fact that this is a concern to me says a lot about who I am. If you were to sit down with me to talk about this, you would want to ask about my family background, my relationship with my parents, siblings, in-laws, wife, daughter, church communities, friends, and other places where I have learned about relationships. You would want to determine why relational openness and honesty is so important to me, and why I find communication that is indirect so problematic. You would want to find out why violations of confidentiality cause me to withdraw and back away. You would want to investigate why I get upset when I am in a conversation where someone relays a problem or concern that someone else has with me. You would want to understand which kinds of relationships I find safe and which ones I find toxic. Through careful listening and processing, you would soon learn about who I am and what is important to me. As I have passed midlife, I have come to realize that I am drawn to certain kinds of relationships and repelled by others, and this is largely due to the dynamics around openness, revealing, and concealing.

If you observed the communities where I have worked, and the relationships I have valued, you would be able to predict with some degree of accuracy where I have experienced burnout and exhaustion and where I was enlivened and buoyant. In the communities where issues were on the table openly and honestly and there was minimal back room politics, I was at ease. Even if the community was in trouble or experiencing difficulty, I found the commitment to reality refreshing. When people had problems with one another, they were open and honest and shared directly. But in the communities where facades ruled the day and secret communication was the major form of relating, I struggled a lot. When confidentiality was violated and it was hard to determine how that came about, I did not find the community safe. And when people would tell me what others thought without having encouraged those people to be open about what they thought, I felt distanced and alienated. I have even noticed that the same community may have started off one way and changed to the other and that resulted in a shift in my comfort.

It is in the interaction between personal and corporate variables where people live the experience of burnout.

**So how can I minister to those who are having problems with burnout?**

*Balance organizational and individual factors.*

One of the easiest things to do with someone who is burned-out is to add to their problems by laying on more responsibility, guilt, and obligation. The last thing someone who is exhausted needs is an extra load to bear. This is particularly important now that we understand the role of communities in the development of burnout symptoms.

Churches, parachurch organizations, factories, corporate business centers, and other workplaces have their own culture and ethos. In some cases this culture can breed overworked, highly stressed, and burned-out staff. I have seen churches and parachurch organizations where the systems and structures are poor, the leadership is weak, and sin has crept into the community's function to such a degree that anyone who is employed there finds themselves stressed out to the extreme. While individuals bring their own baggage and history to the problem, the community plays a major role in the creation of the problem. Similarly, there are workplaces where performance is all that matters, and when quotas are met they are then raised to a higher level. Even if the employee's own mindset is not one that links acceptance with performance, the company will make that link for them.

When someone is burned-out they will probably resort to one of two extremes: either engaging in excessive self-blame or dumping on their employer and holding them fully responsible. Caring persons will walk with the burned-out person to help them find the appropriate place on that continuum. In most cases, people need to arrive at some sense of personal responsibility for the burnout, but also share that responsibility with the community. This will then pave the way for resolution, where some solutions are linked with community and others with the individual.

***Recognize that everyone has a personal threshold that they should not go beyond.***

Will anyone ever swim from London to New York? Will anyone ever run a one-minute mile? Will anyone ever go a year without sleep or food? The answer to each of these questions is obvious. The span of the Atlantic Ocean is too great for anyone to traverse. Beating the four-minute mile was a significant achievement a number of years ago, but it would be impossible to do it in one minute. And our bodies have a particular physiological makeup that requires sleep and food in order to survive. In simple terms, each of these accomplishments exceeds a realistic threshold.

The key with work and burnout is to understand where the threshold is located. When does the person's capacity to perform become so strained that limits are exceeded? When is the saturation level at a point where something must be deleted before depletion sets in? As we talk with friends, fellow parishioners, and family members, we need to help them ascertain where that point is and whether they have already passed it. There is no magical way to determine this limit. It will vary from person to person and it requires careful listening to help the person discern their limit. In so doing, we need to help the person resist comparing themselves with others—"I don't know why I am so exhausted. I don't work half as hard as my husband." We also need to help the person make the distinction between being selfish and looking after oneself—reflecting on where your limits are is not egocentric but rather a thoughtful, preventative course of action.

Most of us do not realize what our limits are until we have passed them and someone else points this out to us. It is very much like being pulled over by the police for speeding. Often we do not know the speed we were driving until the officer stops us or someone in the car makes a comment. That is why burnout, in contrast to other difficulties, is better assessed by a friend, family member, or co-worker. We often have a better sense of when others have exceeded their limits than when we have done so ourselves. But what criterion does one use in assessing limits that relate to burnout?

It may require something as specific as looking at someone's yearly income and spending pattern. If spending exceeds salary, that person's life will exhibit significant exhaustion and weariness. Or the use of time may be the right route into a discussion on thresholds. There are 168 hours in a week. So if work demands and expectations exceed eighty hours and one has a spouse, children, and other responsibilities, there is undoubtedly a violation of thresholds in terms of what one can do in a week. Again, there are seven nights in a week. Find out how many nights the person has been involved in work-related tasks in the past month.

The ideal state in terms of health, well-being, and an absence of burnout, will be found when there is no gap between what a person can handle and what they are handling. If there is a gap, people may need to be gently encouraged to consider cutting their work hours, getting a different job, having one spouse leave the workforce, buying a smaller house, getting rid of one car, relocating to another area, selling a luxury item, or any number of other options. None of these decisions are, in themselves, going to get rid of burnout, but they may help move the person back to a point of saturation before their personal threshold was violated. To use Selye's terms, it will put them in touch with their limited adaption energy.

### Focus on personal identity, not just performance.

When talking to a friend or family member who is either on the path to burnout or has already reached that destination, most of us will tend to focus on what they are doing and encourage them to do less. In many cases, telling an overly committed person to work fewer hours is like telling a person with asthma to stop wheezing. The work and the wheezing are not the problem. They are the symptom, the manifestation of the problem, and the consequence of something more fundamental. So the injunction to "slow down" needs to be replaced with an important question: "Why have you been working so hard?" There will be times when it is good to ask this question directly and openly and, with appropriate encouragement and empathy, to pursue the follow-up issues. At other times, it is important to have this question focused in your own mind. As you listen and process what the individual is telling you, ask yourself, "What are they telling me about why they work so long and hard?" It is difficult to determine when you should speak and when it is better to withhold. In some ways this is in the arena of wisdom, and one needs to ask for God's help to ascertain the right timing.

This line of thinking moves us out of the realm of performance and behavior into the sphere of identity and essence. What factors are moving this person toward drivenness? What is the underlying motivation for working so hard? Why do they constantly work beyond a threshold that is comfortable and appropriate? Apart from their explanations about it being a busy time of year or a financial crunch, what keeps them going endlessly?

Some people have a fragile and insecure identity. They may have come out of brokenness growing up and have never come to feel accepted, loved, and valued. In fact, just as they were treated in a way that reflected a lack of affirmation, they have now turned that in on themselves and have minimal self-compassion and self-appreciation. To unconsciously compensate for those feelings, they overwork to receive the external accolades that come from this behavior. They are promoted and have more people working for them, all of which gives the message that they are valued and appreciated. And then when the salary increase comes, their identity gets quietly tied with money, so being worth more means they have more strength, more influence, and more power. In essence, their value becomes linked with what they can do, with the distant and somewhat futile hope that this will somehow translate into who they are—somehow if I "do" well I will "be" alright.

It is important to remember that motives are not always conscious. Many of us are engaged in particular behaviors but we have no idea what is behind them. So to talk about compensatory behaviors that come from a fragile identity is not to say that the individual understands that this is going on. It is important, then, to approach this area with wisdom and discernment. A comment here or there along with a sensitively raised question may move the person a little further along in self-understanding. Keep in mind that the process of determining motivation can be overwhelming. When the person finally realizes what is driving them, they may be embarrassed, awkward, uncomfortable, or resistant. And depending on the depth and duration of the underlying cause, they may need to pursue formal counseling.

### *Acknowledge the significance of personal physiology.*

Not only are we psychological and spiritual in our basic makeup, we are also physical. The body is constantly in dialogue with every other part of us. In fact, this dialogue is so intimate that each component is constantly sharing its fortunes with the others. In other words, when a person is going through the pain of burnout, we can assume that there are direct relationships among the emotional, psychological, spiritual, and physiological aspects of the experience.

Marguerite has been working long hours at her job while trying to manage a home and three young children. She is completely absorbed by her retail company and you have sensed that she is on the road to burnout. For the past three months, all the telltale signs are present. You phone her at work one morning and she goes on in great detail about getting cut off in traffic on the way to work. You try to listen with compassion, but inside you are taken aback by how much this incident has impacted her. While it is only a minor irritation from your perspective, she seems quite thrown by it. What has gone on in this incident for Marguerite?

She woke up that morning exhausted. As has been the case for the past few months, she did not sleep well (had a number of disruptive dreams), and felt like she had already done a day's work when she got in the car to go to work. When she was cut off, her already depleted body experienced more depletion. As is true for anyone who experiences a stressful shock, the limbic system and the hypothalamus in the brain quickly assess the perceived threat. This activates the sympathetic branch of the autonomic nervous system, which in turn increases the heart rate, and other bodily functions go into motion. Stress hormones are released, particularly adrenaline, and blood pressure goes up so blood flow to the muscles increases. The neurochemical balance in the brain shifts so that emotions and attention are heightened as the body prepares for action. And all of this in a split second when Marguerite is cut off!

This normal physiological response happens to anyone who is presented with a perceived threat. Without choice or decision, the body kicks into action and the entire system begins to respond. It is one of the reasons, in fact, that being cut off is very helpful when you are tired because the adrenaline rush wakes you up! The adrenaline, though, serves a more fundamental purpose: it prepares us to deal with the stress and helps us cope with it. Animals that have their adrenal glands removed usually die in the face of stress because they are unprepared to deal with it.

So what makes this situation so problematic for Marguerite? If her reaction is a normal physiological response, why does it create so much trouble for her? The key is not the presence of this one incident but the degree to which it is part of a cumulative picture. She was stressed physically the day before the incident, woke up exhausted, and started the drive to work with significant depletion. She has been beyond her physical threshold for a number of months, so each stressful incident is layered on top of an already problematic life. If the demands on the body continue and there is little time in between stressful events, it is likely that she will start to develop more symptoms such as high blood pressure and high blood levels of cholesterol, two of the most important risk factors for heart attacks and strokes. She will also start to develop more cold and flu symptoms because habitual stress will weaken her immune system, that part of our physiology that protects us from diseases.

What is significant in Marguerite's story is that these physical reactions—reactions that are very much part of the process of burnout—are going on outside her awareness. She may be saying things like "It's a busy time of the year in our business, so I don't expect this to go on forever." She might even wax eloquent on the driving patterns of people in her area and suggest that mandatory testing should occur every year. As her friend, you might be telling her things like "You need to slow down" or "You need to stop and smell the roses," but all of this ignores a fundamental reality. There really is a close stitching between the mind and the body.

When friends and family members are in this state, and we are not trained as physicians, we need to be careful to stay within our area of expertise. However, some simple education can be helpful. If people understand what happens in a stressful situation like being cut off by another car, they might gain another view of what happens to the body when you rest and replenish. When you sit by a fire in your family room and read a book for a few hours, the body is receiving a different message than when you are driving to work in a state of panic and frenzy.

These realities also speak to the importance of looking at one's physical life when considering various ways to back away from burnout. We know, for instance, that sleep deprivation decreases our efficiency and capacity to deal with stress. This awareness might result in going to bed earlier than normal. We also know that adrenal arousal decreases our perceived need for sleep. In other words, if I am in a panic state a lot of the time, I will not think I need much sleep. My body will be so energized that sleep seems unnecessary. An adrenaline addiction will keep most people going for a long time. However, when there is a less frantic pace, the body will then become more aware of the need for sleep.

Some people who are burned-out experience considerable anger and irritation with others. We know that anger is a tremendous drain on the physiological system that decreases our capacity to deal with stress. Often the problem with people who are driven, competitive, and impatient is the presence of this kind of anger and hostility. This is most detrimental to healthy functioning and speaks to the need to encourage people to deal with their anger directly and immediately.

People who are burned-out also need to make care for the body a key part of their life. It is not appropriate to lay a lot of injunctions on individuals who are severely burned-out, but gentle encouragement along the following lines is appropriate:

Moderate exercise can add two years to your life span and enhance your ability to deal with stressors.

Deep breathing that is conscious, slow, and deep will aid with physical relaxation and prevent short, shallow, and hurried breathing which tends to increase stress.

People who are fifteen pounds overweight have a pulse rate that is ten beats more per minute, or 5,256,000 extra beats per year.

Personal disclosure to someone else usually results in increased immune system functioning and a reduction in symptoms of physical stress.

### Point out the importance of sensuality.

From dealing with my own experiences of burnout, as well as those of others, one thing is very clear: people who are burned-out experience profound sensual deprivation. When you talk to someone who is burned-out, you get the distinct impression that they are feeling flat, weary, unresponsive, and uninterested. They do not display any emotional vitality or life. A deep exhaustion has overcome them and there is no impetus to feel much of anything.

This state is in contrast to what it means to be created. Not only are we created in the image of God, but we are created human. Among many other things, this means that we have the capacity to experience the five senses. While we can reason, think, and process, and so reflect

God's image through these abilities, we can also touch, taste, see, hear, and smell. We can drink in all that the created world has to offer and experience it sensually.

The road to burnout is often a road that does not countenance sensuality. With an emphasis on production, performance, doing, and accomplishing, there is no time for basic things like touching, tasting, seeing, hearing, and smelling. I have asked people who are struggling with depression and burnout to look at the next seven days in terms of five cups, each cup representing one of the five senses. At the end of the week I ask them to describe for me what is in each of their cups. Not surprisingly, many of them will describe five empty cups. At least from a conscious perspective, they have not had any sensual experiences during the course of the week. They have been very busy and productive, but in the process, have neglected a key dimension of who they are as created humans.

I follow up that time of assessment by encouraging people to seek out experiences that help fill the five cups. Consciously touch things and people and allow the tactile stimulation to impact you. Eat a meal consciously, savoring each bite and each course. Go to an area where you live and drink in what you see. Visit a forest, a stream, or a city and listen carefully to all that you hear. Wander through a market or a garden or a dump and absorb the smell. When they begin to address the sensual deprivation, the person soon realizes that there is a whole world out there that they have missed. Slowly and subtly, this orientation begins to challenge and change the mindset that only values production.

It is important to note that Western culture has confused most of us in its pairing of the sexual and the sensual. For men, in particular, it is often hard to distinguish between feelings and sexuality, emotion and sexual behavior. It is no surprise, then, that many men who are on the road to burnout will use sex as a way of combating the rush to production or as the prime way of easing the stress. Whether it is pornography, strip shows, prostitutes, or affairs, sex can become a way of dulling the ache that comes from the burnout. Indirectly, it can be a cheap imitation for true sensuality. It is no surprise, then, that these same men will find it very difficult to engage in sexual relations with their spouse.

### *Acknowledge the significance of the sabbath.*

Although it is a biblical command that is rooted in the character of God and that just makes a lot of practical sense, the concept of the sabbath is simply that for many people, a concept. I grew up in a church environment where the Lord's Day was filled with rules and regulations. Some in our fellowship would not go to restaurants on Sundays, or listen to the radio, or swim, or ride in a boat. But then there were some who would not swim in the lake on Sunday but would "bathe." They would not go in a motorized boat but a canoe was acceptable. As is true with all humanly constructed religious rules, there was so much duplicity in the system that it became humorous. And while I take full responsibility for my own personal life and do not want to blame history, I was given a very poor theological foundation upon which I could build my life of worship, work, and play.

The irony of this legalistic approach to the sabbath is that it misses Scripture completely. As we were speculating about whether being in the water was swimming or bathing, God was calling us to bring rhythm to life, to learn to create a beautiful tapestry of production and replenishment. Many of the people who taught me about the sabbath when I was younger often spent Sunday afternoon sleeping. No doubt for some of them, this was a time of restoration. But for many it was simply recovery from an extremely busy week, not a creative time of rest where people were reveling in replenishment and re-creation.

As with many people who have grown up in a legalistic culture, I have gone to the other extreme. In the presence of theological silliness, I systematically ignored the biblical injunction. Sabbath has been a foreign and distant concept with little practical influence in my life. I have fallen into the trap of believing that sabbath is something you do when you have finished your work. After all, that is what God did, isn't it? He did everything he had to do and then rested. Of course, the problem with this shallow line of argument is that most of us never feel finished with our work. We do not see the sabbath in the way it should be seen, as a predetermined time to rest, independent of where we are with our work. In some sense, sabbath frees us from the need to be finished with our work because another form of termination is built in by God.

When we talk to people who are burned-out, we need to remind them compassionately about God's intent for work and rest. This will not be manipulative sermon-making where people feel guilty. Rather, in the spirit of the sabbath, it will be gentle nudging to let people know that God values being as much as doing, that rest is not simply the absence of work but the presence of sensuality and relationships, that sabbath-keeping is a commandment along with all the other commandments, and that ultimately, like everything else that God requests, our obedience will bring him glory and will benefit us personally in many practical ways.

If we fully grasp this concept it will revolutionize our parenting and our preparation of future parents. There is something profoundly sad about this generation of children of Christian parents that has learned very little about rest, replenishment, and sabbath. Ironically, one might argue that children have lost a sense of play, where sensuality and enjoyment are prized. It appears that being productive and competitive are much more important. The parents of this generation have become chauffeurs to innumerable activities and carriers of the cultural message that doing counts more in life than being. Sadly, the number of activities our children are in has become a new measure of the child's success and, covertly, a sign of genuine parental interest. But one wonders whether this generation will understand sabbath-keeping when they have children of their own.

### Help facilitate proper beliefs.

Because significant spiritual and psychological battles are fought in the mind, it is important to expose the inner beliefs behind the burnout. At times these will actually be verbalized by burned-out people, while at other times you might hear comments that suggest the presence of these lurking beliefs. It is helpful to challenge these thoughts with new and more helpful truths like the following:

- My stress-driven lifestyle is destructive (physically, psychologically, spiritually, etc.).
- I can be responsible for my own stress rather than be victimized, while at the same time I can recognize that there are other external factors influencing the problem.
- I am limited because I am created, not the Creator.
- Carrying a load that is beyond my limit over an extended period of time will create stress.
- My behavior normally reflects underlying issues of identity.
- My physiological system has been wired by God and it requires that I pay attention to it.
- The mind and the body are so linked that nothing I do will separate their connection.

**Summary**

Work is a stressor that makes demands on the body. When work stress is chronic, it is called tedium, but when the stress is directly linked with excessive people involvement, burnout is the more accurate phrase.

How do we understand burnout from a biblical perspective?

1. Work and God
2. Work and sabbath
3. Work and satisfaction
4. Work and employment

To understand people's experience, we need to know that burnout is characterized by:

1. Excessive concern with quantity of work and time, mixed with depersonalizing of others and denial
2. Generalized weariness
3. More intensity in people-related fields
4. Individual and communal variables

When ministering to those who are having problems with burnout:

Balance organizational and individual factors.

Recognize that everyone has a personal threshold that they should not go beyond.

Focus on personal identity not just performance.

Acknowledge the significance of personal physiology.

Point out the importance of sensuality.

Acknowledge the significance of the sabbath.

Help facilitate proper beliefs.

# 6

# Dysfunctional Families

## What is a dysfunctional family?

In the past twenty years, the term *dysfunctional family* has become part of our modern vocabulary. You hear about it in the popular media, listen to friends describe themselves as coming from such a family, and find an increasing number of books and magazine articles focusing on the topic. When such a phenomenon occurs, people's responses fall into two camps. Some are frustrated, arguing that there is no such thing and that the term itself is creating the problem. They say that people just need to get on with their lives. On the other side are those who have embraced this notion. They explain all aspects of their own current existence as being traced to the dysfunctionality of their family of origin.

Like all extremism, these two responses do not help us deal with other people. Those who argue that the term has created problems for people have obviously not spent much time with people from difficult family backgrounds. They are not going to provide much pastoral care and sensitivity to those who are struggling. On the other hand, to use a dysfunctional background as a form of both explanation and justification

125

for all behavior raises ethical concerns around personal responsibility and choice.

Because the term *dysfunctional family* is more descriptive than diagnostic, I want to stay away from a tight definition in this chapter. I would rather like the reader to get a feel for what it is like to be in a dysfunctional family and how that can impact an individual's functioning. But to start, a number of things need to be affirmed.

We were all raised by people who sinned. In some sense this is a very simple and rather obvious statement, but it is important to fold this into our awareness. If we are all tainted by sin because we are the offspring of Adam and Eve, still reside in a body on the earth, and are not fully redeemed, it is inevitable that every parent and parental figure will experience this same influence. No parent, no matter how well intentioned or caring, is perfect. All parental attitudes, words, and behavior are intertwined with sin, and this impacts the lives of their children. And if our parents sinned, we can rightfully assume that their parents sinned as well. By extension, the ultimate family tree will bring us back to our first parents, who started the unhealthy and unhelpful process. While this argument requires a level of theological commitment, it is fair to say that in some sense, all children come from a home that was dysfunctional in that their parents or parental figures were influenced by sin.

However, while the cross-generational expression of sin does speak to the dysfunctionality in all of our families of origin, humanity was also created in the image of God. So while sin has permeated every aspect of our being, it is also true that God's stamp is on the life of every living person. What does that mean practically? It means that almost every parent does some good for their child, expresses some care, and gives some genuine love. And that expression of good, care, and love comes from God, the giver of every good and perfect gift. What is the vehicle through which it comes? The image of God. While sin has impacted us in profound ways, it is also true that everyone is not as bad as they can be. Though some parents have times of hate and disgust with their children, very few actually kill their children. While some parents abuse in cruel ways, they do show infrequent glimpses of genuine, nonviolent love and care. So it is in this interesting relationship between original sin, where we affirm that no parent is perfect, and being created in the image of God, where we acknowledge the presence of some good in every family, that dysfunctionality is understood. In other words, dysfunctionality, the fruit of sin, is intertwined with health and functionality, the fruit of the image of God.

The other aspect of dysfunctionality that needs to be unpacked is the linkage of the term with the past. In common usage, many people are referring to the family of origin when they talk about the dysfunctional family. It is something I came from, a context that has influenced who I am. This emphasis blurs us from another reality. Some people are currently in dysfunctional families. Dysfunctionality is not just in their past, it is an apt description of their current family system, and all the members of that family are being influenced by the present dysfunctionality. Undoubtedly, those influences will spill over into the future. We now see that coping with a dysfunctional family is not just about resolution of the past, but also about ministry in the present, and even about looking at a preventative grid for the future.

When counselors and therapists use the term *dysfunctional family*, they are usually describing a family where there is a lack of healthy functioning in ten areas. In this section we will look at each of these in brief and general terms, while in a later section we will focus more on what it is like for an individual raised in this kind of family.

*Power.* At various points in the life of a family, someone needs to have an influence and take initiative. In healthy families there is an appropriate distribution of power so no one person or set of persons makes all the decisions. All family members believe they have a share in the distribution of power. Dysfunctionality sets in when one or more members dominate to such a degree that other members of the family feel completely powerless to bring about any influence.

*Alliances.* Because a family is a unit that contains a number of individual members, there is always a threat to oneness in a family. This will often play itself out in alliances between certain family members. In dysfunctional families one parent may be in a coalition with one of the children, leaving other children out and alienating their spouse. Or children may be in an alliance against the parents, or vice-versa, leaving the family unit to suffer as a whole. When alliances take place, the family system is threatened and the good of the whole gets lost.

*Intimacy.* Care and affection for one another is part of a healthy family. One could say that in healthy families, people like each other, look out for each other, and have compassion for one another. In dysfunctional families, the intimacy slips to one extreme or the other. Some families are characterized by a lack of affection and intimacy expressed in tangible ways. In others, the intimacy is either smothering, overbearing, or abusive. In this case, the intimacy is neither appropriate nor nuturing for the individuals in the family.

*Self-regard.* As we have seen in the chapter on self-image, families become a mirror for individual members of the family. If they hear positive, encouraging, and realistic things about themselves, they will internalize those statements and will see themselves similarly. This is not to say that healthy families are always positive, but even when they are negative, there is a sense in which the person believes they are regarded positively. In dysfunctional families, individual members are not regarded positively, and they are given this message either through direct words and behavior or through neglect and emotional abandonment.

*Individuality.* When individuals are part of a bigger system, there is always a danger of the needs of the one becoming less important than the good of the whole. The other extreme is just as dangerous. If the family as a unit dominates, it is very easy for individual members to believe that their feelings, gifts, and abilities do not matter. In healthy families, this tension is always in a good balance where the good of individuals is considered important within the broader context of the family.

*Expressiveness.* Healthy family systems are characterized by openness and an absence of secrecy. Individual family members believe that they can express their opinions, feelings, and beliefs with the assurance that they will be heard and respected. In the process, the whole family grows because the members are adding their unique perspective for the good of the whole. In dysfunctional families, parents and children live behind facades where secrecy reigns and appearance dominates.

*Mood.* Apart from what is said, you can often assess whether a family has affection in it. This is often captured in body language, physical touch, and the tone behind the speech. In healthy families, there is an appropriate familiarity in the family and a genuine expression of warmth and affirmation. In dysfunctional families, the air is tense and there is clearly an absence of affection.

*Empathy.* In healthy families, understanding each other's feelings is a key variable in how the family interacts in both formal and informal settings. The key is not whether you agree with the other person or not. What is most important is that you are understood. In dysfunctional families, the individual members do not share openly because there is no confidence that they will be heard or understood by others. As a result, feelings are kept to oneself and they are only shared outside the family, if at all.

*Conflict.* It is inevitable that there will be conflict in a family, whether that family is healthy or dysfunctional. Health is not found in the absence of conflict but in the way the conflict is handled. In healthy families, the fighting is fair and respectful and engaged in with a view toward reconciliation and growth. In dysfunctional families, conflict is usually handled in one of two ways. In some cases, conflict is not allowed. Being happy, up, friendly, and agreeable is the strong message. In other families, conflict is not resolved with respect and understanding but with abuse, violence, and vengeance.

*Openness.* One of the dangers of the family system is that it can shut itself out from other systems. In healthy families, there is an appropriate boundary around the family, where one can find support, intimacy, and care, but there are also gates so that members of the family can connect and relate to other systems. In dysfunctional families, there is a cocooning effect where the family shuts itself out from the rest of the world. Subtly, the family learns that the "world out there" is not to be trusted and they must not engage it. On the other side of the dysfunctionality are families where the family is so involved in the world outside that the family itself is insignificant and unimportant.

## How do we understand dysfunctional families biblically?

### 1. Biblical authority and exhaustiveness

Those of us who hold strongly to the authority of Scripture reflect a faith commitment that indicates we want the Bible to be the key power to influence all aspects of our lives. It is authoritative in its ability to dictate and command as well as to guide and lead. So when it comes to the dysfunctionality of the family, I need to know what the Bible says about warmth in the family, distribution of power, conflict resolution, and the other dynamics that reflect health or lack of health. I also need to search the Bible for answers to questions about marital dysfunction, parenting, abuse, and a myriad of other topics that relate to family life. But in so doing I am going to run into a rather stark reality.

The Bible, while authoritative in its ability to influence our lives, is not exhaustive. It does not cover every problem area. It does not address every family dysfunction. More importantly, it does not provide solutions to every family problem that I will confront. In the face of this reality there are two major options that we can take. The one chosen by many Christians confuses authority and exhaustiveness. Because the Bible does not deal with the minute details of my problems, I am going to ignore it. I will pursue other kinds of help, utilize other resources, and relegate it to devotional reading.

The other option is to recognize that the Bible works hand-in-hand with godly wisdom and discernment and, most importantly, with the work of the Holy Spirit. The Bible does not always provide a verse that I can bring to bear on my marital difficulties or parental weariness. However, I need to thoughtfully read the Bible, seeking to understand its principles, concepts, and ideas. I must also allow the work of the Spirit to use these truths to move me in a wise and insightful direction. If a wife is being abused by her husband and she looks up "abuse" in her concordance she will be disappointed. But if she allows the truth of Scripture to bathe over the problem, God will provide fresh insight that will help chart a course of action.

## 2. Biblical material on marriage and family

Even though the Bible is not exhaustive, it is filled with material that relates to marriage and family issues. Significantly, almost none of the marriages and families in the Bible are presented in lofty terms as illustrations of health and well-being. In fact, one of the most encouraging aspects of the Bible on this topic is that many of the marriages and families are filled with dysfunction. In a culture where some are crying out for a return to "family values," it is interesting that the Holy Scriptures do not present the family in such nostalgic and sentimental terms. Family life in the Bible is rough and raw.

The following are brief examples worth pursuing:

- The book of Genesis is an excellent place to commence a study on the family. Starting with the sin of the first couple and the sibling rivalry of the first children, it moves through an epic of families caught in deception. Reading the book as a unit gives a broad understanding of the nature of family.
- The marriages and families of the following individuals warrant careful study. Read the stories slowly and carefully to pull principles, concepts, and ideas out of the narrative, all the while listening for the experiences of the family members.
  - ▸ Abraham and Sarah—Genesis 11–23; Romans 4; Hebrews 11:8–12; 1 Peter 3:1–7
  - ▸ Aquila and Priscilla—Acts 18:1–3, 18–19, 24–28; Romans 16:3–5; 1 Corinthians 16:19; 2 Timothy 4:19
  - ▸ Ahab and Jezebel—1 Kings 16; 17:1–2; 18–19:3; 20–22; 2 Kings 9
  - ▸ Isaac and Rebekah—Genesis 24–28
  - ▸ Ananias and Sapphira—Acts 4:32–5:12

- ► Hosea and Gomer—Hosea 1–3; 14 (also see Jer. 3:6–20; Mal. 2:10–16)
- ► Jacob, Leah, and Rachel—Genesis 29–33; 35
- ► Moses and Zipporah—Exodus 2:11–3:12; 4:18–26; 18; Numbers 10:29–34; 12:1–3
- ► Nabal, Abigail, and David—1 Samuel 25
- ► Zechariah and Elizabeth—Luke 1

- A number of passages address marital issues by presenting the ideals, the goals, and the ultimate values in marriage and family.
  - ► Deuteronomy 6
  - ► Psalms 127–128
  - ► 1 Corinthians 7
  - ► Ephesians 5:21–6:4
  - ► Colossians 3:18–21
  - ► 1 Peter 3:1–7

- While the Bible presents material on the biological family, there is a stronger emphasis on the significance of the spiritual family. Along with the frequent references to spiritual fathers, mothers, brothers, and sisters, the following passages are important in the context of any study on family.
  - ► Matthew 12:46–50; 22:23–33
  - ► Mark 10:29–30
  - ► Luke 9:59–62
  - ► John 19:25–27

### 3. God's intent and human harm

One of the most significant themes for Christians who have come from dysfunctional families, or are in one currently, is the role of God. What is his posture toward the events and circumstances that have created the dysfunction? Did he cause it all? Did he make someone else do it? Does he care? Because there are no obvious answers to these questions, abused people who ask them are often left hurt and wounded.

The story of Joseph in the book of Genesis is one of the best stories of dysfunctional families that you will ever read. In fact, it is an intriguing exercise to take a look at Joseph's extended family using the tenfold grid above. By any standard, Joseph was reared in an extremely unhealthy environment. But when the story was near its end and Joseph was in front of his brothers, who were very nervous because they had plotted his demise years before, Joseph makes a startling statement in Genesis 50:19–20.

> But Joseph said to them, "Do not be afraid! Am I in the place of God? Even though you intended to do harm to me, God intended it for good, in order to preserve a numerous people, as he is doing today."

Joseph does not gloss over what his brothers did. He makes it abundantly clear that harm was their primary agenda. He also does not guess at their motives or indicate that their motives were pure even though their behavior was wrong. Again, there is clarity in Joseph's simple words. The doing of harm was at the core of the motivation. In the presence of extreme sibling rivalry, Joseph does not negate it, minimize it, or try to explain it away.

What Joseph does, though, is move to God's intent. He does not cancel out the motivation of his brothers by saying that, because of God's intent, their intent was unimportant. Rather, their negative intent to harm was, in fact, used by God for another purpose. Notice that God is not exerting harm and hardship on people because of something cynical or sadistic. Instead, his providential will takes the evil actions of people and turns them into something good. It was through extreme difficulties that Joseph was brought to Egypt, and it was a famine that brought his family to settle there as well. In a larger cosmic sense, God was assembling his people together in Egypt, through human hardship, in preparation for their move out of Egypt and into the promised land. Early in Scripture we get a little glimpse into the heart of God who specializes in bringing joy out of pain. In this case he used the dysfunctionality of one family to accomplish the saving of many lives.

**What is it like to experience a dysfunctional family?**

*1. All families provide a map for navigating life.*

When you are about to embark on a journey to a new location, the purchase of a map is a wise investment. The map will give you a real view of the new location so you do not have to guess and wonder. It will also help you understand what you are seeing. By comparing the map and your own observations, the pattern of things will start to make sense. The map will also provide you with a way to negotiate your way around by letting you know how to go from one place to another with ease.

While there are many ways to view families and family life, one of the most basic is to see the family as the provider of the map for life. When we are living in our family of origin we are taught, implicitly and explicitly, how to navigate through life. Even when we leave our family and live on our own or get married, new situations provide supplemental additions to the map—updates, if you like, to show us how to get around.

Kari grew up in a family that was a very closed system. Both her parents and her siblings had little outside contact of any significance and almost never invited people into the home. This closed system was combined with a strong critical spirit where the family negated and devalued "outsiders" and viewed people suspiciously. As Kari grew up, her map of life took shape. In one corner of the map these words were in large print—"The world is not a good place and people cannot be trusted so stick closely to your family. They are the only ones you can really trust."

Not surprisingly, Kari had major problems with fear and anxiety, and she found herself housebound most of the time. Her historical map provided a view of reality, but following this script created problems.

Darren grew up in a home where his mother and sisters were picked on regularly. From a very young age, he remembers his father yelling at his mother over incidental mistakes and hitting his sisters if they did anything he did not like. In contrast, he and his brothers were valued by his father in ways that were awkward given the way that women were treated. While Darren did not like this blatant sexism, he has found himself struggling in his marriage. While things went well when he and

Marie first got together, there has been a deterioration in the past few years. He loses his temper with her a lot and says things that he regrets later on. His historical map, one that he was not totally comfortable with, has given him a pattern for understanding male-female relationships.

Serena is known by her friends as one of the nicest, friendliest, and most helpful people they have ever met. She always has a smile on her face and goes out of her way to be helpful to everyone. Deep down, however, she has been struggling with low-grade depression and inner bouts of anger. What she does not realize is that her early wiring was oriented in one direction. Her family believed that girls should be helpful, giving, and kind. They should always look out for the well-being of others; being nice was the ultimate virtue. Conflict should be avoided at all costs. Girls who expressed opinions were seen to be self-centered, opinionated, and not very nice. Her historical map gave her a way to negotiate the world, but her struggles with depression and anger were signs that avoiding conflict at all costs may not be the healthiest way to live.

Kari, Darren, and Serena illustrate the power of maps to influence our view of reality, to establish a pattern for understanding, and to provide a way to negotiate the world. They also illustrate that the map can still influence us outside of our awareness. Kari knew that she did not trust others and experienced fear and anxiety in social situations, but she did not link all of these traits with her family of origin. Darren was aware of his mapping and was uncomfortable with it, but this awareness did not seem to stop him from perpetuating old patterns that he observed in his father. Serena was well aware of her depression and anger, but did not link them with any historical issues.

### 2. Dysfunctional family maps create painful journeys.

Most maps, however, do not just describe how to move from one point to another. They are complex and intricate, describing many aspects of navigation and illustrating that there is more than one way to get anywhere. Such complexity is illustrated in the case of Edwin. Reflect on the tenfold grid we looked at earlier.

Edwin was the third of four children. His sister was one year younger and his two brothers were five and seven years older. His father was an accountant by profession and his mother spent her time raising the four children. Believing that "the man runs things in the home and the church," Edwin's father exerted considerable control and dominance in the home. If you visited the home, he did most of the talking, led most of the conversations, and seemed to set himself up as the most important figure in the house. In contrast, his mother was quiet and demure and only spoke when her husband addressed her. They were an evangelical family and his father saw the way the family functioned as appropriate for a Christian family that sought to follow the Bible. For him, the problem with the culture was the fact that wives were not submitting and children were not obeying.

When the children were still young, Edwin found himself aligning with his father, while his sister and two brothers had an alliance with their mother. This was never stated explicitly, but when there was a fight in the home, everyone would retreat into those camps. As the children grew up, these distinctions played out in terms of intimacy and affection. Edwin felt some love and affirmation from his father but almost none from his mother. In contrast, his mother doted on the other three, so he never felt totally understood by her. There was almost no alliance between Edwin's parents. Even though they were married, it seemed like they were isolated individuals.

All four of the children struggled with self-image issues growing up. Even though Edwin felt affection from his father at times, a lot of it depended on Edwin performing the right way. When he showed interest in activities that interested his father, the affirmation seemed to be present. The two older boys struggled because their father seemed so disinterested and passive. Their younger sister, who was valued by her mother for how she looked and dressed, ended up feeling like her appearance gave her value but that who she was at the core was somewhat irrelevant.

It was an interesting family in terms of individuality. In many ways they were a collection of autonomous and independent islands, meeting periodically in the context of the house, but finding their primary identity in activities and relationships outside the family system. When they were together there was minimal expression of feelings and beliefs; personal subjects, like death and sex, were avoided completely. In fact, when Edwin's uncle, who had spent a lot of time with the family, passed away, very little was said about him after the funeral. You just did not talk about these kinds of things in this family. There was little empathy, as everyone believed that the rest of the family members did not really understand or even care about them. It was not worth the risk to open up.

The tone in the family was not negative, but it lacked energy and vitality. A depressive sense hung over most of the family get togethers, even though Edwin's older brother tried to bring humor into it. There was also minimal conflict. When people were unhappy with each other they usually got quiet or went out. If there was fighting it usually consisted of an angry and hostile exchange with little real resolution when it was over. Individual family members would return to their work outside the family and go about their business, literally and figuratively.

Now, as a husband and father in his early thirties, Edwin is battling a number of demons that can be traced to his past. His marriage lacks fulfillment and he finds himself quite distant from his children. He will do things with them, but there is little affection or warmth between them. Work preoccupies his time, but he experiences minimal satisfaction in what he is doing. His peers see him as successful, but deep inside he feels like a failure. His connection with his parents occurs largely at celebratory times of the year like Christmas and birthdays, but the same flatness characterizes these gatherings as was true of his early home experiences. He has almost no significant connection with his siblings and when they do get together it does not seem like there is much to talk about. At some level he is aware that his family of origin is playing a role in his current experiences, but he is not sure when and how. It all seems very complex. He worries that he is perpetuating the same dynamics in his own family.

As we listen to the Edwins of the world, it is clear that their map is complex and intricate. The dynamics in his family of origin have obviously played a significant role in who he is today, but it is not a simple one-to-one relationship. We cannot point to an individual historical fact and link it with some feeling or behavior in the present. It also needs to be noted that Edwin's family illustrates dysfunctionality that is significant but not as severe as homes where one parent is an alcoholic, or sexual abuse is present, or physical violence is part of the picture. Having said that, the principle remains the same. When your roots are influenced by dysfunctionality rather than health, growth is not hampered permanently, but the journey can be painful.

**So how can I minister to those who are having problems with a dysfunctional family?**

*Avoid biblical proof-texting that denies the power of history.*

When it comes to coping with dysfunctionality in family systems, I think one of the most damaging aspects of the evangelical world is our incessant need to deny the importance of history. My own view is that this does not reflect the richness of our biblical and theological tradition but is one of the places where the influence of Western culture comes to the surface. We live in an ahistorical context where words like *history*, the *past*, and *tradition* have been devalued and terms like *contemporary* and *relevant* have been elevated to a lofty status. In the process, we have come to believe that what happened before is not as important or influential as what is happening now or what might happen in the future.

This cultural habit is most problematic when it is done with sloppy proof-texting: "The Bible says you are to forget the past just like God forgot our sins. We are new creations, all things have passed away. The old has gone. All things have become new. The devil wants to drag you back into those old issues. You don't need to deal with this anymore. Just live at peace with those people in your past. Just move on from the evil that happened to you."

If you deal with Christians who are struggling with their past, you can assume that either they believe parts of this line of argument or one of their friends or family members has given them some of this feedback. Because this often deeply held conviction has a Christian aura to it, it will not be easy to break through, but sensitive and gentle instruction and interaction may help move the person to a place where they can have a more compassionate approach to themselves.

In Philippians 3:13, Paul uses the phrase "forgetting what lies behind." Out of context, it seems clear that we should simply put from memory that which preceded today. But a more careful look at the context leads us to a very different conclusion. At the beginning of the chapter (3:1–4), the apostle talks about the danger of putting confidence in the flesh, which for him is a synonym for reliance on human achievement and accomplishment. For Paul, there were seven places where he could engage in self-reliance, the first four were not his choice, but a matter of family—circumcised, of the people of Israel, of the tribe of Benjamin, and a Hebrew (3:5). The next three were choices that he made—Pharisee, zealous, faultless in terms of legalistic righteousness (3:6). He then moves to a balance sheet image and says he has to engage in an assessment of profit and loss (3:7–9). Ultimately, his goal is to know Christ (3:10–11) and to pursue righteousness, not with perfection (3:12), but with an understanding that he is in the process of working toward that lofty goal. In order to make this happen, he does not rely on what happened before but presses forward to the ultimate goal in heaven (3:13–14). Note that Paul does not ignore his history at all. He talks about it, weighs it up, and seeks to move on. He does not want it to unduly influence him, especially if it fosters self-reliance. Whatever else he is saying, he is not encouraging us to obliterate our history from memory.

God is described in Jeremiah 31:34 as the one who "will forgive their iniquity, and remember their sin no more." If God is God, then the notion that he cannot remember something is nonsensical. Jeremiah is not presenting God as someone who ignores sins or wipes them out of his mind, but as someone who does not hold the sins against his people. There is a substantial difference between memory and theology here. God has not forgotten what we have done to him. It would be naive to think otherwise. But he does not hold it against us. As was the case with Paul in Philippians 3, obliteration from memory is not the prime consideration of the passage.

In 2 Corinthians 5:17, the apostle Paul does say, "everything old has passed away," but again the full context is necessary to understand that this is not synonymous with forgetting the past. In the previous verse, Paul talks about two ways to view Christ and people. Prior to our reconciliation to God, through Christ, we saw everyone from a "human point of view." Our perceptions, attitudes, and observations were bound by time and space and our functioning in community reflected that. But because we are in Christ, we are part of a new creation, a community that does not function with a worldly point of view but that sees through Christ's eyes. The old that has gone is the worldly point of view. The new that has come is Christ's point of view. The focus of the section is not whether one should remember the past, but how one should function as a member of the reconciled community.

Is it the devil that is dragging people back into the past? It is interesting that when Paul talks about appropriate and inappropriate ways to handle anger in Ephesians 4:26, he concludes by indicating that all of this is linked with not making "room for the devil" (v. 27). In other words, the person who is struggling with their past and trying to resolve their angry feelings is working hard to not give the devil a foothold. Ironically, the passage does not indicate that it is the devil who is responsible, but that the individual may not deal well with their anger and, in the process, create an opportunity for the devil to do his work.

And what of making peace with those in our past and overcoming the evil they have brought on us? The idea that we can "just live at peace" with those in our past is inconsistent with the biblical view of peacemaking. Hebrews 12:14 provides an injunction that indicates living at peace with people requires energy and work—"Pursue peace with everyone." Similarly, Romans 12:18—"If it is possible, so far as it depends on you, live peaceably with all"—suggests that peace with others is not automatically guaranteed. We need to do all that we can to live at peace with others and take responsibility for our part in it. But that does not ensure that the other parties will do their part. The goal for the Christian, then, is not to be at peace with everyone but to do everything one can to facilitate peace. Those who struggle through the relational issues that are rooted in a dysfunctional past are often trying to bring peace in those relationships, but that desire is not always reciprocated. For that they need not feel guilty. They are only responsible for what depends on them.

At the end of Romans 12, Paul concludes this section on love and relationships with the command in verse 21 that we should "not be overcome by evil, but overcome evil with good." The sense of the word *overcome* in this passage is not an "easy fix, simple steps" approach that helps us negate the evil that has been done to us. Instead, it is a battle term, suggesting struggle, work, energy, courage, and fortitude. When evil has been done to people in the context of their family, it is not easy to "just move on" and have a righteous and good reaction. Again, those who have come out of dysfunctionality or are living in it presently need to be aware of the real nature of the journey. The battle between evil and good is hard work.

I have found it quite paradoxical that some of the Christians who are the most antihistory and the most unsupportive of people who have come out of dysfunctionality are the worst offenders when it comes to a clear and careful use of Scripture. They use jargon and phrases that have a theological aura to them that, at first blush, sound godly and spiritual. However, as this analysis has shown, they are using the Bible superficially; rather than letting it speak for itself, they are using it to support their superficial solutions. In the process, the church of Jesus Christ is not well served. When a caricature of the Bible is used against people who are in pain because of their personal histories, they not only feel alienated by the Christian community but they also see the Bible as a weapon that can be used against them rather than a source of hope and life.

### *Recognize the diversity in the counseling literature on the role of history.*

If you are a person who reads Christian counseling literature you will notice that there is considerable disagreement about the role of history and the way it should be dealt with. Even Christian writers present varied paradigms for how one should understand a dysfunctional background. Jay Adams encourages us to live responsibly in spite of our background, while Neil Anderson suggests that we need to break the bonds that are rooted in history. Leanne Payne and John and Paula Sanford argue that we need to have our memories healed, while Gary Smalley and John Trent indicate that we need to receive a blessing from those in our past. Walter Wink sees the influence of principalities and powers in our history, while Charles Solomon argues for the appropriation of Galatians 2:20.

While you should not avoid this literature, you should be aware that there are many dangers in wading into it. Unfortunately, in the evangelical world there is a bandwagon effect where people join the parade toward the one model they consider to be "the answer." It is sad that even though as Christians we have found "the way," we are still searching for "the" answer. Often the problem is not with the writer of the book or the leader of the system, but with the disciples who, in their enthusiasm, affirm this approach as the only approach.

The fact is that people who are struggling historically or presently with a dysfunctional family are not going to find one simple answer that will solve all their difficulties. Finding a healthy map for life is not easy, and one system rarely provides all the appropriate navigation skills. Caring listeners will bring this mindset into interactions with hurting people, to help them work through the ambiguity that comes from trying to change maps from one that is unhelpful to one that will give them a better sense of reality.

***Bring clarity to history, reasons, excuses, consequences, intent, and impact.***

As you seek to care for friends and family members who have experienced various forms of dysfunctionality, it is important to be clear in your own mind about how you understand history and its influence in our lives. To the degree that you have clarity, you will be able to teach and encourage others with compassion and sensitivity. As a result, it is important that certain terms are unpacked with care.

History, as the term connotes, is simply a word to describe what happened in the past. It is not a bad term, or an inaccurate term, even though some want to give it negative value. The Bible is filled with history. In fact, a substantial portion of the Hebrew Scriptures is devoted to God telling his people what he has done in the past, while the New Testament is heavily reliant on arguments from what happened in history. God, one might say, is very much a God of history. So to admit that one has a history, whether it is good or bad, is an appropriate and necessary admission.

But what do we do with that history? To use history as an explanation for what is going on in the present is to utilize it as a reason. Why does Edwin find it difficult to be closely connected with others? Partially because his family of origin gave him a life map that he is following. Why do some men treat women like slaves? Possibly because as they were growing up they never saw men give women genuine respect. Why are some people extremely uncomfortable with social situations? Quite likely because they came from a family where being open and expressive was not valued. In all of these situations, history forms an explanatory backdrop for behavior in the present. It is not a foolproof explanation, either, which is why words like "partially," "possibly," or "quite likely" need to be used. We don't know for sure that there is a relationship between history and any particular present behavior, but we can be sure that there is a context of some sort that contributed to it.

When people are stopped for speeding, they will often tell the police officer the reason they were speeding was because they were late. In response to such explanations most will receive a somewhat interested acknowledgment and a ticket. In other words, the reason does not function as an excuse. While the behavior may be explained, it is not justified. This distinction is very important when it comes to how one understands history. To say that Edwin came from dysfunctionality and that has influenced the way he is today is to provide a reason. That is legitimate and appropriate. However, to argue that all his behavior is now justified is quite another matter.

For example, a high percentage of prostitutes have been sexually abused in their past. To make that statement is to provide a reason and a historical backdrop for their prostitution. But that does not justify or excuse the behavior. We cannot ignore the ethical, moral, physical, and spiritual problems inherent in this lifestyle. But here is where many people make a mistake. They want to choose between reason and excuse. Some will argue that we should accept and understand prostitutes because of their histories and not worry about the moral and ethical dimensions of their behavior. These people argue that because prostitutes have been sexually abused and are working through many dimensions of their own sexuality, prostitution makes sense for them at this point. Others will go on the antihistory bandwagon and say it does not matter whether they have been sexually abused or not: prostitution is wrong and they should stop it. Such people don't want to hear about why prostitutes are the way they are. They simply want the prostitutes to live righteously.

It seems to me that neither of these options is appropriate. The one turns the reason into an excuse and, in the process, ignores the importance of an ethical-moral grid for understanding life and God and behavior. The other ignores the reason completely and assumes that anyone who cites a reason is implicitly making an excuse. The better course is to look at the behavior and determine if there is a moral component that needs ethical reflection. For instance, the case of prostitution is fairly clear. While past sexual abuse may have predisposed the individual to get involved in this lifestyle, it is not one that should be condoned or encouraged. Even though the struggle to get past one's current lifestyle may be painful and require intense counseling and help of various sorts, it is a necessary struggle. On the other hand, if a person is shy because they came from a family where they were squelched and unappreciated, one would not want to say to that person that they have no excuse and need to just stop being shy. Because there is no inherent ethical dilemma, we may decide to live with the fact that their reason from the past does excuse the fact that they simply cannot share in a Bible study group. However, we may encourage them to share in a one-on-one context or in a very small group, so they can slowly move toward having more confidence in the larger group.

Implicit in the argument is the fact that history has consequences. It is the sowing what you reap principle of Scripture. What happened then affects what happens now. And in some technical sense, if what happened then is impacting what happens now, it is not really "in the past." It is very much in the present experience of the person. So to argue that we should "move on," a favorite expression of ahistorical types, is to deny the sowing-reaping principle. It would be like telling David that he should just move on from his sin with Bathsheba, the death of the child, and the murder of Uriah. Even though he was forgiven by God, he could never move on because the human and personal consequences of his historical behavior were intimately connected. While he wrote Psalm 51 in response to his sin, I can imagine that David had some nights when he lay awake thinking about the whole situation. Forgiveness does not lead to obliteration from memory any more than an apology from a driver after hitting a pedestrian results in the immediate healing of the broken leg.

And what of intent and impact? Just as the pedestrian can fully embrace the driver's apology and the leg will remain broken, so too the intent of the driver has very little to do with the impact. The driver might have been doing everything just right, took his mind off the road for a moment, and hit the pedestrian. He could easily say, "I didn't mean it," but that will not lessen the pain experienced by the person who was injured. Understanding the positive intent does not negate the negative impact. At times, people will try to minimize the anguish of those who are struggling with painful families by saying, "I am sure your parents meant well." While that is probably true, more than likely the parents were misguided, misinformed, or poorly influenced by their own family of origin. Those deficits, while not their own fault per se, still have an impact on the family.

While many people do not navigate this road very well, I have found much wisdom in the brief interchange between two characters in the movie *The Lion King*. Simba, the lion cub, has a decision to make: "I know what I have to do but going back means I have to face my past."

Rafiki, the eccentric ape, hits him with a stick.

"Ouch. That hurt. What did you do that for?"

Rafiki responds sarcastically, "It doesn't matter. It's in the past."

Simba's simple retort reflects the truth about the role of history in all of our lives: "Yeah, but it still hurts."

### *Recognize the sociocultural pressures on marriage and family.*

Understanding the dysfunctionality of a family and the nature of the maps that have been created as a result is a complex process. One of the compounding factors is the changing nature of marriage and family. In early history, marriages and families were largely physical and economic units. Families worked together in agricultural contexts, so the larger the family, the greater the likelihood that you would make a decent living. Notions of romance, love, and affection were not strong factors in family life. By the Middle Ages, noblewomen living in castles had more leisure since others did the work, so their appearance, rather than their ability to produce and reproduce, became important. As a result love and infatuation entered into the marriage equation. But it was AD 1200 before dating actually commenced and marriages were an expression of personal choice. Prior to that time all marriages, world-wide, were arranged. In light of these realities, it is interesting to note that all the biblical material on marriage and family was written in an agricultural context where the economic paradigm was more influential than the romantic and affectionate one.

In most of contemporary Western culture, we select our own spouse, love precedes marriage rather than follows it, and psychological and emotional survival are important. The result is that pressures change substantially. In the past, a wife might be unhappy with her spouse because he was not working hard enough to secure sufficient produce from the farm. Currently, a husband might be unhappy with his spouse because she does not make him feel safe, does not listen to him sensitively, doesn't treat him with respect, or doesn't meet his needs. Children move from being expressions of economic success and well-being to functioning as significant parts of a family unit where trust, intimacy, and empathy are expected to be given and received.

While all of us live in a modern world and most of us are in or close to urban centers, these changing sociocultural factors play a significant role in our confusion about marriage and family. For example, what does it mean to love your spouse? The Bible commands me to love my spouse after marriage—and this was written in a context where I may not have seen my spouse until the day I married her. In that sense, love is premised on marriage and not marriage premised on love. How does that translate into contemporary culture, where love precedes marriage and becomes the key variable in the engagement? Obviously, you get engaged to someone you love. But what does that mean? Many of us got married because of sex drive, fear, a need for affirmation, or social acceptability. We may have called it love, but most of us had no idea what love was about prior to marriage. What does love mean in a family when you are in the stage of building a career? What does love mean in marriage when children come along? What does it mean to truly love your children? What kind of love do we expect from our children? And of course the big question, what is love? Is it emotional, cognitive, behavioral, all three? Does it change as the relationship develops? Can you fall out of love? Can you lose love? And if you fall out of love does it mean you made a mistake when you married that person?

When people are experiencing difficulties related to their marriage and family dysfunction, it is important to remember that there are many forces at work. While personal and family issues play a significant role, the power of sociocultural factors cannot be minimized. How we define marriage and family in contemporary culture is a confusing subject, and the confusion is intensified for those of us who are Christians. We are trying to allow the truths of Scripture to penetrate this area of our lives, but we recognize that the culture of the Bible, particularly in the area of family, is completely different from our own. It is not an easy task to take the principles of Scripture and have them wash over all aspects of our family life, both present and past. However, it is a task we need to pursue with passion as we seek to care for those who are experiencing the impact of dysfunction.

*Refer if the dysfunctionality requires further insight or if it is significantly limiting the person's well-being.*

Since we all have a history and were raised by people who sin, it would be inappropriate to suggest that everyone with dysfunctionality in their background needs formal counseling. However, counseling has many different facets, and if dysfunction is present, formal help is worth pursuing for a number of different reasons. Not all counseling is about behavioral change. Some of us have a disposition that seeks to understand our roots and wants to put current issues in a historical context. For these people, counseling can provide insight and wisdom. While actual behavioral change may not occur, there is value in having greater self-understanding. It fills out one's picture of oneself and can be very helpful in processing how others view you. If the friend or family member you are talking to has dysfunctionality in their past or present, and they are the kind of person who is introspective and reflective, a nudge toward formal counseling might be advisable.

On the other hand, there are those who are experiencing so much impact from the dysfunctionality that it has become a threat to their well-being. Both in their inner life and in their behavior, they are experiencing significant paralysis and limitations. As was noted earlier, their history is not past; it is having an impact on them in the present. People in this situation need help not just for insight and self-understanding, but they need to work through changes so their lives are less hampered by the lack of health in their family system.

**Summary**

Dysfunctional families do not function in a healthy way in terms of power, alliances, intimacy, self-regard, individuality, expressiveness, mood, empathy, conflict, and openness, with the result that they provide family members with a poor map for navigating the journey of life.

How do we understand dysfunctional families biblically?

1. Biblical authority and exhaustiveness
2. Biblical material on marriage and family
3. God's intent and human harm

In understanding people's experience of a dysfunctional family, we need to know:

1. All families provide a map for navigating life.
2. Dysfunctional family maps create painful journeys.

When ministering to those who are having problems with a dysfunctional family:

Avoid biblical proof-texting that denies the power of history.

Recognize the diversity in counseling literature on the role of history.

Bring clarity to history, reasons, excuses, consequences, intent, and impact.

Recognize the sociocultural pressures on marriage and family.

Refer if the dysfunctionality requires further insight or if it is significantly limiting the person's well-being.

# 7

# Wounded Healers

One of the great dangers in a book of this nature is that the reader can adopt a posture of "me" and "them." "Them" are those who are in trouble with problems related to self-image, grief, depression, burnout, or dysfunctional families. "Me," in contrast, is somewhat removed and unaffected by such trials. But as Henri Nouwen so powerfully argues, the starting point for service is not the suffering of others.

> After all attempts to articulate the predicament of modern man, the necessity to articulate the predicament of the minister himself became most important. For the minister is called to recognize the sufferings of his time in his own heart and make that recognition the starting point of his service. Whether he tries to enter into a dislocated world, relate to a convulsive generation, or speak to a dying man, his service will not be perceived as authentic unless it comes from a heart wounded by the suffering about which he speaks.[1]

We commence not with the need of the other, or the problem they are experiencing. Rather, we look first at ourselves.

151

This approach flies in the face of our normal view of help. We tend to see those who are in trouble as weak and in need of the resources we can bring to the situation. Sensing that we are supposed to be experts, we then feel the need to provide answers, solutions, and prescriptions. Ironically, even though we are lay people, we try to act like professionals. But then we experience anxiety because we know that we do not have a specialized body of knowledge and skills. Nouwen suggests that our starting point is wrong. We need to begin with our own heart. It is when we identify with the other that we will begin to truly care.

Our best window into this kind of understanding is the ministry of Jesus, who is described as "a man of suffering and acquainted with infirmity" (Isa. 53:3). The "me" and "them" paradigm is shattered when we understand the argument put forth by the writer to the Hebrews (4:15–16).

> For we do not have a high priest who is unable to sympathize with our weaknesses, but we have one who in every respect has been tested as we are, yet without sin. Let us therefore approach the throne of grace with boldness, so that we may receive mercy and find grace to help in time of need.

The reason we are able to go to Jesus with boldness, knowing that we will find mercy and grace, is because he is a wounded healer. He is able to sympathize with our weakness. His identification with our struggles makes him credible, authentic, and full of integrity. He truly is a suffering Savior.

So when the psalmist (34:15) describes God's response to our struggles—"The eyes of the LORD are on the righteous, and his ears are open to their cry"—this is not a distant or impersonal reaction, but one where the eyes and ears of God are present to our vulnerability, seeing and listening intently. The incarnation of Jesus and his life of suffering that culminated in death on a cross is a witness that God not only knows about the journey of pain, but has experienced it. Dorothy Sayers says it well:

> For whatever reason God chose to make man as he is—limited and suffering and subject to sorrows and death—He had the honesty and courage to

take His own medicine. Whatever game He is playing with His creation, He has kept His own rules and played fair.[2]

At the end of a Bible study, when a man tells me he is struggling with depression, it is easy for me to distance myself and act as if I have never experienced this problem; I might even begin to patronize him, in both my attitude and behavior. At the back of church it is easy to quickly dismiss the widower who has just lost his wife, or the young mother who is struggling with self-image. However, the co-pilgrim does not see the other as inferior. In contrast, when I see myself as a co-pilgrim, I will seek to identify with brokenness and vulnerability and make that the foundation upon which I will demonstrate care.

Does this mean that I need to have experienced depression to care for those who are depressed? Or gone through burnout to really connect with someone in the midst of it? No. But I do need to be in tune with my own brokenness in order to understand the brokenness of others. This is not easy. My colleague Maxine Hancock points out the difficulty of this position when she suggests that the

> greater strength we have in some area of human excellence—intellect, beauty, physical strength—the harder it is to embrace the reality of our vulnerability, which is a condition of being human.[3]

It is in understanding our own frailty and sinfulness that we learn we are in need of Christ, both at conversion and during the Christian journey. It is when we are experiencing weakness that we are reminded of our lack of sufficiency. When we are in this sphere of existence, it is then that we are more in tune with God and his people. The reason?

> But we have this treasure in clay jars, so that it may be made clear that this extraordinary power belongs to God and does not come from us. . . . So death is at work in us, but life in you. . . . For whenever I am weak, then I am strong.
>
> 2 Corinthians 4:7, 12; 12:10

How does this work out at the end of the Bible study, when the depressed man comes to me? If I see myself as an expert, I will tend to rely on my own resources and strengths and see myself as needing to have the answers. I am not there to care and understand, but rather to be The Helper. That mindset will put me on the continuum of arrogance and anxiety. If I believe I do have the answers, in my arrogance I will control, push, and prescribe without any attempt to understand or genuinely care for the depressed man. If I don't believe I have the "answers" but feel that I should, in my anxiety I will struggle and fret, feeling like I have nothing to offer. How interesting that in our desire to be strong with the weakness of others, we often end up feeling weak.

In contrast, if I adopt the approach of Paul in 2 Corinthians, I will be able to resonate with my friend's depression because I know that the treasure is in a jar of clay. A jar of clay is fragile and frail, susceptible to bruising and breaking. He is no different than me. We both participate in the brokenness of creation. And the only way that God's great power can be demonstrated is when I learn to live in the weakness, rather than seeking to flee from it.

Without this mindset, we are threatened by the difficulties of others. The grief of the widow, the pain of the burned-out executive, the insecurity of the teenager, the angst of the person struggling with a dysfunctional family, all seem to be things that need to be fixed. But if we participate as co-pilgrims in the struggles of life we don't need to fix. We are there to understand, to care, to listen.

When we do engage in the ministry of understanding, care, and listening, it is hard work. To really pay attention to another is to live sacrificially and humbly. In a sense it is a death. And to borrow Paul's image, it is a death of self so the other can live.

This means that the experience of both the person who is struggling and the co-pilgrim who is walking alongside is not a movement from weakness to strength. It is not that the person with the problem is weak and as a result of my strength he becomes strong. Rather, we are both living the reality captured in 2 Corinthians 12:10, that it is in the embracing of weakness that we become strong. It is not that I once was weak and now I am strong, but it is in my weakness that I am strong. So I do not speak into my friend's supposed weakness with my strength, but recognize that cure and complete healing are God's sole prerogative, while care and understanding are my deep privilege as a wounded healer.

And so with Eugene Peterson, we pray:

Teach us to be reverential in all these occasions of need that are the agenda of our work, aware that you were long beforehand with these people, creating and loving, saving and wooing them. Teach us the humility of not caring, so that we do not use anyone's need as a workshop to cobble together makeshift, messianic work that inflates our importance and indispensability. Teach us to be in wonder and adoration before the beauties of creation and the glories of salvation, especially as they come to us in these humans who have come to think of themselves as violated and degraded and rejected. Teach us the reticence and restraint of not caring, so that in our eagerness to do good, we do not ignorantly interfere in your caring. Teach us not to care so that we have time and energy and space to realize that all our work is done on holy ground and in your holy name, that people and communities in need are not a wasteland where we feverishly and faithlessly set up shop, but a garden, a rose garden in which we work contemplatively.[4]

# Notes

## Chapter 2  Self-Image

1. C. S. Lewis, *The Screwtape Letters* (Old Tappan, Revell, 1976), 74.

## Chapter 3  Grief

1. C. S. Lewis, *A Grief Observed* (New York: Bantam Books, 1976), 28.
2. Harold S. Kushner, *When Bad Things Happen to Good People* (New York: Avon Books, 1981), 25–26.

## Chapter 7  Wounded Healers

1. Henri J. M. Nouwen, *The Wounded Healer: Ministry in Contemporary Society* (Garden City, NY: Image Books, 1979), xvi.
2. Dorothy L. Sayers, *Christian Letters to a Post-Christian World* (Grand Rapids: Eerdmans, 1969), 14.
3. Maxine Hancock, "To Be Fully Human," *Crux* 36 (December 2000): 37.
4. Eugene Peterson, *Subversive Spirituality* (Grand Rapids: Eerdmans, 1997), 168.

**Rod J. K. Wilson** is president and professor of counseling and psychology at Regent College in Vancouver, British Columbia, author of *Counseling and Community*, and coauthor of *Exploring Your Anger* and *Helping Angry People*. Along with his professional counseling and consulting work, he has spent his career in academia in both teaching and administrative posts and in pastoral ministry. He and his wife, Bev, live in Burnaby, British Columbia.